JMX: Managing J2EE with Java Management Extensions

Juha Lindfors, Marc Fleury, and The JBoss Group, LLC

SAMS

201 West 103rd St., Indianapolis Indiana, 46290 USA

JMX: Managing J2EE with Java Management Extensions

Copyright ©2002 by Sams Publishing

International Standard Book Number: 0-672-232288-9

Library of Congress Catalog Card Number: 2001092343

Printed in the United States of America

First Printing: Month, 2000

03   02   01   00   4   3   2   1

Trademarks

Warning and Disclaimer

EXECUTIVE EDITOR
Michael Stephens

DEVELOPMENT EDITOR
Christy A. Franklin

MANAGING EDITOR
Matt Purcell

PROJECT EDITOR
George E. Nedeff

COPY EDITOR
Pat Kinyon

INDEXER
Ginny Bess

PROOFREADER
Kay Hoskin

TECHNICAL EDITOR
Kevin Farnham

TEAM COORDINATOR
Pamalee Nelson

INTERIOR DESIGNER
Anne Jones

COVER DESIGNER
Aren Howell

PRODUCTION
Brad Lenser

Overview

Contents

About the Authors

Juha Lindfors got involved with the JBoss J2EE application server in early 2000. While digging into the source, he got a crash course in the JMX API, which was already part of the server core. Today, apart from trying to learn to write, he spends a lot of his time writing free software and training people in JMX and J2EE. The rest of his time is spent trying to figure out what to do when he grows up while studying Computer Science at the University of Helsinki, Finland.

Marc Fleury, Ph.D., was born in Paris in 1968. Marc started in Sales at Sun Microsystems France. A graduate of the Ecole Polytechnique, France's top engineering school, and an ex-Lieutenant in the paratroopers, he has a master in Theoretical Physics from the ENS ULM and a Ph.D in Physics for work he did as a visiting scientist at MIT (X-Ray Lasers). Marc currently serves as the President of the JBoss Group, LLC—an elite services company based out of Atlanta, GA.

The JBoss Group LLC, is a service company dedicated to support, training, and consulting around the free JBoss platform. Based in Atlanta, GA, this LLC regroups core JBoss programmers around the world. *JBoss* is an open-source, standards-compliant, J2EE application server implemented in 100 percent pure Java. The JBoss/Server and complement of products are delivered under a public license. With 50,000+ downloads per month, JBoss is arguably the most downloaded J2EE-based server in the industry.

Dedication

To my Mom.

Acknowledgments

I'd like to thank Marc Fleury for his excellent insights into JMX and for kicking my arse to keep me moving. I also much thank Andreas Schaefer for his help in covering some of the difficult parts of the book. My thanks to all the folks at Sams who made this book real, especially Christy Franklin for her help and comments to get the chapters finished, and the Technical Editor, Kevin Farnham, for putting up with my buggy Java command-line instructions. To Mikko and Tuomo, thanks for dragging me out for an occasional movie or a game of squash. There are numerous other people to thank I can't remember right now. JBoss developers—you should be proud of your work. And of course, I would like to thank the Academy.

Tell Us What You Think!

As the reader of this book, *you* are our most important critic and commentator. We value your opinion and want to know what we're doing right, what we could do better, what areas you'd like to see us publish in, and any other words of wisdom you're willing to pass our way.

As an Executive Editor for Sams Publishing, I welcome your comments. You can fax, e-mail, or write me directly to let me know what you did or didn't like about this book—as well as what we can do to make our books stronger.

Please note that I cannot help you with technical problems related to the topic of this book, and that due to the high volume of mail I receive, I might not be able to reply to every message.

When you write, please be sure to include this book's title and author as well as your name and phone or fax number. I will carefully review your comments and share them with the author and editors who worked on the book.

Fax: 317-581-4770
E-mail: feedback@samspublishing.com
Mail: Michael Stephens
         Executive Editor
         Sams Publishing
         201 West 103rd Street
         Indianapolis, IN 46290 USA

Introduction

The Java Management Extensions defines architecture for software and network management in the Java programming language. This book will cover the JMX specification and show you how resources can be managed using JMX.

What is JMX?

JMX is a unified framework to instrument the disparate pieces of Java code in a modern IT infrastructure. Before JMX, there was no standardized approach in the Java programming language to start, manage, monitor, and stop different software components or applications. Management of software has been achieved through an ad-hoc collection of procedures and custom management code. JMX promises to remove the need for expensive application-specific management solutions by defining an architecture that allows more generic management applications to be built.

Why JMX for J2EE?

The Java 2 Enterprise Edition is a complex, distributed, service-based enterprise platform. It consists of many different kinds of resources that are dynamically created, distributed, moved across nodes, redeployed, and destroyed. The management of such a platform calls for an isolation layer between the management applications and the managed resources. The management architecture must be generic enough to allow a wide variety of different kinds of resources and components to be managed. The management architecture must be able to cope with the dynamics and distribution of the platform and provide a management model that allows increasingly long uptimes and 24x7 service. JMX can provide all this.

Part I: Java Management Extensions Specification

The first part of this book will cover all the aspects of the JMX specification. Several examples will be implemented to demonstrate how to build management components, discuss the different types of components the JMX specification defines, and look at the management architecture established by the JMX implementations.

After finishing the first section of the book, you should be familiar with the concept of *managed beans* (MBeans). You will understand the different approaches to implementing such managed beans, how to control their life cycle, and how the managed beans are able to communicate with each other and with other management applications. You will also understand the role of an agent in the management architecture and how it is used to decouple the managed resources from the management applications.

You will also learn about the standard services defined in the specification and how they can be used when implementing resources. The standard services include functionality for scheduling events, loading MBeans over the network, monitoring the managed resources, and creating relationships between different management components.

MBeans are used to represent resources that can be managed. In Chapter 1, "Getting Started," you will start right off with a classic Hello, World example and walk through instrumenting a resource. You will also be shown, with help of a code example, how the management interfaces are created. You will learn to deploy the MBean and will see how it can be accessed via a management application.

Chapter 2, "Architecture," will give you a detailed look at the management architecture the JMX specification defines. You will see where the different parts of the architecture, the agent, the MBeans, the management applications, and the various connectors and protocol adaptors fit.

Chapter 3, "Standard MBeans," Chapter 4, "Dynamic MBeans," and Chapter 5, "Model MBeans," describe the different types of MBeans in detail, covering all the aspects of the resource instrumentation. Standard MBeans, Dynamic MBeans and the Model MBeans will be covered, including examples of implementing each type of MBean.

In Chapter 6, "MBean Server," and Chapter 7, "Standard Agent Services," you will concentrate on the JMX agent layer, taking an in-depth look at the different components that form the agent and covering all the standard agent services that the specification defines.

After you have finished Part I, "Java Management Extensions Specifications," you will have gained all the necessary information to build JMX-compliant management solutions as defined in the specification.

Part II: JMX in the J2EE Platform

In the second part of the book, you will concentrate on the distributed services level of JMX and how they can be implemented with the help of the J2EE platform. In most cases, you will go into detailed implementation of features that are discussed in Part I, extending the ideas and functionality present in the specification.

Part II will start by building a specialized Model MBean implementation in Chapter 8, "XMBean: Model MBean Implementation." You will see how many of the features of Model MBeans can be implemented. Specifically, you will implement a Model MBean that is able to retrieve its management interface from an external source, in our case, from an XML file.

Chapter 9, "Connectors and Protocol Adaptors," concentrates on the basics of JMX distributed services level—the connectors and protocol adaptors. You will implement a basic RMI connector and look at some of the existing legacy integration options through an SNMP adaptor.

In Chapter 10, "JMX Distribution Layer with J2EE Services," you will move on to more advanced distribution implementations for JMX. Specifically, you will leverage the J2EE platform to implement location transparency for MBeans, build an asynchronous connector with JMS, and build another synchronous connector with SOAP.

Chapter 11, "JMX for the Administrator," will cover some of the future directions in management and focuses on the work done by the JSR-77 expert group to define a management model for the J2EE platform.

In Chapter 12, "JMX as Server Architecture," you will see how JMX can be used as a core infrastructure to implement application servers. You will take a detailed look at how JBoss, the open source J2EE server, leveraged the architecture and modularity provided by JMX to implement a fully-modular server architecture.

After you are finished with the book, you should have a very solid understanding of the JMX specification and how to implement management solutions on the JMX architecture. In addition, you should have a solid view of how to use the JMX with the J2EE platform and how the future of the J2EE management will look.

Java Management Extensions Specification

IN THIS PART

Getting Started

IN THIS CHAPTER

This chapter will give you step-by-step instructions to writing a managed bean (MBean). It will also show you how to deploy the MBean to an agent. If you have no previous knowledge of the JMX specification or MBeans, you should take the time to read through the chapter. However, if you are already familiar with the MBean concept and the JMX API, feel free to use this chapter as a review and just quickly glance through it.

In the following examples, both the Sun JMX Reference Implementation and the IBM Tivoli JMX Implementation are used. Two different implementations are used to illustrate the portability of the MBeans across the implementations but also to point out the differences of the two implementations when using features the JMX specification does not define. Such features include the JMX connectors and protocol adaptors.

After you have finished reading this chapter, you will have the basic knowledge required for JMX development using Standard MBeans. You will also know how to register an MBean to an agent and will have the basic knowledge of how to work with at least two different JMX implementations.

MBean Component Types

MBeans are components that implement a management interface, either statically, in which case the management interface is a Java interface, or dynamically, in which case the management interface is defined through a set of metadata classes.

The JMX specification defines four different MBean component types, three of which are mandatory in the current 1.0 version of the specification. The different component types are as follows:

> Standard MBean
> Dynamic MBean
> Model MBean
> Open MBean

The Standard, Dynamic, and Model MBeans are mandatory and must be implemented by all compliant JMX implementation. The Open MBeans were not finished for the 1.0 version of the specification and are not required. However, at the time of this writing, a maintenance release of the specification is in the works and that might change the status of the Open MBeans from optional to mandatory as well.

Standard MBeans are created by declaring a Java interface with the management information that the MBean must implement. The other three component types describe their management interfaces through a set of metadata classes. Model MBeans extend the Dynamic MBeans by allowing additional descriptors to be added to the management interface. Open MBeans restrict the object types used in the management interface to a predefined set of classes representing the basic types.

The MBeans are registered to an agent that is able to manipulate the registered management components. The agent acts as a registry for MBeans offering a means to query and modify the managed components via their management interface. The relationship between the agent and the MBean components is shown in Figure 1.1.

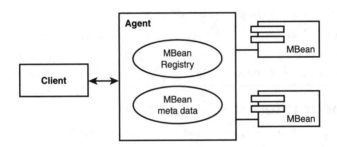

FIGURE 1.1

Overview of the agent and MBean components.

Another important aspect to notice in Figure 1.1 is that management clients are always decoupled from the actual managed resources represented by the MBeans. All communications between the clients and the MBeans are carried through the agent level, and no direct references to the MBean components are ever exposed outside the agent. This is a significant feature of the JMX-based management architecture, and you will study it more in the Chapter 2, "Architecture," when we go through all the details of the architecture.

Writing Your First MBean

You will start by writing a *Standard* MBean using the traditional "Hello, World" example. For now, you need not to worry about all the details of the specification or the rules and requirements for MBeans. Concentrate on this specific example. We will cover the specification in the next chapters, but for now it is important for you to familiarize yourself with the basics of JMX development.

You will build a managed bean where we expose a single attribute that is both readable and writable by the management application. We will also expose one management operation of our MBean. What you will notice during this example is that writing a Standard MBean implementation is no different from implementing a normal Java interface. In fact, writing the MBean implementation is very close to writing a regular JavaBean component with setter and getter methods for manipulating the attributes.

The MBean interface design follows similar naming conventions to those described in the JavaBeans component specification. The difference between your MBean and JavaBean component is that you'll explicitly define and implement an interface that describes the management attributes and operations of the MBean. This results in a Standard MBean, which is often the easiest and most straightforward way to enable Java classes to management.

The following example consists of three different parts.

- Management interface declaration
- Implementation of the resource you want to manage
- Application code to instantiate the agent and register the managed bean

After you are done with the example, you will have an MBean deployed to the agent and can manipulate its attributes and operations through a Web management interface.

Management Interface Declaration

The first part of the example follows the traditional "Hello, World" approach to learning new technologies. First, you will define the management interface and call it HelloMBean. The interface declares three methods: two for accessing a management attribute Name and one management operation print(). The code for the management interface is shown in Listing 1.1.

LISTING 1.1   HelloMBean.java

```
package book.jmx.examples;

public interface HelloMBean {

        // management attributes
        public String getName();
        public void setName(String name);

        // management operations
        public void print();

}
```

As you can see in the HelloMBean.java, declaring a management interface does not differ from declaring an ordinary Java interface. However, you should pay attention to some of the details in the declaration. First, notice how the interface has been named.

```
public interface HelloMBean {
```

The suffix `MBean` is significant. The agent, to which the MBean is registered (see Figure 1.1), uses the introspection features of the Java programming language to look for an interface named with the `MBean` suffix. The interface name identifies the class implementing it as a Standard MBean. When developing standard MBeans, you must follow this naming convention to name all of your management interfaces. In the example, we have named the interface as `HelloMBean`, which the JMX agent will automatically recognize as a Standard MBean interface. The agent will then use introspection to find the MBean attributes and operations from the interface. The actual implementation class, or managed resource as it is called in JMX terminology, will be called `Hello`. Notice the relationship between the classname and the management interface name.

In the management interface, we also declare a read-write attribute `Name`. To declare a management attribute, and to let the agent know it is a read-write attribute, we declared two accessor methods—`getName()` and `setName()`.

```
// management attributes
public String getName();
public void setName(String name);
```

The attribute's name is recognized by the agent that looks for methods matching the MBean attribute naming convention in the interface. In this example, the MBean attribute `Name` is readable because you have defined a method `getName()`. The attribute is also writable because you have defined a setter method `setName()`. You could also declare just one accessor method for the `Name` attribute, resulting in either a read-only or write-only management attribute.

Last, you declare one management operation in the interface. It is a simple operation that doesn't require parameters or return any values when invoked.

```
// management operations
public void print();
```

You are free to name your management operations as you want. In fact, all the methods declared in the MBean interface not matching the naming convention of a management attribute, such as `getName()` and `setName()`, are interpreted by the JMX agent as management operations. Therefore, in this case, the method `print()` is interpreted as a management operation instead of an attribute.

That is all there was to writing the management interface. If you were to enable a management of existing classes via the means of Standard MBeans, you would write the interface exposing the attributes and operations and name the interface after the MBean naming convention. If you are already following the common Java naming practices, there is little you need to change in your existing code. In the optimal case, all you need to do is declare your class to implement the MBean interface that tells the JMX agent which methods and operations you are exposing to the management from your class.

Implementing the MBean

Because you are not exposing a management interface to an existing class but creating a new managed resource, you will also write the class implementing the Standard MBean interface. The Hello class in Listing 1.2 is a public, non-abstract class that implements the HelloMBean interface you saw in HelloMBean.java file in Listing 1.1.

LISTING 1.2   Hello.java

```java
package book.jmx.examples;

public class Hello implements HelloMBean {

        private String name = "";

        public String getName() {
                return name;
        }

        public void setName(String name) {
                this.name = name;
        }

        public void print() {
                System.out.println("Hello, " + name + "!!" );
        }

}
```

The Hello class stores the attribute state in the name field whenever the setName() method is invoked and returns the contents of name when getName() is called. We don't explicitly declare a constructor but rely on the Java default constructor to provide a public constructor required by compliant MBeans.

Again, it's worth it to notice the relationship between the classname Hello and the corresponding name of the management interface HelloMBean that it implements. This naming convention is required for all Standard MBeans.

The Hello class is very trivial Java class by any measure, but it will serve as an example when deploying the MBean and testing it. You will be able to use a Web-based interface to set the attribute value and invoke the print operation. Next, you will look at how to instantiate the agent, register the managed bean, and set up a Web interface to manage it.

Deploying the `HelloMBean`

You have now declared the management interface and written the resource class you want to manage. The third part of the example involves instantiating the agent and registering the managed bean to it. You will set up the agent, called MBean server, and use its programming interface to register your management component. The MBean server implementation is provided with the JMX implementation. At the time of this writing, there are at least three JMX implementations publicly available. Sun Microsystems provides a reference implementation of the JMX specification at `http://java.sun.com/products/JavaManagement/index.html`. In addition, the IBM Tivoli team offers a JMX implementation at `http://www.alphaworks.ibm.com`. The third implementation is provided by AdventNet at `http://www.adventnet.com`.

Regardless of which JMX implementation you decide to use, the agent level implements the same `MBeanServer` interface. All access to the managed beans is invoked through this interface, so the example in this chapter is portable across both the Sun and IBM Tivoli JMX implementations. It should also work on any other compatible JMX implementation. You should note that the MBeans and their interfaces are never directly exposed to the management applications. From the MBeans' point of view, all invocations arrive from the agent to which it is registered. From the client application's point of view, all invocations are made to the `MBeanServer` interface. Remember that there is never a direct object reference between the client and the managed resource.

Listing 1.3 shows the details of creating the agent and registering the MBean. The JMX agent implements the `MBeanServer` interface. You will use this interface to add new MBeans, register them to the JMX infrastructure, and query the existing MBeans in the agent. You will get an in-depth look at the classes and interfaces of the agent in Chapter 6, "MBean Server." For now, all you need to do is create an agent instance and register the example MBean.

To create an instance of the agent, use the `MBeanServerFactory` class available in the `javax.management` package. This factory class contains a static method `createMBeanServer()` that will return a reference to an object implementing the agent. In the case of a Sun Microsystems reference implementation, you get back a reference to Sun's implementation of the agent; in the case of the Tivoli JMX implementation, you are returned a reference to Tivoli's JMX agent.

After you receive the agent reference, you can use it to register the `Hello` MBean implementation. The `MBeanServer` interface contains a `registerMBean()` method that you will use to register the Hello MBean component to the agent. The code to accomplish this is shown in Listing 1.3.

LISTING 1.3   Agent.java

```java
package book.jmx.examples;

import javax.management.*;


public class Agent {

    // the main method of the class
    public static void main(String[] args) {

        try {
            // create the agent reference
            MBeanServer server =
                MBeanServerFactory.createMBeanServer();

            // create reference to the MBean
            ObjectName name =
                new ObjectName("example:name=hello");

            // register Hello MBean
            server.registerMBean(new Hello(), name);
        }
        catch (MBeanRegistrationException e) {
          e.printStackTrace();
        }
        catch (NotCompliantMBeanException e) {
          e.printStackTrace();
        }
        catch (MalformedObjectNameException e) {
          e.printStackTrace();
        }
        catch (InstanceAlreadyExistsException e) {
          e.printStackTrace();
        }
    }
}
```

Listing 1.3 creates the agent and registers the MBean but does little else. To manipulate the MBean, you can either write more Java code to programmatically invoke methods of the MBean interface, or you can use existing management tools to change the attributes and invoke management operations on the Hello MBean.

For this example, you will use the tools provided by the Sun and Tivoli JMX implementations to view and manipulate the registered MBean. The MBean server itself is a local object to the Java Virtual Machine (JVM) and does not offer means to remotely connect to it. For all calls coming outside the JVM, remotely or from another process in the local machine, the JMX connectors or protocol adaptors are used. These components are often implemented as MBeans themselves, and registered as part of the agent, allowing a wide variety of connectivity to the MBean server. We will cover the architectural view of connectors and protocol adaptors in Chapter 2 and then implement some of them in the second part of the book.

You will use an HTTP protocol adaptor that both implementations provide to remotely manage the Hello MBean. Something you need to be aware of at this point is that the JMX specification, in its 1.0 version, does not define any standard protocol adaptors or connectors. This means that every time we discuss or use either an adaptor or a connector in this book, we have moved outside the scope of the current specification and are using JMX implementation specific features. Work is currently under way in the Java Community Process to define specifications for standard connectors, and it is likely that some of those will end up in the future versions of the JMX specification.

NOTE

JMX protocol adaptors and connectors are not part of the current 1.0 version of the JMX specification.

Java Specification Requests for JMX Connectors

Even though the current 1.0 version of the JMX specification does not specify the distributed services level of the management architecture, there is currently work under way in the Java Community Process (JCP) to standardize some JMX Connectors.

The JSR-070 proposes an IIOP-based protocol adaptor for JMX. The IIOP protocol-based adaptor would allow any CORBA-enabled application to connect and manage JMX-based management systems. This enables many existing management tools to connect to the JMX-based systems without complete rewrite, thus adding to the portability of the platform.

The JSR-148 proposes a specification describing how to map JMX instrumentation to the WBEM Common Information Model (CIM). The CIM model describes the management information in an implementation-neutral schema.

There are also plans to start the second phase of the JMX specification process that includes the client side of the distributed services level—how the client discovers and connects to remote JMX agents. At the time of this writing, no specification request had been submitted yet.

> For an up-to-date list of ongoing JSR efforts, check the Java Community Process (JCP)
> Web site at http://www.jcp.org. The list of all JSRs is available at
> http://www.jcp.org/jsr/all/.

Deployment with Sun JMX Reference Implementation

Sun provides an HTTP protocol adaptor with its JMX Reference Implementation in a class
com.sun.jdmk.comm.HtmlAdaptorServer. As you can see from the package name, it is not
part of the JMX API but a class from Sun's Java Dynamic Management Kit (JDMK) that is a
commercial product offered by Sun Microsystems.

You can download the reference implementation that includes the specification classes and some
additional classes, such as the HTTP adaptor, from Sun's Web site at http://java.sun.com/
products/JavaManagement/index.html. Download the reference implementation binary code
release and save and extract the zip onto your hard drive. The zip file contains the usual
JavaDoc API documentation, library jar files, and some sample code. For our example, we are
interested in two jar files in the jmx-1_0_1-ri_bin/jmx/lib directory—jmxri.jar and
jmxtools.jar.

The jmxri.jar file contains the JMX API classes required to compile the Java sources. It also
contains the implementation classes for the JMX agent. The jmxtools.jar file contains the
classes required by the Sun HTTP adaptor.

Extract the required files and compile the three classes you wrote (Hello.java, HelloMBean.java,
and Agent.java). Copy the three Java files and the Sun reference implementation zip package
to your working directory and execute the next set of commands.

The first command will unzip the archive using the Java archive tool to your working directory.
The second command will compile the three files we wrote for this example, using the libraries
in the archive that should be found under directory jmx-1_0_1-ri_bin/jmx/lib after the archive
is extracted. The third command will run the agent application.

For more detailed instructions on how to set up the Java development environment, the JMX
implementations, and other libraries needed in examples later, please refer to Appendix A,
"Environment Setup."

```
C:\Examples> jar -xf jmx-1_0-ri-bin.zip

C:\Examples> javac -d . -classpath .;jmx-1_0_1-ri_bin/jmx/lib/jmxri.jar;jmx-
➥1_0_1-ri_bin/jmx/lib/jmxtools.jar Hello.java HelloMBean.java Agent.java

C:\Examples> java -classpath .;jmx-1_0_1-ri_bin/jmx/lib/jmxri.jar; jmx-1_0_1-
➥ri_bin/jmx/lib/jmxtools.jar  book.jmx.examples.Agent
```

Unix and Linux users should notice that you will need to use a colon : separator in your classpath instead of the semicolon.

If everything worked correctly, you should have three compiled classes. If you encountered an error, please see the detailed setup instructions in Appendix A.

When you started the agent, you probably noticed that it did not do anything visible. It started and then immediately stopped. We will change that behavior next by adding a few lines to the agent that will create and register the Sun HTTP protocol adaptor implementation. The protocol adaptor itself is an MBean, so we will use the registerMBean() method call to register it to the MBean server. Again, remember that the adaptor is not part of the current 1.0 version of the JMX specification.

The code changes to the Agent.java file to register the HTTP adaptor are highlighted in Listing 1.4.

LISTING 1.4   Agent.java

```
...

    try {
      // create the agent reference
      MBeanServer server =
      MBeanServerFactory.createMBeanServer();

      // create reference to the MBean
      ObjectName name =
      new ObjectName("example:name=hello");

      // register Hello MBean
      server.registerMBean(new Hello(), name);

      // create the adaptor instance
      com.sun.jdmk.comm.HtmlAdaptorServer adaptor =
      new com.sun.jdmk.comm.HtmlAdaptorServer();

      // register the adaptor MBean to the agent
      server.registerMBean(adaptor,
      new ObjectName("adaptor:protocol=HTTP"));

      // start the adaptor
      adaptor.start();
    }
    catch (MBeanRegistrationException e) {
      e.printStackTrace();
    }

...
```

Compile the Agent.java file again and run it. Notice that the execution did not end immediately this time. This time, an HTTP adaptor instance was created, registered and started. The agent now has a thread waiting for incoming HTTP requests from the network. By default, the thread is listening for HTTP requests on port 8082. You can now open your Web browser and point it to the address http://localhost:8082. It should open the page shown in Figure 1.2.

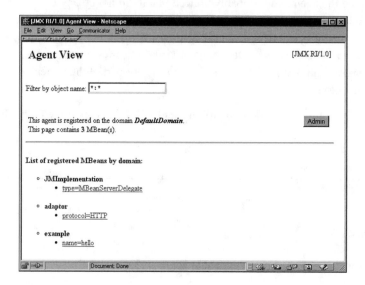

FIGURE 1.2
The HTML page generated by the Sun HTTP Adaptor.

Figure 1.2 shows the HTML page generated by the protocol adaptor. It lists the registered MBeans, including the HTTP adaptor MBean as well. The last entry on the page in Figure 1.2 shows your Hello MBean under the example domain with the name property set as hello. Click the link under Example and you will be able to manipulate the MBean.

On the next HTML page shown in Figure 1.3, you will see a list of the MBean's attributes. The attribute Name that we added as a read-write attribute to the Hello MBean is shown here with its type, access (RW), and value. The default value for Name is an empty string. You can change it by typing a new value in the text field, for example World, as can be seen in Figure 1.3. Click the Apply button and the Web browser will refresh the page displaying the new value in the text field. You have just changed the value of a managed attribute in the MBean.

Also one management operation is exposed in the MBean, the print() method. At the end of the HTML page in Figure 1.3, you will see the HTTP adaptor listing the MBean's management operations. The adaptor has included a Print button for the operation in the Web page. Click the button and the page will change to say Print Successful. Now go look at the console from which you started the agent and you should see it has printed the string

```
Hello, World!!
```

This is the result of executing the management operation on the MBean through a Web browser from a local machine. It could have just as easily been remotely over the network. You can try the remote access with a Web browser from another machine if you have a local network set up.

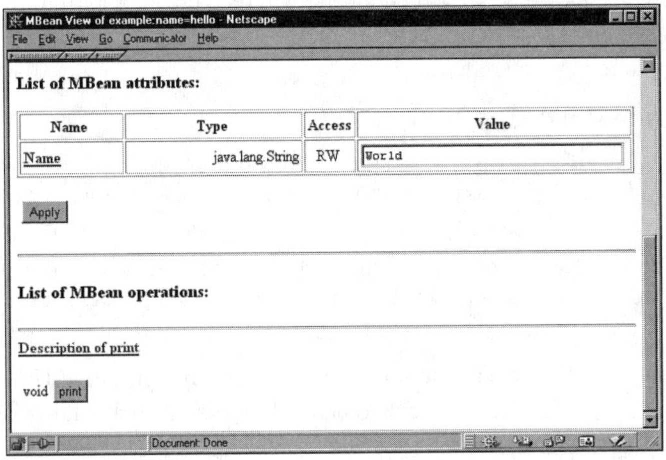

FIGURE 1.3
HTML View of the HelloMBean.

You have now created an MBean, registered it to the agent, manipulated its attributes, and invoked a management operation remotely via a Web page. As you hopefully noticed, creating the MBean was quite effortless and, in return, you have gained the ability to remotely manage a software component over the network via a Web browser.

Deployment with Tivoli JMX Implementation

The Tivoli JMX implementation works similarly to the Sun reference implementation. Remember that all of the MBean code you wrote is portable between the implementations. What you need to change is the Agent.java file to use a different HTTP adaptor class.

First download the Tivoli JMX implementation from IBM alphaWorks Web site at http://www.alphaworks.ibm.com. At the time of this writing, there are two distributions available, one for Windows NT and another for Sun Solaris. The packages contain some platform-specific code, but you are not going to need that so either one of the downloads should work. The following installation instructions are for the Windows NT package.

Extract the files from the zip. The `jmxc.jar` and `jmxx.jar` files contain the JMX API classes and the Tivoli JMX implementation classes. Inside the `jmxext.jar`, you can find the HTTP adaptor implementation in addition to other connector classes, for example the RMI connector. In the example, you will use only the HTTP adaptor.

To compile the agent using the Tivoli JMX implementation, execute the next sequence of commands. If you modified the `Agent.java` source to include references to Sun HTTP adaptor class earlier, remember to remove them first. Again, the first command will unzip the archive using the Java Archive tool. The second command will recompile all the Java files, this time with the Tivoli JMX libraries that can be found in the `tmx4j/base/lib` and `tmx4j/ext/lib` directories after extracting the archive.

```
C:\Examples> jar -xf tmx4j_NT_1_2.zip

C:\Examples> javac -d . -classpath .;tmx4j/base/lib/jmxc.jar;tmx4j/base/lib/
➥jmxx.jar;tmx4j/ext/lib/jmxext.jar Hello.java HelloMBean.java Agent.java


C:\Examples> java -classpath .;tmx4j/base/lib/jmxc.jar;tmx4j/base/lib/jmxx.jar;
➥tmx4j/base/lib/log.jar;tmx4j/ext/lib/jmxext.jar book.jmx.examples.Agent
```

You should be able to run the agent and it will execute once and then exit. Unix and Linux users need to remember to replace the semicolon in classpaths with a colon.

Now let's add the Tivoli HTTP adaptor to the agent code. The changes to add the adaptor to the original `Agent.java` file are in bold in Listing 1.5.

LISTING 1.5 `Agent.java`

```
...

    try {
        MBeanServer server =
            MBeanServerFactory.createMBeanServer();

        ObjectName name = new
            ObjectName("example:name=hello");
        server.registerMBean(new Hello(), name);

        // create the adaptor instance
        com.tivoli.jmx.http_pa.Listener adaptor =
            new com.tivoli.jmx.http_pa.Listener();
```

1

LISTING 1.5 Continued

```
    // register the adaptor MBean to the agent
    server.registerMBean(adaptor,
        new ObjectName("adaptor:protocol=HTTP"));

    // start the adaptor
    adaptor.startListener();
}
catch (IOException e) {
    e.printStackTrace();
}
catch (MBeanRegistrationException e) {
    e.printStackTrace();
}
```

...

Recompile and run the agent. This time the execution will not end immediately, and you can point your Web browser to the `http://localhost:6969` page. Notice that the default port number is different from the Sun reference implementation. When you start the agent, you should see the following message on the console.

```
The HTTP Adaptor started on port number 6969
```

When you open the browser, you will see a Find an MBean link on the front page. Click the link and it will open another page that will allow you to query the registered beans in the agent. In the query field, type the name of the MBean, `example:name=hello`. Be aware that the query string is case sensitive (see Figure 1.4).

After you submit the query, you will see a list of MBeans matching the `object name` filter. In this case, the result set has only one MBean, the Hello example. Click the link and a new page with the MBean's details will open. Notice that the agent has recognized the MBean's type as *standard (*see Figure 1.5*)*, it lists the attributes we have exposed in the MBean and it displays the `print()` operation that we declared in the MBean interface as a management operation. Click the `Name` attribute and change its value to **World**. Then click the `print()` operation and press the Invoke Operation button on the page that the browser opened. You should see the hello message in the agent console window.

```
Hello, World!!
```

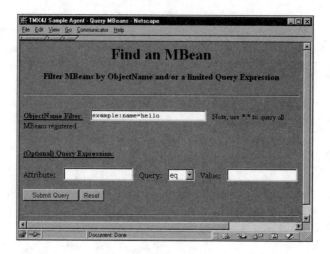

FIGURE 1.4

The HTML View generated by the Tivoli HTTP Adaptor.

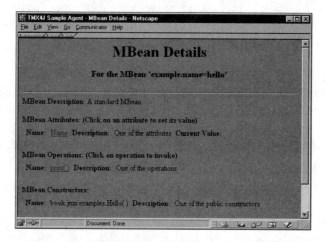

FIGURE 1.5

HTML View of the Hello *MBean.*

That is all there is to it to make the Hello MBean work with another JMX implementation. The only change we needed to make was to register a different HTTP protocol adaptor in the agent. The actual MBean code was portable and worked unchanged with both implementations using their specific Web-based management applications.

Summary

In this chapter, you saw how to define an interface for a Standard MBean, had a brief look at the JMX API, and created an instance of a management agent. You then proceeded to deploy the MBean on both Sun Microsystems' JMX reference implementation and Tivoli's JMX implementation. In both of these cases, you also saw how to start the implementation-specific HTTP adaptors and how they can be used to query and manipulate the MBean attributes and remotely invoke the management methods.

By now, you should have some basic idea how MBeans can be built and how generic management tools, such as the HTTP adaptor, can be used to manage resources without having to build custom management solutions and user interfaces for them. This gives you a solid base to proceed to the following chapters, which will take you into the details of the JMX specification.

For those curious to take a peek at the specification before continuing, you can download it from Sun's Web site at http://java.sun.com/products/JavaManagement/index.html. Also, there is a mailing list available for discussion of the specification that you can read at http://archives.java.sun.com/jmx-forum.html.

Architecture

IN THIS CHAPTER

The JMX specification divides the architecture of a JMX-based management system into three separate levels. Each level has a distinctive role in the architecture and addresses separate aspects of the architecture of a management system.

In this chapter, you will look at each level of the JMX architectural model, identifying the role of each level and how it should be used as part of the management system. Two of the levels—the agent level and the instrumentation level—are defined in the current 1.0 version of the JMX specification (see Figure 2.1). The third level—the distributed services level—is mostly unspecified at the time of this writing. However, you will still look at how the distributed services level fits into the JMX architecture model and later, in the second part of the book, go into detail on some possible implementations of the distributed services of the JMX architecture.

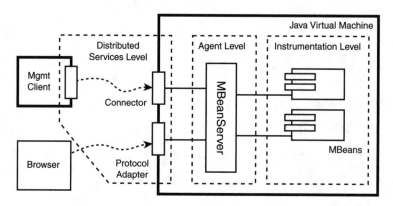

FIGURE 2.1

JMX Management Architecture.

The instrumentation level defines how to implement the MBeans to make the resources manageable by JMX-compliant management tools. The instrumentation level defines the MBean and four different types of MBeans—Standard MBean, Dynamic MBean, Model MBean, and Open MBean.

You will learn about the first three MBean types in detail in Chapters 3, "Standard MBeans, 4, "Dynamic MBeans, and 5, "Model MBeans." The Open MBean specification was still not finished in the 1.0 release of the JMX, so it is not a mandatory part of the JMX implementation and is subject to change. Consequently, none of the current JMX implementations can claim compliance with the Open MBean specification. A quick overview of Open MBeans is given in Appendix B, "Open MBeans."

In the agent level, the JMX specification defines the role of an MBean server. The MBean server is a key component in the management architecture and is responsible for delegating all the invocations between the management applications and the managed resources—acting as a communication bus between them. This isolates the managed resource from the management client, which creates flexibility in managing systems requiring high availability.

MBeans can be updated, redeployed, and moved between MBean servers without having to necessarily detach the client communication from the server. The management applications never directly reference the resource they manage. Instead, the agent level introduces a concept of *object names* that the client software uses as an indirect reference to the resource. You will see in later chapters that this is one of the key architectural designs in the JMX-based management solutions.

Finally, the distributed services level defines how the communication between the management applications and a remote agent or agent-to-agent communication should be implemented. This level is not yet specified by the current 1.0 version of the JMX specification, leaving most of the details open for interpretation. This is unfortunate because all remote communication between the clients and the MBean server becomes dependent on a specific JMX implementation. The distributed services level will be defined in the second phase of the JMX specification. At the time of this writing, there are some plans to get this second phase started. You will spend a good portion of the second part of this book in looking at implementation options for the distributed services of JMX.

2

ARCHITECTURE

History

The problem of managing applications partly stems from the wide variety of different types of software in existence today. There are applications ranging from simple helper tools, such as the infamous Notepad, to applications that handle critical business transactions. However, not all types of applications need a full-blown management system behind them. Notepad is quite an unlikely candidate to need a management system, whereas middleware servers handling the flow of business processes are very likely candidates for requiring a management infrastructure. The complexity, size, and criticality of the application are often the deciding factors.

Today, you increasingly see software that has become more and more distributed in nature. More software is being transformed from the traditional client/server two-tier architectures to three-tier or n-tier architectures. Many envision a future where software is run on a set of distributed servers on the network. Applications are built from components that support advanced, and somewhat complex features including transactions, clustering, fail-over, location transparency, and so on. New service-based platforms, such as the J2EE, are being designed and built, adding new services and component types to applications. The new development is focused on techniques to maximize the potential for scalability. By breaking functions into smaller components, the application can be spread across many servers, in many different ways. This will result in increased reliability.

However, all this adds to the complexity of managing an application. The application has become more dynamic. It changes during its lifetime, new software components and plug-ins are added, old ones are removed and the existing ones replaced and patched. The application can exist in various, highly different environments, from the client desktop to the server machine, from a cell phone to an air traffic control system. The architecture, the size and the runtime environment among different types of software in use today varies enormously.

Often, you find that many of the different types of applications have one thing in common—they somehow need to be managed. You need to enable the administrator to make adjustments to the application's configuration, fine-tune it, update it, and monitor its performance. You also want to provide the tools for administrators to do this easily. And more than likely, you do want to build the management system that allows all this just once, instead of implementing it individually per application.

Some standards have emerged during the years, some were designed by committees, some were picked up out of necessity. For example, the Simple Network Management Protocol (SNMP) is currently the *de facto* standard for network and device management. The Distributed Management Task Force (DMTF) has defined a Common Information Model (CIM) and a Web-based Enterprise Management (WBEM) using XML schemas. Big industry names, such as IBM and Computer Associates among others, offer their own proprietary technology and solutions to manage the IT infrastructure.

JMX offers uniformity to implementing management systems in Java programming language. The MBeans are generic enough to be able to represent many different types of manageable resources: applications, services, software components, and even devices. The JMX management architecture is independent of any specific network protocol, supporting several different connector implementations. Tools can be built to interoperate with existing management applications that support different management models, such as the Management Information Base (MIB) used with SNMP based management or CIM/WBEM models. Most notably, you can easily enable the management of your existing applications to JMX compliant management tools by exposing the management properties of your application via the JMX MBeans.

Overview

The management architecture proposed by the JMX specification aims to provide the management capability to Java applications with as little development effort as possible. The core of the architecture is the agent that is a fairly lightweight invocation bus between the management applications and the managed resources. The agent can be configured, as necessary, with a set of connectors to provide the remote access and a set of different agent service MBeans. The component-based approach to building the management agent allows greater scalability between different operating environments. The core component of the agent, the MBean server, is simple enough to be implemented for different runtime environments, ranging from J2ME to J2EE platforms. In addition to the core agent services defined in the specification, other additional services can be developed by JMX implementers. These agent services, like all MBeans, can be dynamically loaded, updated, and unloaded in the JMX management architecture.

Also, the JMX specification defines the instrumentation of resources in a generic fashion that allows any Java object to be managed. There are no specific management models for known component types but one generic way to enable all management of Java resources—servlets, EJBs, users, and so on. New component types, as well as the existing ones, can use the same methods to expose a management interface.

Instrumentation Level

The instrumentation level defines how you can create JMX manageable resources. JMX manageable resources can be managed by using any JMX-compliant management application. A managed resource can be a Java object representing an application, a software component, service, a device, and so on.

The manageable resources are created through MBeans. The instrumentation level defines two basic MBean types—Standard MBeans and Dynamic MBeans. In addition, two extensions of the Dynamic MBeans are defined—Model MBeans and Open MBeans. The Standard, Dynamic, and Model MBeans are a mandatory part of the specification and are implemented by all compliant JMX implementations. The Open MBeans are not mandatory or fully-defined in the 1.0 version of the JMX specification.

MBeans can represent not only the application resources (such as a servlet, a user, or a modem) that you want to manage, but also a number of services and JMX infrastructure components that can also be managed. The agent level can add connectors, protocol adaptors, or agent services and register them as MBeans, making parts of the agent level itself manageable through the instrumentation level. MBeans can discover and invoke other MBeans registered to the server and use the services offered by other MBeans to help in management of the resource.

In addition to the MBeans, the instrumentation level defines a notification mechanism. The notifications can be used between MBeans, MBean servers, and management applications to broadcast information to interested listeners. Notice that the distribution of the notifications to remote systems is not specified in version 1.0 of JMX.

2

ARCHITECTURE

All MBeans expose a management interface via the JMX agent. The management interface consists of management attributes, operations, notification, and constructors. The management interface is described by a set of metadata classes. The management applications can discover the management interface of an MBean by querying the MBean server at the agent level.

Standard MBeans are built by declaring a Java interface that the MBean implements. The Standard MBean interface uses a set of naming conventions that allows the agent to discover and build the metadata of the management interface. Standard MBeans are often the simplest type of MBean to design and implement. However, they do lack in their ability to extend the management interface with behavioral properties (see Chapter 5, "Model MBeans") and cannot be used to create the management interface dynamically at runtime.

Dynamic MBeans are created by implementing a generic `DynamicMBean` interface. This interface allows the agent to retrieve the management interface metadata from the MBean at registration. The `DynamicMBean` interface also declares the methods for invoking management operations and manipulating the management attributes. Dynamic MBeans do not have the compile-time restriction on declaring their management interface that Standard MBeans do. This allows for greater flexibility in creating the management interface at runtime, for example, by retrieving the relevant information from a database.

Model MBeans extend the Dynamic MBeans by the introduction of descriptor objects. The descriptors allow the developer to extend the management interface metadata by defining behavioral properties that can be attached to each individual element of the metadata. Model MBeans provide a generic management template that can be used to create and configure management of existing classes.

Agent Level

The agent level consists of the MBean server and a set of agent services that build on the instrumentation level. The agent level itself does not address the distribution or remote access but uses the distributed services described in "Distributed Services Level" section later in this chapter.

The JMX agent acts as a communication channel between the management applications and MBeans representing the managed resources. One of the responsibilities of the agent level is to decouple the management applications from the resource implementation. The management applications never reference the resources they manage directly; they always invoke all management operations through the JMX agent using *object name* references.

The central component in the agent level is the MBean server. The MBean server acts as a registry for MBeans and allows management applications to discover the management interface of the registered MBeans. The `MBeanServer` interface also declares the required methods for creating and querying MBeans and the methods for invoking and manipulating MBean operations and attributes.

The agent level also consists of a set of agent services. Four such services are defined by the JMX specification—M-Let service, Timer service, Monitoring service, and Relation service. All of these standard agent services are implemented as MBeans themselves. This allows parts of the agent level to become manageable as well.

The M-Let service allows MBeans to be loaded from the network and included to the agent dynamically at runtime. The Timer service can be used as a scheduler that sends notifications to MBeans or management applications at a given date and time or at intervals. The Monitoring service includes MBeans that can act as observers of other MBeans' management attributes and send notifications on attribute changes. The Relation service allows associations to be created between MBeans and maintains the consistency of created relations. All of the four aforementioned standard services are mandatory, so you can expect to find them in all compliant JMX agent implementations (see Figure 2.2).

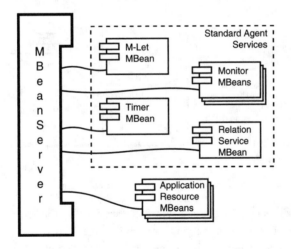

FIGURE 2.2
Agent services are specified as MBeans, which allows them to be managed from outside the agent's JVM.

In addition to the potential agent service MBeans, the agent, in most cases, is accompanied by at least one JMX connector or protocol adaptor. The connectors and protocol adaptors are part of the distributed service level discussed in the "Distributed Services Level" section later in this chapter. In practice, all JMX implementations provide at least one connector or protocol adaptor that can be registered to the agent as an MBean, thus adding the remote access possibilities to the agent.

The MBean server and standard agent services are discussed in Chapter 6, "MBean Server," and Chapter 7, "Standard Agent Services."

Invocation Mechanism

The management applications are decoupled from the managed resources by introducing *object names* references that represent registered MBeans in the agent. The management applications reference the MBeans by passing an object name reference to the agent with each operation. The MBean server that contains the registry of the MBeans will then look up the corresponding MBean Java reference from its internal repository and invoke the corresponding operation or attribute on the MBean, as shown in Figure 2.3.

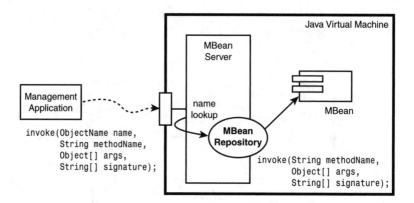

FIGURE 2.3

Invocation sequence from the management application to the managed resource.

Because the invocation is generic and not typed to a specific Java interface, there is no need to redistribute new Java classes when the management interface evolves. In the case of a large graph of components with dependencies to the services provided by other components, the changes occurring due to maintenance will have a much less widespread effect on the system. Notice, however, that this requires you to give up the type checking provided by the Java compiler. You should carefully consider when and where to apply the JMX invocation semantics. JMX allows a lot of flexibility from decoupling the managed resource and introducing the detyped invocation, but in doing so, you nullify some of the assets of the compile time type checking.

Distributed Services Level

The 1.0 version of the JMX specification does not address the distribution of the JMX archi-tecture. However, a brief overview of the distributed services level is given and is described in this section.

As was mentioned previously in the "Agent Level" section, the MBean server in the agent level does not implement remote access methods. The remoteness in the agent is achieved by con-figuring the JMX agent with one or more JMX connector or protocol adaptor MBeans. The connectors and protocol adaptors allow the management applications to access a remote JMX agent via specific protocols. This allows the management applications from different JVMs to invoke management operations on the MBean server, get or set management attributes, instan-tiate and register new MBeans, and register and receive notifications from the managed resources.

JMX connectors are split into two different components. On the server side, the agent registers a connector server that is able to receive remote method invocations from the management client. On the client side, the connector provides an object that implements a remote view to the MBean server that the client can use to transparently invoke an operation on a remote MBean server. Both the connector client and server are specific to a certain protocol. However, the management client can switch between different connector implementations because the different implementations should ideally implement the same remote interface to the MBean server. What the remote MBean server interface will be like exactly is determined by the sec-ond phase of the JMX specification.

Protocol adaptors adapt the operations of the MBean server into a representation of a given protocol or possibly into a different information model altogether, such as the SNMP Management Information Base (MIB) or DMTF Common Information Model (CIM) models. The management applications that connect to protocol adaptors are typically legacy manage-ment solutions or non-Java management tools interoperating with the JMX-based management systems.

Connectors and protocol adaptors are discussed in more detail in Chapter 9, "Connectors and Protocol Adaptors," and Chapter 10, "JMX Distribution Layer with J2EE Services."

Summary

The JMX architecture divides the management system implementation into three separate lev-els. The instrumentation level defines the mechanisms for creating manageable resources with as little impact to the development effort as possible. The instrumentation level is also generic enough to enable the management of applications, software components, services, and devices.

The agent level decouples the management applications from the resources. The MBean server is the core component of the agent level—a lightweight invocation bus between the management clients and the resource. The agent level can be configured dynamically to meet the needs of the management system by registering agent services to the MBean server. These services benefit from the instrumentation level, adding manageability to the agent level as well.

The distributed services level defines how management clients can connect to the agent and how agent-to-agent communication is implemented. The MBean server itself is not accessible through any remote invocation mechanism; it needs at least one connector or protocol adaptor registered to it for remote manageability. Remember that the distributed services level is not fully defined in the first phase of the JMX specification.

Standard MBeans

IN THIS CHAPTER

In this chapter, we will discuss all the aspects of instrumentation using Standard MBeans.

First, you will look at the formal definition of an MBean, as defined in the JMX specification. You will then go through the naming conventions and properties of Standard MBeans and see how to implement the management interface using the Standard MBean mechanism. At the end of this chapter, you will look at the notification mechanism defined in the JMX specification and see how it can be used for communication between the managed component and the management application.

In this chapter, you will write example code to demonstrate the features of Standard MBeans. You will later use the same base example to implement Dynamic MBeans and compare the two different kinds of instrumentation of managed components. Also, familiarizing yourself with the JMX notification mechanism is important at this point, because it will be featured in the subsequent chapters of the book.

MBean Definition

MBeans must be concrete Java classes. That is the first requirement for all MBeans, regardless of their type. The MBean must be declared as a public, non-abstract class. Classes with package-only visibility or abstract classes are not compliant MBeans. The public, non-abstract class requirement is to ensure that the agent is able to instantiate the MBean on request.

For this same reason, an MBean must have at least one public constructor. An MBean is allowed to have any number of constructors that can be defined using the usual Java visibility rules with keywords `public`, `private`, or `protected`. Nevertheless, at least one of the constructors must be public. Also, the constructor is allowed to have any number of parameters of any type. However, remember that it is the developer's or the administrator's responsibility to make sure all the classes used in the constructor parameter list are available to the agent when it needs to instantiate the MBean.

In the Hello MBean example we built in Chapter 1, "Getting Started," you didn't declare any constructors at all. However, both of the agent implementations you used accepted the component as a valid MBean. In the example, a default constructor was used. A default constructor is a `public` constructor that takes no arguments. Therefore, the `Hello` class was a valid MBean. However, keep in mind that the default constructor is only guaranteed when you do not explicitly declare any other constructors, regardless of their visibility.

The `MBean` class must implement its own corresponding MBean interface or a `DynamicMBean` interface. If an MBean implements its own statically-typed Java interface, it is called a Standard MBean. Dynamic MBeans implement the `DynamicMBean` interface. We will cover the Dynamic MBeans in detail in the next chapter.

These are the three rules you need to remember when developing your MBeans.

- An MBean must be a public, non-abstract class.
- An MBean must have at least one public constructor.
- An MBean must implement its own corresponding MBean interface or implement the `DynamicMBean` interface.

Implementing Standard MBeans

The main constraint for writing a Standard MBean is the requirement to declare a statically typed Java interface that explicitly declares the management attributes and operations of an MBean. In some cases, having to declare such a rigid programmatic structure to expose the management interface may not be desirable. Usually, however, the Standard MBean mechanism is the simplest and most convenient method for bringing new Java classes into the JMX realm.

The naming conventions used in the MBean interface follow closely the rules set by the JavaBeans component model. To expose the management attributes, you declare getter and setter methods, similar to JavaBean component properties. There are some differences however, especially in the way the JMX agent takes into consideration the inheritance structure of the MBeans, which makes the naming conventions used by the Standard MBeans specific to the JMX specification. We will go through the naming conventions and see examples of the inheritance patterns in the next few pages.

The Hello MBean example used in Chapter 1 was a Standard MBean. We declared a statically typed Java interface called `HelloMBean` that was implemented by the resource class `Hello`. It is important to notice that the suffix of the interface name, `MBean`, is significant. The agent uses introspection on the MBean class to determine which interfaces the class implements. The agent will recognize the class as a Standard MBean type if it finds it implementing an interface with a corresponding MBean suffix in the name. For example, a `User` class implementing a `UserMBean` interface is recognized by the agent as a Standard MBean.

Let's take a closer look at the attribute naming conventions next.

Standard MBean Attributes

Management attributes are named characteristics of an MBean. With Standard MBeans, attributes are defined in the MBean interface via the use of naming conventions in the interface methods. There are three kinds of attributes, read-only, write-only, and read-write attributes. The agent determines what kind of attribute has been declared by introspecting the method naming in the MBean interface.

Read-only attributes are defined by declaring only a getter method in the interface. The naming for the getter follows the same rules as with the JavaBeans component model. In other words, a `getAttribute()` method defines a read-only attribute named `Attribute`. Similarly, you define a write-only attribute by declaring only a setter method in the MBean interface, for example, `setAttribute()`. If you declare both the getter and setter method, the agent will determine the attribute `Attribute` is a read-write type.

The naming convention for MBean attributes is as follows:

```
public AttributeType getAttributeName();
public void setAttributeName(AttributeType value);
```

Attributes can be any valid Java type. You can use the standard Java classes such as `String`, `Integer`, and `Boolean`, or you can use your own classes as attribute types. Java primitive types, such as `int` or `byte`, are acceptable as well. You can also use an array of any valid Java type. Remember that if you use your own classes, the classes need to be available to the agent at runtime.

There are some restrictions to defining the MBean attributes. You cannot overload attribute accessor methods. For example, you cannot declare an MBean attribute of Java type `int` that has overloaded setter method, such as follows:

```
public void setAttributeName(int value);
public void setAttributeName(String value);   // NOT COMPLIANT!
```

Overloading an attribute setter method will lead to a non-compliant MBean.

Another restriction worth noting is the fact that attributes based on arrays can only have getter and setter methods that deal with the entire array all at once. In other words, you cannot declare a setter method for an attribute of Java type `int[]` that will set, for example, the value of the first item in the array. You will have to declare a setter method that operates on the entire array of integers instead. A workaround for this is to declare a management operation that will manipulate single entries in the array. You will see an example of how to do this in the "Standard MBean Example" section later in the chapter.

For `boolean` types, the Standard MBean naming conventions allow two alternative ways to declare the getter method. For example, for a management attribute named `Active`, you can declare either a getter method, `getActive()` or `isActive()`, in the management interface. Both methods will be recognized as accessors to the `Active` attribute. The `isActive()` form of declaration also implies the `boolean` type for the given management attribute.

The naming convention for `boolean` types can be expressed as follows:

```
public boolean isAttributeName();
```

Note, however, that you cannot use both the getAttributeName() method and isAttributeName() method for the same attribute in the MBean interface. You will have to pick one of the two methods.

MBean attribute names are case sensitive. Declaring two accessor methods for attributes that differ in capitalization will lead to two separate MBean attributes exposed by the agent.

Management Operations

Management operations for Standard MBeans include all the methods declared in the MBean interface that are not recognized by the agent as being either a read or write method to an attribute. The operations don't have to follow any specific naming rules as long as they do not intervene with the management attribute naming conventions.

The management operations can have return values. The returned values can be of any valid Java type, either primitive type or reference type. In case of the generic management tools, such as the two HTTP protocol adaptors we used earlier, it is up to the adaptor to decide how to deal with the return value. If the management application is aware of the semantics of the return value of the operation it has invoked, it may react to the return value in a specific way. Depending on the return value, the management application may attempt to display the returned object to the user, send a notification based on the value of the returned object, or execute other management code or business logic.

Exceptions in the Management Interface

When creating the Standard MBean interface, you can declare the methods to throw any type of exception as per the rules of Java programming language. The exception types can be those included in the Java standard libraries, such as the java.io.IOException, or they can be custom application exceptions declared by the application developer.

When the agent invokes a method of the management interface, whether a management operation method or management attribute's accessor method, it will catch all the instances of java.lang.Throwable and its subclasses if thrown. The agent will wrap the checked exceptions in a javax.management.MBeanException class and then proceed to propagate this exception to the originating caller. Unchecked exceptions—subclasses of RuntimeException—will be wrapped in a javax.management.RuntimeMBeanException class. Similarly, all errors thrown by the MBean implementation will be wrapped in javax.management.RuntimeErrorException.

Both the RuntimeMBeanException and MBeanException implement a getTargetException() method that allows you to access the original exception that was thrown in the MBean. The RuntimeErrorException implements a getRuntimeError() method for retrieving the error thrown by the MBean.

The methods in the MBeanServer interface used for accessing the MBeans, such as setAttribute(), getAttribute() and invoke(), declare the checked exception class MBeanException to be thrown, and, therefore, require a try–catch block in the management client. In the exception handling code, the client can extract the actual target exception and react accordingly.

Standard MBean Example

So far, you have learned several details about Standard MBeans, and now it is time to put that knowledge into practice with a code example. In the next few pages, you will define and implement a User resource and create a management interface for it. The User resource is not specific to any existing system. It is an abstract construct that stores the user ID, name, address, and phone numbers. It should be easy to see a User resource as part of many information systems. Managing users is a common administrative task in many environments.

You will define five attributes for the management interface of the user object. First, the user has a read-only attribute ID. The ID represents a unique identifier for this particular user, such as a primary key in the database. You will also define read-write attributes Name and Address. These two string attributes can be used to store the user's name and address.

```
public long getID();
public String getName();
public void setName(String name);
public String getAddress();
public void setAddress(String address);
```

To demonstrate the use of arrays, define an array-based attribute PhoneNumbers. It's a string array containing a maximum of three telephone numbers.

```
public String[] getPhoneNumbers();
public void setPhoneNumbers(String[] numbers);
```

Last, there is a write-only attribute Password. Because you only declare a setter method for this attribute, which makes it write-only, you can set a new password for the user via the management interface. But you are unable to read the stored password after you've set it. This prevents the HTTP adaptor from displaying the contents of the Password attribute on the Web page.

```
public void setPassword(String passwd);
```

Naturally, any management operation dealing with sensitive information, such as passwords, must be properly secured. The JMX specification does not currently define security features for MBeans. In practice, this responsibility is left mostly to the distributed services level and agent level of the JMX architecture—the connectors, protocol adaptors and the JMX agent.

In addition to the five attributes, you declare three operations for this MBean component. Two of the operations, addPhoneNumber() and removePhoneNumber(), are used for modifying individual elements of the PhoneNumbers array. The third operation, printInfo(), is used for printing the contents of the User object—name, address, and phone numbers. This time, you won't print the information to the console, as you did with the Hello example in Chapter 1. Instead, you declare the printInfo() operation to return a string value.

Listing 3.1 is the complete declaration of the management interface.

LISTING 3.1 UserMBean.java

```
package book.jmx.examples;

public interface UserMBean {

    // read-only attribute 'ID'
    public long getID();

    // read-write attribute 'Name'
    public String getName();
    public void setName(String name);

    // read-write attribute 'Address'
    public String getAddress();
    public void setAddress(String address);

    // read-write array attribute 'PhoneNumbers'
    public String[] getPhoneNumbers();
    public void setPhoneNumbers(String[] numbers);

    // write-only attribute 'Password'
    public void setPassword(String passwd);

    // management operations
    public String printInfo();
    public void addPhoneNumber(String number);
    public void removePhoneNumber(int index);
}
```

3

STANDARD MBEANS

In the MBean implementation, you will store the attribute values to object fields id, name, address, password, and numbers. This is a very straightforward assignment from parameters to fields. However, there are a couple of things you should notice.

In the example, the setID() method of the User class is implemented. Notice that you did not declare this method in the MBean interface. This is a usual practice in cases where the methods in the resource class are not meant to be exposed for management applications. In the User class, the reading of the ID attribute is allowed for management applications, but the ability to write the ID value is reserved for the application's internal methods only. The user of the management application will not be able to change the value of this attribute. For the ID value, the creation time of the object instance is used because a database or directory is not set up for this example.

The methods addPhoneNumber() and removePhoneNumber() have been implemented and exposed for management. They allow you to modify individual entries in the array attribute PhoneNumbers. The addPhoneNumber() method tries to add the string given as parameter to the first entry in the array containing a null reference. The removePhoneNumber() method will set the array entry to null for the given index.

Listing 3.2 is the full source code of the managed resource.

LISTING 3.2   User.java

```java
package book.jmx.examples;

public class User implements UserMBean  {

    private long id          = System.currentTimeMillis();
    private String name      = "";
    private String address   = "";
    private String password  = null;
    private String[] numbers = new String[3];


    // read-only attribute 'ID'
    public long getID() {
        return id;
    }


    // application method, not exposed to management
    public void setID(long id) {
        this.id = id;
    }


    // read-write attribute 'Name'
    public String getName() {
        return name;
    }
    public void setName(String name) {
```

LISTING 3.2   continued

```
      this.name = name;
   }


   // read-write attribute 'Address'
   public String getAddress() {
      return address;
   }
   public void setAddress(String address) {
      this.address = address;
   }


   // read-write array attribute 'PhoneNumbers'
   public String[] getPhoneNumbers() {
      return numbers;
   }
   public void setPhoneNumbers(String[] numbers) {
      this.numbers = numbers;
   }


   // write-only attribute 'Password'
   public void setPassword(String passwd) {
      this.password = passwd;
   }


   // management operations
   public String printInfo() {
      return
        "User: " + getName() +"\n"+
        "Address: " + getAddress() +"\n"+
        "Phone #: " + getPhoneNumbers()[0] +"\n"+
        "Phone #: " + getPhoneNumbers()[1] +"\n"+
        "Phone #: " + getPhoneNumbers()[2] +"\n";
   }

   public void addPhoneNumber(String number) {
      for (int i = 0; i < numbers.length; ++i)
         if (numbers[i] == null) {
            numbers[i] = number;
            break;
         }
```

3

STANDARD
MBEANS

LISTING 3.2 continued

```
    }

    public void removePhoneNumber(int index) {
        if (index < 0 || index >= numbers.length)
            return;

        numbers[index] = null;
    }
}
```

User Client

Next, you will build a simple management client for the MBean to demonstrate the use of the User MBean. The client will operate in the same Java Virtual Machine as the JMX agent but will be useful to show the programmatic invocation of the MBeans. Later, after you have read about the JMX connectors in Part II, "JMX in the J2EE Platform," you can also invoke the same MBeans using a wide variety of different protocol and messaging mechanisms.

As was shown in Chapter 2, "Architecture," where management architecture was covered, the MBeans themselves are never directly exposed to the management clients. What the management applications have access to is the agent layer of the JMX architecture, which offers the programmatic interface to manipulate the managed resources. This layer of indirection between the management application and the managed resource creates the decoupled nature of the JMX-based management systems. The only static information known to the management application about the resource is its name, which was used to register the component to the agent, and is represented by the ObjectName instance. Any change to the management interface of the resource is kept local between the resource and the agent. In effect, this decouples the management applications from the resources, and changes to the resources, as they evolve and go through maintenance, can be isolated.

Listing 3.3 should clearly explain this nature of the Java Management Extensions. As you will see, the name of the managed resource is involved in all invocations to the agent, which will then proceed to propagate the invocation to the correct managed resource known to it. Notice that you never at any point have a direct Java reference to the resource on which you invoke the operations. You should also notice that all the invocations to management operations are generic, and all the type information—in other words, the operation's signatures—are passed to the agent as string types instead of statically-typed method calls. This type of invocation is crucial to systems built for very long uptimes where new components are introduced to the system dynamically and the old ones are upgraded by hot-deploying the software components.

The whole agent API will be covered in Chapter 6, "Mbean Server," but for now look at two methods of the `MBeanServer` interface needed to use in the client—the `setAttributes()` and `invoke()` methods.

The `setAttributes()`, as the name implies, is used to set the management attributes of an MBean. The `setAttributes()` method takes an `ObjectName` instance and an `AttributeList` instance as its parameters, where the `ObjectName` is the name of the MBean registered to the agent, and the `AttributeList` is a collection of `Attribute` objects representing the management attributes.

The `invoke()` method of the MBeanServer is declared as follows (exceptions have been left out for the sake of brevity).

```
public Object invoke(ObjectName name, String operationName,
                     Object[] params, String[] signature)
```

As you can see, there is no static type information involved in the invocation. The return value and parameters are passed as generic objects, the MBean instance to receive the invocation is identified by its object name, and the operation name and its signature are passed as strings. On the one hand, this kind of detyping of the invocation leads to a system capable of dynamically changing while maintaining high-availability capabilities. On the other hand, it puts you, the developer, in a position where extra rigor is needed in implementation. You should be extra careful when writing the invocations to avoid simple typos or disarranged signatures. Smart use of refactoring techniques to avoid replicating the invocations and use of constants and other measures are recommended.

Now that you are aware of the double-edged sword of the invocation and can handle it with care, take a look at the `UserClient` code. The management code to handle the programmatic invocation of management operations is shown in Listing 3.3.

LISTING 3.3   `UserClient.java`

```java
package book.jmx.examples;

import javax.management.*;
import java.util.List;

public class UserClient {

    public void run() {

        // Find an agent from this JVM. Null argument will return
        // a list of all MBeanServer instances.
        List srvrList = MBeanServerFactory.findMBeanServer(null);
```

LISTING 3.3   continued

```
MBeanServer server =
    (MBeanServer)srvrList.iterator().next();

try {
   // register the MBean
   ObjectName name = new ObjectName("example:name=user");
   server.registerMBean(new User(), name);

   // Invoke the printInfo operation on an
   // uninitialized MBean instance.
   Object result = server.invoke(
                    name,           // MBean name
                    "printInfo",    // operation name
                    null,           // no parameters
                    null            // void signature
                );

   System.out.println("Non-initialized User object:");
   System.out.println(result);

   // Create the list of management attribute value pairs
   AttributeList list = new AttributeList();
   list.add(new Attribute("Name", "John"));
   list.add(new Attribute("Address", "Strawberry Street"));
   list.add(new Attribute("PhoneNumbers", new String[]
                    {
                      "555-1232",
                      null,
                      null
                    }
                ));

   // Init the MBean instance by calling setAttributes()
   server.setAttributes(name, list);

   // Invoke the printInfo to retrieve the updated state
   result = server.invoke(
                    name,           // MBean name
                    "printInfo",    // operation name
                    null,           // no parameters
                    null            // void signature
                );

   System.out.println("Initialized User object:");
```

LISTING 3.3   continued

```
        System.out.println(result);
    }
    catch (MalformedObjectNameException e) {
        e.printStackTrace();
    }
    catch (InstanceNotFoundException e) {
        e.printStackTrace();
    }
    catch (MBeanException e) {
        e.getTargetException().printStackTrace();
    }
    catch (ReflectionException e) {
        e.printStackTrace();
    }
    catch (InstanceAlreadyExistsException e) {
        e.printStackTrace();
    }
    catch (NotCompliantMBeanException e) {
        e.printStackTrace();
    }

}

/**
 * Main method for the client. This will instantiate an agent
 * and register the User MBean to it.
 */
public static void main(String[] args) {

    MBeanServer server =
            MBeanServerFactory.createMBeanServer();

    new UserClient().run();
}
}
```

At the main() method, the JMX agent instance is created with the createMBeanServer()
method of the MBeanServerFactory class. Then the run() method is invoked, which implements the client logic. The client first tries to find a reference to the MBeanServer. This is
achieved by using the MBeanServerFactory class and its findMBeanServer() method. The
findMBeanServer() method will return an agent reference based on either an agent identifier,
which can be passed as a parameter, or a list of all known MBean server instances found in the

JVM. The UserClient code uses the latter option, and picks the first reference from the returned list, knowing that, in the case of this specific example, the only MBean server instance in the JVM is the one created in the main() method.

Next, you create the ObjectName instance that identifies the MBean in the agent. The object name represents the reference to the MBean, which the agent will know how to map to a Java reference to the managed resource. Remember that this is the mechanism keeping the management client decoupled from the resource implementation.

After you have created the ObjectName instance and registered the MBean to the server, you can use the MBean server to invoke the printInfo() operation. It returns a formatted string containing the managed resource's state.

To compile and run the code using Sun reference implementation, execute the following two commands:

```
C:\Examples> javac -d . -classpath .;jmx-1_0_1-ri_bin/jmx/lib/jmxri.jar
➡ UserClient.java User.java UserMBean.java

C:\Examples> java -classpath .;jmx-1_0_1-ri_bin/jmx/lib/jmxri.jar
➡ book.jmx.examples.UserClient
```

The client should output the following:

```
Non-initialized User object:
User:
Address:
Phone #: null
Phone #: null
Phone #: null
```

As you can see, none of the fields in the resource have been initialized yet. Next you build an AttributeList object containing the attributes you want to set on the MBean. The AttributeList contains instances of Attribute objects that represent the management attributes in our managed bean—Name, Address, and PhoneNumbers.

When the AttributeList has been created and initialized, you set all of the attributes with the setAttributes() call and invoke the printInfo operation again. This time, the output contains the attribute values you passed to the agent.

```
Initialized User object:
User: John
Address: Strawberry Street
```

```
Phone #: 555-1232
Phone #: null
Phone #: null
```

You can also try the User MBean with the JMX HTTP adapter that was tested in Chapter 1. You will need to alter the `Agent.java` from the `Hello` example (Listing 1.4 in Chapter 1) to register the User MBean component to the agent. The changes are shown in Listing 3.4.

To compile and run execute the following commands (using Sun Reference Implementation), use the following:

```
C:\Examples> javac -d . -classpath .;jmx-1_0_1-ri_bin/jmx/lib/jmxri.jar;
➡jmx-1_0_1-ri_bin/jmx/lib/jmxtools.jar
➡User.java UserMBean.java Agent.java

C:\Examples> java -classpath .;jmx-1_0_1-ri_bin/jmx/lib/jmxri.jar;
➡jmx-1_0_1-ri_bin/jmx/lib/jmxtools.jar
➡book.jmx.examples.Agent
```

LISTING 3.4   Agent.java

```
...

    try {
        // create the agent reference
        MBeanServer server =
            MBeanServerFactory.createMBeanServer();

        // create object name reference
        ObjectName name =
            new ObjectName("example:name=user");

        // register Hello MBean
        server.registerMBean(new User(), name);

        // create the adaptor instance
        com.sun.jdmk.comm.HtmlAdaptorServer adaptor =
            new com.sun.jdmk.comm.HtmlAdaptorServer();

        ...

    }
```

Enter the query for the User component name, `example:name=user` and click the link to open the management view of the MBean (see Figure 3.1).

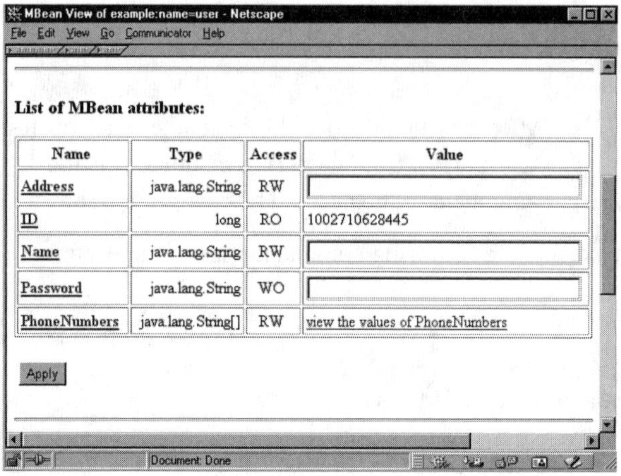

FIGURE 3.1

HTTP Adaptor view of the User MBean.

Now fill in some attribute values for Name, Address, and Password. Try viewing the values of PhoneNumbers and use the management operations addPhoneNumber() and removePhoneNumber() to add and remove single entries to the array.

The User MBean example covers the most common features of the Standard MBeans. You have written a simple management client and programmatically invoked operations on the MBean. You have seen, at the code level, the implications of decoupling the management applications from the managed resources and the agent's role in providing the said indirection. You have also seen examples of all three kinds of management attributes—read-only, write-only and read-write—as well as an example of an array-based attribute.

Next, you will look at how the inheritance of the Standard MBean management interfaces are interpreted by the agent, and how inheritance can be used to enable management of existing Java resources.

Inheritance Patterns

In the case of Standard MBeans, the management interface can be inherited from the super-class. It is also possible for the subclass to override the management interface of its ancestor by declaring its own management interface. You will now see how the agent determines the actual management interface of a Standard MBean and then investigate the inheritance patterns.

The most common case, which you have seen with the two Standard MBean examples so far, is to have the MBean class directly implement its own management interface. However, it is also possible for an MBean to inherit its management interface from a superclass. For example, you could create a subclass of the User class—implemented in the previous chapter—and call it Guest. In this case, the Guest class inherits the methods and fields of its superclass as per the usual Java language inheritance rules, but it also inherits the management interface of its superclass. When the Guest component is registered to the agent, the agent will first look for a management interface matching the naming conventions for the Guest class. If the agent does not find the GuestMBean interface, it will traverse the inheritance tree of the Guest class to find the ancestor User. For the User class, the agent will find the matching management interface declaration. Therefore, the Guest class is a compliant MBean and exposes the same attributes and operations as its ancestor User. The management applications will be able to manipulate the Guest instances by using the same interface as for the User instances.

Figure 3.2 shows the inheritance pattern for the Guest class. When the Guest component instance is registered to the agent, it will expose the UserMBean management interface.

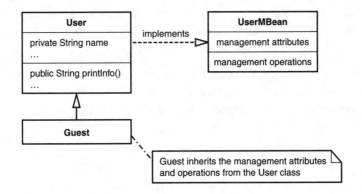

FIGURE 3.2
Class structure of the Guest *MBean.*

It's also possible for the Guest class to override the management interface of its ancestor class. If the Guest class implements a management interface GuestMBean, the agent only exposes the attributes and operations specified in that specific interface. The management interface of all the ancestor classes will be overridden, and nothing of the ancestor classes is exposed to the management. You could use this feature to turn the Guest component instances to strictly read-only in terms of management by defining the interface in Listing 3.5.

LISTING 3.5 GuestMBean.java

```java
public interface GuestMBean {

    // read-only attributes
    public long getID();
    public String getName();
    public String getAddress();
    public String[] getPhoneNumbers();

    // operations
    public String printInfo();
}
```

When implementing the Guest resource, you would declare the class as follows:

```java
public class Guest extends User implements GuestMBean {
    // implementation
}
```

This declaration would hide the UserMBean management interface completely and only allow the management application to read the Guest object's state.

In case the Guest should inherit the management interface of its ancestor User and expose additional attributes and operations, you must have the GuestMBean extend the management interface of the superclass, in this case the UserMBean interface.

As Figure 3.3 shows, this leads to two parallel inheritance trees—one of the implementation and another one of the management interface. Of course, it is also possible for the Guest in this case to implement the entire management interface, instead of inheriting the implementation from the User superclass.

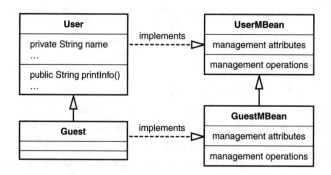

FIGURE 3.3

Management interface inheritance.

MBean Notification Mechanism

Building a component-based system often requires the ability for the components to communicate between parts of the system, sending important events and state changes. The JMX architecture defines a notification mechanism for MBeans that allows management events or notifications to be sent to other MBeans or management applications.

The JMX notification mechanism is based on the Java event mechanism. It involves listener objects that are registered to the MBeans emitting notifications, called *broadcaster* MBeans. The broadcaster MBeans send out notification objects to all interested listeners whose notification filters accept the notification's type.

The JMX notification mechanism builds upon the following four classes:

- `Notification`
- `NotificationBroadcaster`
- `NotificationFilter`
- `NotificationListener`

The `Notification` object is a generic event object sent to the listeners when an event occurs. It extends the `java.util.EventObject`, which is the standard Java event class. The listener object implements the `NotificationListener` interface that contains one method, `handleNotification()`. This is a generic event handler used for all JMX notification listeners, regardless of the notification type.

The `NotificationBroadcaster` interface is implemented by the MBeans emitting management events. The `NotificationBroadcaster` interface declares methods for registering (`addNotificationListener`) and unregistering (`removeNotificationListener`) listeners and an additional method for retrieving the notification metadata (`getNotificationInfo`). It is important to notice that the notifications sent by the broadcaster MBeans are part of the management interface. The management applications can query the agent for information about what types of notification the MBean emits.

The `NotificationFilter` interface is passed to the broadcaster MBean as an argument when the listener is registered. The interface contains one method, `isNotificationEnabled()`, which must always be invoked by the broadcaster MBean before the management event is sent. This allows the object registering as a listener to select which notifications to receive of all the possible notifications the MBean is emitting.

3

STANDARD MBEANS

The registering of the listener to the broadcaster MBean is done through the agent layer. As with all the other MBean invocations, the MBean server sits between the consumer and the producer of the notifications. The `MBeanServer` interface exposes two methods for adding a listener to an MBean, and two for removing the listener. The declarations of the four methods are shown next. Exceptions have been left out for the sake of brevity.

```
public void addNotificationListener(
            ObjectName name,
            NotificationListener listener,
            NotificationFilter filter,
            Object handback)

public void addNotificationListener(
            ObjectName name,
            ObjectName listener,
            NotificationFilter filter,
            Object handback)

public void removeNotificationListener(
            ObjectName name,
            NotificationListener listener)

public void removeNotificationListener(
            ObjectName name,
            ObjectName listener)
```

Both the `addNotificationListener()` method and the `removeNotificationListener()` method are overloaded to take a listener argument either as a direct implementation of the `NotificationListener` interface, or an `ObjectName` reference to a registered listener MBean. If the `ObjectName` reference is used, the listener MBean must implement the `NotificationListener` interface.

Next, we will look at each of the notification interfaces in a little more detail.

Notification

The `Notification` class represents a generic event sent by an MBean. It is a subclass of the standard Java `EventObject` class that should be familiar to those who have worked with Java's event mechanism before. The `Notification` class can be used for any type of management event the MBean wants to broadcast, or it can be subclassed to provide more specific event notifications.

The JMX `Notification` class extends the `EventObject` class by adding fields for the event's type, a sequence number, time stamp, message, and an optional user data. The type string is used to convey the semantics of the notification and is formed by adding string components separated by dots. This is not to be confused with the Java class type and a fully-qualified classname that is a dot-separated string of package structure. A type string can be freely formed and contain as many parts as necessary. Notice, however, that all type strings prefixed with `jmx.` are reserved for the JMX implementation. The following are some examples of notification type strings.

```
MyApp.MyEvent
Acme.Application.User.CreateEvent
Acme.Application.User.RemoveEvent
jmx.modelmbean.general// RESERVED !!
```

As you can see, the type string can be used to build a hierarchical structure for the different types of management events.

The sequence number can be retrieved from the `Notification` object by calling the `getSequenceNumber()` method. This field allows individual notifications to be identified by the receiver, acting as a serial number. The sequence number is valid in the context of a broadcaster MBean instance. Constructing the `Notification` object requires you to supply the sequence number as an argument.

The `getTimeStamp()` method allows access to the date and time the notification was sent. The time stamp can also be set in the constructor, but it is also possible to leave the time stamp creation up to the Notification implementation.

In addition to the `message` field that can be used for an explanation of the notification, the `Notification` object allows the broadcaster to attach a user data object to the management event. The user data object can contain any additional information the broadcaster wants to relay to its consumers. There are no specific restrictions to what kind of object can be attached to the notification. However, it is probably a good idea to have the user data objects implement the `Serializable` interface, making it considerably easier for the connectors to send notifications with user data attached to remote management applications.

NotificationBroadcaster and NotificationFilter

The `NotificationBroadcaster` interface must be implemented by those MBeans broadcasting management events. The interface declares three methods that the MBean implementation must provide. The declaration of the `NotificationBroadcaster` interface is shown in Listing 3.6.

LISTING 3.6   NotificationBroadcaster Interface

```
package javax.management;

public interface NotificationBroadcaster {
  public void addNotificationListener(
          NotificationListener listener,
          NotificationFilter filter,
          Object handback)
        throws IllegalArgumentException;

  public void removeNotificationListener(
          NotificationListener listener)
        throws ListenerNotFoundException;

  public MBeanNotificationInfo[] getNotificationInfo();

}
```

The addNotificationListener() registers an event consumer with the MBean. It takes a NotificationListener reference as its first argument and two other arguments—the NotificationFilter object and a hand-back object reference.

The removeNotificationListener() method of the NotificationBroadcaster interface removes the given listener instance from the notification broadcaster. If the given listener instance was not found, a ListenerNotFoundException should be thrown.

The last method of the NotificationBroadcaster interface is a method to return the metadata of the broadcaster MBean to the agent. We will take an extensive look at the metadata structures of the JMX architecture in the Chapter 4, "Dynamic MBeans," when we investigate the Dynamic MBeans. The getNotificationInfo() method is part of the metadata that is being passed to the agent. It returns an array of MBeanNotificationInfo objects, each of which describe a notification class emitted from the broadcaster MBean. In turn, each MBeanNotificationInfo object describes all the notification types for the given notification class. Remember that the Notification class can be used to deliver several different types of notifications. It is very easy to get your classes and types mixed up here, so be careful.

The NotificationFilter interface allows the listener to communicate to the broadcaster MBean which notifications it is interested in receiving. The broadcaster MBean may be sending several different types of notifications. The listener can register to receive all or just some of them. When passing the filter to the broadcaster MBean, you can select which events you want to receive and avoid registering for each individual event type separately, or avoid having to handle dozens of notifications from the MBean when you're only interested in one particular type. It is also possible to implement more sophisticated logic in the filter that selects the notifications based on the time stamp, sequence number, or possibly the user data object of the notification.

The `NotificationFilter` is a very simple interface to implement. It only contains one method, `isNotificationEnabled()`, which returns a Boolean value `true` or `false`, depending on whether the broadcaster MBean should send the given `Notification` instance to the listener. The declaration of the `NotificationFilter` interface is shown in Listing 3.7.

LISTING 3.7   `NotificationFilter Interface`

```
package javax.management;

public interface NotificationFilter
            extends java.io.Serializable {

  boolean isNotificationEnabled(Notification notif);

}
```

The broadcaster is required to check the notification against the filter before sending it to the notification consumer. If the filter is a `null` reference, all notifications from the MBean will be delivered to the registered consumer.

The hand-back object is provided as an argument with the `NotificationListener` reference when the consumer is registered. It can be used to provide the listener instance an object reference that it can use to retrieve required context information with every broadcast notification. The hand-back object must be stored by the `NotificationBroadcaster` implementation and passed back to the listener with each notification. In addition, the hand-back object must not be changed by the broadcaster.

The same listener object can be registered more than once to the broadcaster with different hand-back objects. This will cause the listener to receive the notifications as many times as it has registered itself, each time with a different hand-back object.

Broadcaster MBean Example

The implementation of the `NotificationBroadcaster` interface can become quite complex compared to the usual JavaBeans event mechanism. You need to store a triplet of objects with each added listener— `NotificationListener` reference, the `NotificationFilter` reference, and the hand-back object. In addition, you will have to generate the sequence number for each `Notification` object and remember to invoke the `isNotificationEnabled()` method of the filter before sending the event to the registered listener.

Luckily, there is a NotificationBroadcasterSupport class available that implements the NotificationBroadcaster interface. You can either have your MBean extend the support class or delegate to it to gain the registration management and notification invocation support. In Listing 3.8, you will use the broadcaster support class to add notifications to the User MBean implementation. The example shows the implementation of the NotificationBroadcaster interface and adds notification to a new management operation remove(). Let's call this new MBean a BroadcastingUser and have it implement a corresponding management interface that extends from the UserMBean interface.

The management interface for the BroadcastingUser is shown in Listing 3.8.

LISTING 3.8   BroadcastingUserMBean.java

```
package book.jmx.examples;


public interface BroadcastingUserMBean extends UserMBean {

    public void remove();

}
```

Remember that the Standard MBean inheritance patterns will expose all properties and operations declared in the ancestor interfaces to the management.

Next, you will write the MBean implementation. Most of the implementation will be inherited from the User class that already implements the attributes and all operations of the MBean, except for the remove() operation. You will use the NotificationBroadcasterSupport class to help implement the NotificationBroadcaster interface. Because you already used up the inheritance tree by extending the User class, you will delegate the NotificationBroadcaster method calls to a support class instance.

The notificationSequence field in the BroadcastingUser class is used for keeping track of the sequence numbers of sent notifications. The implementation of the remove() management operation uses the sendNotification() method of the support class to emit the Notification object. Each Notification object is created with example.user.remove as its type, notificationSequence as its sequence number, and the current BroadcastingUser instance as its source.

Notice that the source reference in the Notification instance will be converted by the agent to represent the ObjectName reference of the broadcaster MBean. This allows the notification consumer to reference the broadcasting MBean through the MBean server and also ensures the decoupling of the Notification objects from the broadcaster MBean. Remember that no direct references to the MBean instances should exist outside the agent. All communications must go through it.

The NotificationBroadcaster is implemented by delegating the functionality of the addNotificationListener() and removeNotificationListener() methods to the notification support object. In addition, you provide the metadata about the notification by returning an MBeanNotificationInfo object from the getNotificationInfo() method.

The complete source for the BroadcastingUser class is provided in Listing 3.9.

LISTING 3.9   BroadcastingUser.java

```
package book.jmx.examples;

import javax.management.*;

public class BroadcastingUser extends User implements
      BroadcastingUserMBean, NotificationBroadcaster  {

   // broadcaster support class
   private NotificationBroadcasterSupport broadcaster =
            new NotificationBroadcasterSupport();

   // sequence number for notifications
   private long notificationSequence = 0;


   // management operations
   public void remove() {

      broadcaster.sendNotification(
         new Notification(
            "example.user.remove",        // type
            this,                          // source
            ++notificationSequence,        // seq. number
            "User " +getName()+ " removed." // message
         )
      );
   }


   // notification broadcaster implementation
```

LISTING 3.9   continued

```
public void addNotificationListener(
        NotificationListener listener,
        NotificationFilter filter,
        Object handback) {

    broadcaster.addNotificationListener(
            listener, filter, handback);
}

public void removeNotificationListener(
        NotificationListener listener)
        throws ListenerNotFoundException {

    broadcaster.removeNotificationListener(listener);
}

public MBeanNotificationInfo[] getNotificationInfo() {
  return new MBeanNotificationInfo[] {
    new MBeanNotificationInfo(
      new String[]
        { "example.user.remove" },  // notif. types
        Notification.class.getName(), // notif. class
        "User Notifications."         // description
    )
  };
}

}
```

The `remove()` operation implementation was left empty apart from the notification send implementation. In a real-world case, you would add any necessary code to clean up the database records if a user was removed from the system.

NotificationListener

The `NotificationListener` is implemented by all classes wanting to act as management event consumers. The `NotificationListener` interface is a generic listener interface that can be used to receive several different types of notifications from different sources.

The interface defines only one method, `handleNotification`, which is declared as follows:

```
public void handleNotification(Notification notification,
                               Object handBack)
```

The same listener can be registered to receive notifications from different notification broadcasters. In addition, the same listener can receive several different types of notifications from the same notification broadcaster, depending on the notification filter. There are several ways for the implementation of the NotificationListener interface to determine the source and meaning of the received notifications.

- Use the getSource() method of the Notification class to determine the source of the notification. The object returned by the getSource() method is an ObjectName reference to the MBean that broadcast the notification.

- Use the getType() method of the Notification class to retrieve the notification type information. This is a dot-separated string of the notification's semantic information.

- Use the handBack object to map the notifications to a registered listener. The handBack object is guaranteed to be returned to the listener with every notification and can be used to pass any type of context information.

- Optional use of user data objects. The broadcaster can attach additional data to the notifications. The user data can be retrieved via the getUserData() method call of the Notification class.

Notification Listener Example

Listing 3.10 will show how to register and receive the notifications from the BroadcastingUser MBean. You will register three instances of the BroadcastingUser class to the agent and add a listener object to each one of them, implemented as an inner class UserListener in the code. The notification listener registration is accompanied by a filter object and implemented as an inner class UserFilter, which only accepts notifications of type example.user.remove to be sent to the listener. In addition, you will use the ObjectName instance as a hand-back object with each registration. You will use the hand-back to reference the notification producer MBean in the listener code to unregister it when a notification to remove the user is received. Normally, you would use the getSource() method of the Notification object to retrieve the ObjectName reference to the broadcaster. Unfortunately, the JMX RI version 1.0 has a bug in how it handles the listener instance that is registered to more than one notification producer. This causes the getSource() to return the same ObjectName reference with each notification, regardless of which MBean instance sends it. We use the hand-back to work around this quirk in the reference implementation.

Listing 3.10 is the complete code for the ListenerClient class. After registering the MBeans and adding listeners to them, it invokes the remove() method of the BroadcastingUser objects that will cause a notification to be received in the listeners. The listeners will then unregister the MBeans.

LISTING 3.10   ListenerClient.java

```java
package book.jmx.examples;

import javax.management.*;
import java.util.List;

public class ListenerClient {

  private NotificationListener listener = null;
  private NotificationFilter filter     = null;
  private MBeanServer server            = null;

  public void run() {

    // Find an agent from this JVM. Null argument will
    // return a list of all MBeanServer instances.
    List list = MBeanServerFactory.findMBeanServer(null);
    server    = (MBeanServer)list.iterator().next();

    // create the listener and filter instances
    listener = new UserListener(server);
    filter   = new UserFilter();

    // Register three different instances of Broadcasting
    // User MBean to the agent. The single UserListener
    // instance is registered to each MBean. MBean
    // ObjectName is used as a hand-back object.
    try {
      ObjectName john = new ObjectName("user:name=John");
      ObjectName mike = new ObjectName("user:name=Mike");
      ObjectName xena = new ObjectName("user:name=Xena");
      Attribute jName = new Attribute("Name", "John");
      Attribute mName = new Attribute("Name", "Mike");
      Attribute xName = new Attribute("Name", "Xena");

      server.registerMBean(new BroadcastingUser(), john);
      server.registerMBean(new BroadcastingUser(), mike);
      server.registerMBean(new BroadcastingUser(), xena);

      server.addNotificationListener(
              john, listener, filter, john);
      server.addNotificationListener(
              mike, listener, filter, mike);
      server.addNotificationListener(
```

LISTING 3.10 continued

```
                xena, listener, filter, xena);

    server.setAttribute(john, jName);
    server.setAttribute(mike, mName);
    server.setAttribute(xena, xName);

    // Invoke remove on each MBean instance. This
    // will broadcast a notification from the MBean.
    server.invoke(john, "remove", null, null);
    server.invoke(mike, "remove", null, null);
    server.invoke(xena, "remove", null, null);
  }
  catch (JMException e) {
    e.printStackTrace();
  }
}


//
// Notification listener implementation.
//
class UserListener implements NotificationListener {

  MBeanServer server = null;

  UserListener(MBeanServer server) {
    this.server = server;
  }

  public void handleNotification(Notification notif,
                                 Object handback) {

    String type = notif.getType();

    if (type.equals("example.user.remove")) {
      try {
        System.out.println(notif.getMessage());

        server.unregisterMBean((ObjectName)handback);
        System.out.println(handback + " unregistered.");
      }
      catch (JMException e) {
        e.printStackTrace();
      }
    }
```

LISTING 3.10   continued

```java
    }
  }


//
// Notification filter implementation.
//
class UserFilter implements NotificationFilter {

  public boolean isNotificationEnabled(Notification n) {
    return (n.getType().equals("example.user.remove"))
            ? true
            : false;
  }
}


//
// Main method for the client. This will instantiate
// an agent in the JVM.
//
public static void main(String[] args) {

  MBeanServer server =
      MBeanServerFactory.createMBeanServer();

  new ListenerClient().run();
}

}
```

When you compile and run the BroadcastingUser MBean and the ListenerClient, you will see the following output on the console.

```
User John removed.
user:name=John unregistered.
User Mike removed.
user:name=Mike unregistered.
User Xena removed.
user:name=Xena unregistered.
```

The user removed messages are the contents of the Notification object's message field and retrieved with getMessage() method. The unregistered messages are generated by the listener after it has invoked the unregisterMBean() method on the MBeanServer.

Attribute Change Notifications

The JMX specification defines a specific `AttributeChangeNotification` class for MBeans that send notifications on change in their management attribute.

The `AttributeChangeNotification` class extends the `Notification` class by adding four new fields to the notification—`name`, `type`, `oldvalue`, and `newvalue`. The `name` field should contain the name of the management attribute whose value has been changed, and the `type` field should contain the runtime type of the management attribute. The `oldvalue` and `newvalue` fields should contain the old and new value of the attributes, respectively. All the new fields are accessible via respective getter methods for retrieving the values—`getAttributeName()`, `getAttributeType()`, `getNewValue()`, and `getOldValue()`.

In addition, the `AttributeChangeNotification` class defines the notification type string that must be exposed as notification metadata in `getNotificationInfo()` method of the `NotificationBroadcaster` interface. The notification type is exposed as a static string `ATTRIBUTE_CHANGE` in the `AttributeChangeNotification` class.

The `AttributeChangeNotificationFilter` class is an implementation of the `NotificationFilter` interface. It contains methods for configuring the filter to accept or deny a pattern of attribute change notifications.

The methods of the `AttributeChangeNotificationFilter` are described in Table 3.1.

TABLE 3.1   Methods of the `AttributeChangeNotificationFilter` Class

Method	Description
`enableAttribute(String name)`	The attribute change notifications for the given attribute name will be enabled in the filter and sent to the listener.
`disableAttribute(String name)`	All of the attribute change notifications for the given attribute name will be denied by the filter.
`disableAllAttributes()`	All attribute change notifications for all management attributes in the filter will be disabled.
`getEnabledAttributes()`	Returns a vector of the enabled attributes in the notification filter.

The `AttributeChangeNotification` allows you to easily configure which attribute notifications you want the listener instance to receive.

Attribute Change Notification Example

Listing 3.11 will extend the previous `BroadcastingUser` example. You will add one attribute change notification to its management interface. It doesn't require many code changes, so only the changed parts are highlighted.

In the `BroadcastingUser` class, you will override the `setUser()` method of the superclass `User` to send an attribute change notification after its `setUser()` method has been called. In addition, you need to add the new notification type to your metadata in the `getNotificationInfo()` method. These changes are shown in Listing 3.11.

LISTING 3.11   `BroadcastingUser.java`

```
...


public class BroadcastingUser extends User implements
    BroadcastingUserMBean, NotificationBroadcaster  {


    // broadcaster support class
    private NotificationBroadcasterSupport broadcaster =
            new NotificationBroadcasterSupport();

    // sequence number for notifications
    private long notificationSequence = 0;

    // override the 'Name' management attribute
    public void setName(String name) {
        String oldValue = super.getName();
        String newValue = name;
        String attrType = String.class.getName();
        String attrName = "Name";

        super.setName(name);

        broadcaster.sendNotification(
          new AttributeChangeNotification(
            this,                           // source
            ++notificationSequence,         // seq. number
            System.currentTimeMillis(),     // time stamp
```

LISTING 3.11   continued

```
            "User's name has been changed.", // message
            attrName, attrType,
            oldValue, newValue
          )
        );
    }

...

    public MBeanNotificationInfo[] getNotificationInfo() {
        return new MBeanNotificationInfo[] {

          new MBeanNotificationInfo(
            new String[]
              { "example.user.remove" },  // notif. types
            Notification.class.getName(), // notif. class
            "User Notifications."         // description
          ),

          // attribute change notification type
          new MBeanNotificationInfo(
            new String[] {
              AttributeChangeNotification.ATTRIBUTE_CHANGE
            },
            AttributeChangeNotification.class.getName(),
            "User attribute change notification."
          )
        };
    }

...

}
```

3

Also, you need to change the `ListenerClient` class to accept the new notifications in the notification filter object and change the `NotificationListener` implementation to process the attribute change notifications. The code changes to `ListenerClient` are shown in Listing 3.12.

LISTING 3.12   ListenerClient.java

```java
...

//
// Notification listener implementation.
//
class UserListener implements NotificationListener {

  ...

  public void handleNotification(Notification notif,
                                 Object handback) {

    String type = notif.getType();

    if (type.equals("example.user.remove")) {
      try {
        System.out.println(notif.getMessage());

        server.unregisterMBean((ObjectName)handback);
        System.out.println(handback + " unregistered.");
      }
      catch (JMException e) {
        e.printStackTrace();
      }
    }

    // process attribute change notifications
    else if (type.equals(
        AttributeChangeNotification.ATTRIBUTE_CHANGE)) {

      AttributeChangeNotification notification =
        (AttributeChangeNotification)notif;

      System.out.println(notification.getMessage());
      System.out.println(
        "  New value=" + notification.getNewValue());
    }
  }
}

//
```

LISTING 3.12   continued

```
// Notification filter implementation.
//
class UserFilter implements NotificationFilter {

  public boolean isNotificationEnabled(Notification n) {
    return
      (n.getType().equals
          ("example.user.remove") ||
       n.getType().equals
          (AttributeChangeNotification.ATTRIBUTE_CHANGE)
      )
          ? true
          : false;
  }
}

...

}
```

3

Now, if you compile and run the changed classes, you should see the following output on the console.

```
User's name has been changed.
  New value=John
User's name has been changed.
  New value=Mike
User's name has been changed.
  New value=Xena
User John removed.
user:name=John unregistered.
User Mike removed.
user:name=Mike unregistered.
User Xena removed.
user:name=Xena unregistered.
```

The User's name has been changed messages are printed when the listener receives a notification from the MBean that has had its setName() method called to initialize it with a new value.

Notifications to Remote Systems

The JMX notification mechanism discussed so far is strictly a local one, notifying only the MBeans or management applications that are located in the same JVM. For most practical purposes, you will need the notifications to be able to propagate from the JVM to others that are possibly located on a different machine across the network.

The distributed services level of the JMX architecture is currently, at its 1.0 version, left mostly unspecified. The distribution in the management architecture is the responsibility of the JMX connectors and protocol adaptors. Therefore, these same components are the most likely candidates to take care of the propagation of management events to remote systems as well.

Because the distribution of the notifications is left unspecified, there are several possibilities how to implement them. The notifications can be sent to the management applications synchronously or asynchronously, they can be persisted, and so on. The actual functionality will often be dictated by the underlying connector implementation that is used to distribute the notifications. We will see some implementation possibilities in the second part of the book, which is more concentrated on the distributed services of the JMX architecture.

Summary

We have now covered one instrumentation approach in detail—the Standard MBean. MBeans were defined, the naming conventions involved with declaring a management interface with the Standard MBean were discussed, how management attributes and operations are declared, and how the agent finds them introspecting the MBean interface.

The naming conventions allow you to declare read-only, write-only, and read-write access to the management attributes. Also important to remember are the inheritance rules that the agent uses to determine the exposed management interface.

In the last part of this chapter, you had an in-depth look into the notification system defined by the JMX specification and all the related classes. Notifications are an important mechanism used to implement some of the standard agent services that will be covered in Chapter 7.

Standard MBeans are fairly easy to create and useful when creating new resources for management. They are quick to implement and offer statically typed interfaces for robustness. However, they might become inflexible when the management interface is expected to change often, or when you need to be able to determine the management interface at runtime instead of compile time. In those cases, Dynamic MBeans might suit your needs better. We are going to look at the Dynamic MBeans in Chapter 4.

Dynamic MBeans

IN THIS CHAPTER

Dynamic MBeans, as the name implies, provide a more dynamic definition of the management interface compared to Standard MBeans. Instead of relying on a statically typed Java interface, the Dynamic MBeans implement a generic interface that provides methods for the agent to discover the management interface. This allows the management interface to be changed without a recompilation of the class files and enables the management attributes and operations to be created dynamically at runtime.

Due to their dynamic nature, Dynamic MBeans are quite useful for situations in which you anticipate that the management interface will change often. In addition, the Dynamic MBeans enable you to define the management interface declaratively, for example in an XML file, and create the management interface at runtime. If the exposed management interface is determined depending on an external information source, you might want to postpone the creation of the management interface until such information is available.

One possible case for using Dynamic MBeans is enabling the Java management on existing resources or classes that do not follow the Standard MBean naming conventions. Dynamic MBeans lend themselves to act as adapters exposing a consistent management view to the agent level and delegating the agent's requests to correct methods or even to entirely different components not directly seen by the agent.

Another aspect of the Dynamic MBeans is that they expose the metadata that describes the management interface to the developer. With Standard MBeans, the metadata is generated by the agent that used introspection to discover the management interface. With Dynamic MBeans, the developer is responsible for providing this metadata.

In this chapter, you will first look at all the details of how to implement the methods of the DynamicMBean interface. Then you will go through the metadata structures and see what type of information the developer needs to provide with each Dynamic MBean. In the end, you'll build the equivalent of the standard User MBean as a Dynamic MBean and then see how the JMX management architecture allows you to use the different implementations interchangeably.

DynamicMBean Interface

To be recognized as a Dynamic MBean by the agent, the MBean must implement the DynamicMBean interface. The agent will use the methods defined in this interface to interact with the MBean to determine the management attributes and operations of the MBean, to query the attribute values, and to invoke the MBean operations. The DynamicMBean interface contains six methods (Listing 4.1) that you, as a developer, are responsible for implementing.

The methods described in the interface are generic and detyped, so some extra discipline is in order when implementing Dynamic MBeans. The generic definition of the Dynamic MBean interface provides increased flexibility but should be handled with care.

The `DynamicMBean` interface is shown in Listing 4.1 (the exceptions declared in the interface have been left out for the sake of brevity).

LISTING 4.1 DynamicMBean interface

```
package javax.management;

public interface DynamicMBean {

    public MBeanInfo getMBeanInfo();

    public Object getAttribute(String attribute);

    public AttributeList getAttributes(String[] attributes);

    public void setAttribute(Attribute attribute);

    public AttributeList setAttributes(AttributeList attributes);

    public Object invoke(String actionName,
                         Object[] params,
String[] signature);
}
```

Notice the declaration of the `invoke()` method. All the type information is passed as strings, forming the invocation's signature. The `params` and `signature` arrays must be of the same length and a parameters type is retrieved from the same index location in the corresponding signature array.

The `getMBeanInfo()` method returns an object that fully describes the management interface of the Dynamic MBean. This includes the MBean's attributes, operations, constructors, and notifications. Each of the metadata elements has its own class in the JMX API, which you will examine in detail later in this chapter, in the section "MBean Metadata Classes."

GetAttribute and GetAttributes

The `getAttribute()` and `getAttributes()` methods are used by the agent to retrieve the values of the management attributes from the Dynamic MBean. When you create a Dynamic MBean, it is up to you to map the named attributes to their corresponding values in the MBean

4

**DYNAMIC
MBEANS**

implementation and then return these values to the agent on request. The full declaration of the getAttribute() method is as follows:

```
public Object getAttribute(String attribute) throws
    AttributeNotFoundException, MBeanException, ReflectionException;
```

The returned object must contain the value of the attribute. The runtime type of the returned object must also match the Java type defined in the Dynamic MBean's metadata classes. You can use the AttributeNotFoundException class to indicate to the agent that the named attribute was not found or its value could not be retrieved. The MBeanException class can be used for wrapping any checked exceptions that may be thrown by the getAttribute() implementation, such as the java.io.IOException. The ReflectionException class can be used to propagate exceptions resulting from the use of the java.lang.reflect package back to the agent. You will learn more about the JMX agent exception mechanism and each declared exception in Chapter 6, "MBean Server."

Listing 4.2 is an example implementation of the getAttribute() method that processes the attributes of the User MBean you built as an example for Standard MBeans. This code snippet shows how you would deal with readable attributes for dynamic User MBean.

LISTING 4.2   DynamicUser.java

```
...

public Object getAttribute(String attribute) throws
                           AttributeNotFoundException,
                           MBeanException,
                           ReflectionException {

    if (attribute == null || attribute.equals(""))
        throw new IllegalArgumentException(
            "null or empty attribute name"
        );

    // map the named attributes to fields
    if (attribute.equals("Name"))
        return name;

    if (attribute.equals("Address"))
        return address;

    if (attribute.equals("PhoneNumbers"))
        return numbers;

    if (attribute.equals("ID"))
```

LISTING 4.2   continued

```
        return new Long(id);

    throw new AttributeNotFoundException(
        "Attribute " + attribute + " not found."
    );
}

...
```

In Listing 4.2, you first check the attribute parameter for a `null` reference and empty strings. An attempt to retrieve an attribute with a `null` or empty name will yield an `IllegalArgumentException` being thrown from the implementation. The agent will catch this and other runtime exceptions and will wrap them in a subclass of `javax.management.JMRuntimeException`.

If the given attribute parameter is valid, a simple comparison for the parameter string is made next. Remember that the MBean attribute names are case sensitive, so don't confuse the MBean attribute names with the field names in the implementation class. In a more robust implementation than that shown here, it would be a good idea to define the attribute names as constants to eliminate the possibility of simple typing errors.

Again, notice that the management attribute names can be independent of the underlying implementation names. You can use names in the management interface that are more self-explanatory and consistent than the names used in the resource implementation. With Dynamic MBeans it is up to you to map the attribute name to the object field names.

The `getAttributes()` method returns the values of several MBean attributes. The return type is an `AttributeList` class defined in the JMX API, which is a subclass of the `ArrayList` class in the Java Collections framework. The returned list must contain a set of `Attribute` objects that hold the name and the value of the requested attribute.

The `getAttributes()` method does not signal errors using the Java exception mechanism. Instead, any attributes whose value retrieval caused an error condition should be left out of the return list.

SetAttribute and SetAttributes

The `setAttribute()` and `setAttributes()` methods are the corresponding setter methods to the getter methods in the Dynamic MBean interface. Again, `setAttribute()` is used for setting a single MBean attribute value, and it is up to the MBean implementation to map the

4

**DYNAMIC
MBEANS**

given attribute name in the implementation and set the attribute value. The setAttribute()
method uses the Attribute class as a wrapper for passing the attribute name and value. The
full declaration of the setAttribute() method defines several exceptions that can be used for
signaling error conditions.

```
public void setAttribute(Attribute attribute) throws
        AttributeNotFoundException, InvalidAttributeValueException,
        MBeanException, ReflectionException;
```

The AttributeNotFoundException class can be used to indicate if the given attribute does not
exist in the MBean. InvalidAttributeValueException should be used to indicate the value
given in the Attribute object is not acceptable for the given attribute or the value is of the
wrong type. The use of MBeanException class is similar to that seen with the getAttribute()
method. If the attribute-set operation causes a checked exception to be thrown in the MBean
implementation, it can be caught, wrapped into an MBeanException object, and rethrown to be
managed by the agent. Similarly, the ReflectionException class can be used to wrap exceptions resulting from using the operations of java.lang.reflect package in setting the
MBean's state.

Listing 4.3 is an example implementation of the setAttribute() method. It implements the
attributes for the example User MBean you built as a Standard MBean example and shows how
similar functionality is achieved with Dynamic MBeans. Each attribute name is matched individually and cast to String or to an array of String objects. In case there is a type mismatch
between the provided attribute type and the expected type, the resulting ClassCastException
is caught and rethrown as an InvalidAttributeValueException.

LISTING 4.3   DynamicUser.java

```
...

public void setAttribute(Attribute attribute) throws
                    AttributeNotFoundException,
                    InvalidAttributeValueException,
                    MBeanException,
                    ReflectionException {

    if (attribute == null) throw new
        AttributeNotFoundException("null attribute");

    // map the attributes to fields
    try {
        if (attribute.getName().equals("Name"))
```

LISTING 4.2   continued

```
        this.name = (String)attribute.getValue();

    else if (attribute.getName().equals("Address"))
        this.address = (String)attribute.getValue();

    else if (attribute.getName().equals("PhoneNumbers"))
        this.numbers = (String[])attribute.getValue();

    else if (attribute.getName().equals("Password"))
        this.passwd = (String)attribute.getValue();

    else
        throw new AttributeNotFoundException(
            "attribute "+attribute.getName()+" not found."
        );
    }
    catch (ClassCastException e) {

        // In case of the type mismatch, throw an
        // InvalidAttributeValueException
        throw new InvalidAttributeValueException(
            "Invalid attribute type " +
            attribute.getValue().getClass().getName()
        );
    }
}

...
```

The setAttributes() method takes an AttributeList as a parameter and allows for the setting of several MBean attributes at once. Similar to getAttributes(), this method does not indicate error conditions using the exception mechanism but returns a list of attributes whose values were successfully set. In case there were errors in setting some of the attributes, they will not be added to the returned result set. You can quickly determine if all attributes were successfully set by comparing the sizes of the input list and return list.

The invoke() method is called by the agent when a request to invoke a management operation has been made. The parameters passed with the call include the operation's name, an array of objects containing the values for the operation parameters, and an array of strings declaring the types of the parameter values. Again, the MBean implementation is responsible for parsing all of this information and mapping the invoke call to the appropriate methods in the implementation. The checked exceptions thrown by the implementation can be passed back to the agent by wrapping them with the MBeanException class. The return type from the invoke operation must match the type declared in the management operation metadata for this Dynamic MBean.

Listing 4.4 shows a code snippet that handles the management operation invocation of a Dynamic MBean. Notice that each of the management operations are mapped from their names to method calls in the implementation class.

LISTING 4.4   DynamicUser.java

```
...

public Object invoke(String actionName, Object[] params,
                     String[] signature) throws
                     MBeanException, ReflectionException {

  if (actionName == null || actionName.equals(""))
    throw new IllegalArgumentException("null operation");

  // map management operations
  if (actionName.equals("printInfo")
    return printInfo();

  else if (actionName.equals("addPhoneNumber")) {
    addPhoneNumber((String)params[0]);
    return null;
  }

  else if (actionName.equals("removePhoneNumber")) {
    removePhoneNumber(((Integer)params[0]).intValue());
    return null;
  }

  else throw new IllegalArgumentException(
          "unknown operation " + actionName);
}

...
```

You have now seen how to implement the basic mechanisms for readable and writable management attributes with Dynamic MBeans and how management operation invocations are implemented. Next, you'll look into the metadata structures of the Dynamic MBeans.

When creating Dynamic MBeans, the metadata needs to be explicitly declared by the programmer. In the case of the Standard MBeans, the metadata was automatically built by the agent via

Java language introspection. Now you will see what it is that the agent actually created from the Standard MBean's interface.

MBean Metadata Classes

The Dynamic MBeans expose their management interface via metadata classes defined in the JMX API. The metadata is retrieved by the agent using the getMBeanInfo() method of the DynamicMBean interface. The returned object, an instance of the MBeanInfo class, is an aggregate of several metadata classes. The metadata classes describe all elements of the MBean's management interface—attributes, operations, constructors, and notifications. In addition, the parameters for operations and constructors are represented by their own metadata class. The corresponding metadata classes are

- MBeanAttributeInfo
- MBeanOperationInfo
- MBeanConstructorInfo
- MBeanNotificationInfo
- MBeanParameterInfo

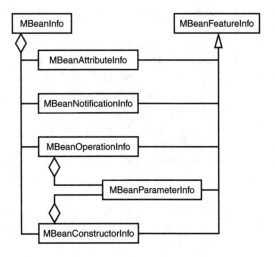

Figure 4.1 shows the structure of the metadata classes in the javax.management package.

FIGURE 4.1

JMX metadata classes.

As you can see from the figure, the MBeanInfo acts as a collection class for all metadata elements that inherit common features from the MBeanFeatureInfo class. The MBeanOperationInfo and MBeanConstructorInfo classes also use the MBeanParameterInfo to construct the metadata that describes the signature of these methods.

The MBeanInfo object is available to the management applications via the getMBeanInfo() method of the MBeanServer interface. Through the agent, another MBean or a management application can discover the management interface of an MBean and its metadata description.

The metadata can also be extended to supply additional information to what is described here. You will see an example of how to do this when the Model MBeans are discussed and see how they attach additional information to the metadata that the agent or the management application can utilize.

MBeanInfo

The MBeanInfo class fully describes the management interface of an MBean. Using the methods of this class, you can retrieve metadata for the attributes, operations, constructors, and notifications of the MBean.

Table 4.1 lists the methods of the MBeanInfo class with short descriptions of their use.

TABLE 4.1   List of the Methods of the MBeanInfo Class

Method Name	Description
getClassName()	Returns the classname of the MBean this MBeanInfo object describes.
getDescription()	Returns a description of the MBean this MBeanInfo object describes. The returned string should be in human readable form. Management applications can use this information in their user interfaces.
getAttributes()	Returns an array of MBeanAttributeInfo objects. The MBeanAttributeInfo objects describe the management attributes including the attribute name, the type of the attribute and the access mode (read-only, write-only, read-write). MBeans with no attributes return an empty array.
getOperations()	Returns an array of MBeanOperationInfo objects. The MBeanOperationInfo objects describe the management operations, including the operation name, its return type, and its parameter types (signature). MBeans with no operations return an empty array.
getConstructors()	Returns an array of MBeanConstructorInfo objects. The MBeanConstructorInfo objects describe the public constructors of an MBean.
getNotifications()	Returns an array of MBeanNotificationInfo objects describing the notifications emitted by the MBean.

The metadata classes are available to all clients through the `MBeanServer` interface. The metadata can also be extended to provide a richer description of the management interface to the agent and the management applications. You will see an example of this in Chapter 5, "Model MBeans."

MBeanFeatureInfo

The `MBeanFeatureInfo` class is a superclass for all the metadata classes in the `javax.management` package, except the `MBeanInfo` class. This class provides an access to two fields, the `name` and the `description` of an MBean metadata object. The subclasses use the name to return the name of the MBean attribute, operation, parameter, constructor, or notification. The description is used to return a human readable string describing the purpose and effects of the MBean metadata element. This is often a string that gives a short description of the management operation or describes the semantics of an attribute, parameter, or a notification. The description string can be used by the management tools to describe the managed resource and its properties to the user.

Notice that when creating Standard MBeans, it is not possible to set the descriptions for the management interface elements. The agent created the metadata structures automatically by introspecting the Standard MBean interface and had no access to any descriptive information. Unfortunately, there isn't a mechanism defined in the JMX specification that would allow the Standard MBeans to relay this type of information to the agent. You need to use Dynamic MBeans or their extensions to be able to provide additional metadata, such as the attribute and operation descriptions.

MBeanAttributeInfo

The `MBeanAttributeInfo` class is used to describe the attributes of an MBean. The class contains the information about the attribute's runtime type, name, description, and its access type. The `name` is the programmatic name of the management attribute. The `description` should be a human readable description of the attribute and its intended use.

The runtime type string must be a fully qualified name of the class, meaning that the package declaration must be included in the classname, such as `java.lang.String`. Also note that this rule applies to the Java array types as well as the primitive types. For example, the fully qualified classname of an array of `String` objects is `"[Ljava.lang.String;"`, and a two-dimensional array of `String` objects is `"[[Ljava.lang.String;"`. For arrays of primitive types, it gets even hairier. For example, the fully qualified classname of an array of `long` types is `"[J"`.

Table 4.2 shows examples of some fully qualified class names.

TABLE 4.2   Some Java Types and Their Fully Qualified Class Names

Type	Fully Qualified Name	Type	Fully Qualified Name
byte	"byte"	byte[]	"[B"
char	"char"	char[]	"[C"
double	"double"	double[]	"[D"
float	"float"	float[]	"[F"
int	"int"	int[]	"[I"
long	"long"	long[]	"[J"
short	"short"	short[]	"[S"
boolean	"boolean"	boolean[]	"[Z"
Object	"java.lang.Object"	Object[]	"[Ljava.lang.Object;"
void	"void"	—	—

More details on the string representation of the classnames can be found in the API documentation of the `java.lang.Class.getName()` method.

Because trying to remember the fully qualified names can be difficult and error-prone, especially in the case of arrays, there's a workaround you can use when creating the metadata classes. The Java language specification defines an expression called a *class literal*. You can use the class literal with all types in the Java language, including primitive types and type void, to access the Class object. This is useful, because the Class object implements the getName() method, which returns a fully-qualified name of the class. For example, when creating the MBeanAttributeInfo object for the array attribute PhoneNumbers in the User MBean, you could write the code as follows:

...

```
MBeanAttributeInfo numbers = new MBeanAttributeInfo(
    "PhoneNumbers",
    String[].class.getName(), // fully qualified class name
    "User's phone numbers.",
    true, true, false
);
```

...

So, instead of using the cumbersome textual representation of `"[Ljava.lang.String;"` for an array of strings, you can let the Java class libraries do the work for you by accessing the array class and then calling its getName() method. The same approach works for a multidimensional array of primitive types, for example, long[][][] or even for type void. You can test it with the following snippet of Java code:

```
System.out.println(void.class.getName());
System.out.println(long[][][].class.getName());
```

MBeanParameterInfo

The `MBeanParameterInfo` describes the parameters for MBean constructors and operations. As with the other metadata classes, the `MBeanParameterInfo` inherits the name and description properties from its superclass `MBeanFeatureInfo`. The name property, along with the description string, is often displayed to the user with generic management tools and should contain the required information for the user to be able to either create a new instance of the MBean or invoke one of its operations. In addition, the `MBeanParameterInfo` class contains the type of the parameter, again a fully qualified classname of the type. This string is accessible through the `getType()` method of the `MBeanParameterInfo` class.

MBeanOperationInfo

The `MBeanOperationInfo` class describes the management operations of an MBean. The object contains information about the operation's name and the description, both inherited from the `MBeanFeatureInfo` class, the type of the method's return value, the method's signature, and the impact of the operation on the MBean.

The signature consists of an array of `MBeanParameterInfo` objects that distinguishes overloaded methods from one another. The return type, as usual, must be a fully qualified classname of the returned object instance. The impact value can be used by the MBean developer to give the management application some idea how the invocation of the operation is going to affect the MBean's state.

The JMX API defines four values that can be used to describe the method's impact. The constants shown in Table 4.3 are declared in the `MBeanOperationInfo` class.

4

TABLE 4.3 The Impact of the `MBeanOperationInfo` Class

Impact	Description
INFO	The management operation is read-only, not affecting the state of the MBean.
ACTION	The management operation does affect the state of the MBean. This usually means changing the values of the MBean object's fields, changing the persistent state of the MBean or changing its configuration.
ACTION_INFO	The management operation implements both read-only types of functionality and also changes the state of the MBean in some way.
UNKNOWN	The effect of the operation is unknown. This is reserved for the operations of the Standard MBeans.

The impact field can be used to implement a coarse-grained scheme of determining which operations should be exposed to the user in the client. It is the responsibility of the Dynamic MBean developer to assign the correct impact values in the MBeanOperationInfo metadata objects. The class provides the accessor method getImpact() for querying the impact of the operation.

Listing 4.5 shows the metadata implementation of one of the User MBean operations, addPhoneNumber(), as it would be implemented with a Dynamic MBean. Notice that the signature of the management operation is built using an array of MBeanParameterInfo objects, each of which will include the name of the parameter, its runtime type, and a description of its purpose. The impact value is set to MBeanOperationInfo.ACTION as the addPhoneNumber() changes the state of the DynamicUser object.

LISTING 4.5   DynamicUser.java

```
...

// addPhoneNumber operation metadata
MBeanOperationInfo addPhoneNumber =
  new MBeanOperationInfo(
     "addPhoneNumber",                 // operation name
     "Add a new phone number.",        // description

       // parameters
       new MBeanParameterInfo[] {
         new MBeanParameterInfo(
            "number",                   // parameter name
            String.class.getName(),     // parameter type
            "The number to add."        // parameter descr.
         )
       },

     void.class.getName(),             // return type void
     MBeanOperationInfo.ACTION          // impact: ACTION
);

...
```

MBeanConstructorInfo

The MBeanConstructorInfo class describes the constructors of an MBean that are exposed to management. The MBeanConstructorInfo contains a name for the constructor, a description string for the management applications to display to the user, and an array of metadata objects describing the parameters of the constructor. The parameters make up the signature of the constructor that is used to differentiate a set of constructors from each other. You build up the parameters by using the `MBeanParameterInfo` objects and can query the array by calling the `getSignature()` method of the `MBeanConstructorInfo` class.

For example, to define a default, no-args constructor for the User MBean, create the metadata object in Listing 4.6.

LISTING 4.6   `DynamicUser.java`

```
...

MBeanConstructorInfo defaultConstructor =
    new MBeanConstructorInfo(
        "Default Constructor",          // name
        "Creates a new user instance.", // description
        null                            // parameters
    );
...
```

MBeanNotificationInfo

Notifications are part of the MBean's management interface, so the `MBeanNotificationInfo` class is required to describe the notifications broadcast by the MBean. The management applications can use the `MBeanNotificationInfo` object to discover the details of the notifications emitted by the MBean.

The use of the `name` field in the `MBeanNotificationInfo` class differs slightly from the other metadata classes in the JMX API. In the case of the notifications, the meaning of the field is restricted to contain the fully qualified classname of the actual notification object that is being broadcast. The `description` can be freely formed to describe the purpose of the notification to the management applications.

In addition to the name and description, the `MBeanNotificationInfo` class describes all the notification types that are sent using the class declared in the `name` field. The notification types are accessible to the management applications via the `getNotifTypes()` method of the `MBeanNotificationInfo` class.

You may remember from Chapter 3, "Standard MBeans," where notifications were discussed, that the `MBeanNotificationInfo` is used with both the Standard MBean and Dynamic MBean implementations.

In the `BroadcastingUser` MBean, you created the following `MBeanNotificationInfo`
instances (see Listing 4.7).

LISTING 4.7   Notification Metadata

```
new MBeanNotificationInfo[] {

  // notification for the remove operation
  new MBeanNotificationInfo(
    new String[]
      { "example.user.remove" },  // notif. types
    Notification.class.getName(), // notif. class
    "User Notifications."         // description
  ),

  // attribute change notification type
  new MBeanNotificationInfo(
    new String[] {
      AttributeChangeNotification.ATTRIBUTE_CHANGE
    },
    AttributeChangeNotification.class.getName(),
    "User attribute change notification."
  )
};
```

This code snippet creates the metadata for two different notification class types, `Notification`
and `AttributeChangeNotification`, each of which is used for sending one notification type.

Attribute and AttributeList

The `Attribute` class is a convenience class in the JMX API for representing the management
attributes of an MBean. The class associates the attribute name with its value and provides the
accessor methods for reading these values. It is used in the JMX interfaces, such as the
`DynamicMBean` interface in `getAttribute()` and `setAttribute()` methods.

The `AttributeList` class is a subclass of the `ArrayList` class in the Java Collection framework. It has been extended to accept `Attribute` object instances in its insertion methods to
ensure type safety in the collection. The `AttributeList` is used in the `DynamicMBean` interface
`setAttributes()` and `getAttributes()` methods.

Inheritance Patterns

Similar to Standard MBeans, Dynamic MBeans can inherit their management interface definition from the superclass. This follows from the normal rules of Java inheritance. If the resource
class does not directly implement either the Standard MBean interface or the DynamicMBean
interface, the inheritance tree is searched for the first ancestor implementing either one of the
interfaces. This interface is then used to expose the management attributes and operations of an
MBean. Remember, the same class is not allowed to implement both the Standard MBean and
the DynamicMBean interfaces. Such resources are not compatible with the JMX specification.

DynamicUser Example

The next example completes the code snippets you have seen in this chapter so far with a full
Dynamic MBean implementation of the User resource. You will build an identical managed
resource to the User MBean to demonstrate the differences between instrumenting a resource
using either the Standard MBean mechanism or the Dynamic MBean mechanism.

You will find that the Dynamic MBean requires quite a bit of extra code to implement the
same management interface as was used with the Standard MBean. This time, you cannot rely
on the agent to discover the management interface of the MBean automatically via introspection. You must provide the management interface metadata to the agent explicitly via the
getMBeanInfo() method. With non-trivial management interfaces, this can become quite a burden to the programmer. Later, in Part II, "JMX in the J2EE Platform," you will see how to alleviate the problem by introducing an MBean implementation that can read its management
interface definition from an XML file.

In addition, what is different with the Dynamic MBean from the Standard MBean implementation is that you no longer have a statically typed Java interface that describes the management
attributes and operations of an MBean. Instead, the developer is left with the responsibility of
correctly mapping the management attribute and operation names to their corresponding fields
and methods in the resource class. The developer must explicitly handle the type casts between
the invocations and the actual runtime types. Again, this places the burden on the programmer
to ensure the correct implementation.

However, for these same reasons, Dynamic MBeans do allow for increased flexibility in how
they implement the management attributes and operations. You can define the management
interface declaratively by implementing a Dynamic MBean that reads an XML file describing
the management interface. You could also implement a Dynamic MBean that retrieves its management interface from a database. This is possible because the management interface of
Dynamic MBeans can be determined at runtime instead of compile time, which is a requirement for Standard MBeans. In addition, with Dynamic MBeans you gain access to the

4

DYNAMIC
MBEANS

MBean's metadata elements that you can extend for the application purposes. You will see more examples of this in Chapter 5.

The code example in Listing 4.8 shows you a full Dynamic MBean implementation, in detail, of a resource that has a matching management interface to the User MBean from Chapter 3. The implementation starts with the code of the getAttribute() and getAttributes() methods. After the getter method implementations is the corresponding implementation of the setAttribute() and setAttributes() methods. These methods map the management attribute names to the actual fields in the resource implementation.

After the management attribute getter and setter method implementations, you have an implementation of the invoke() method. The principal is the same as the management attribute accessor methods; the management operation names are mapped to the actual methods in the resource implementation.

Last, you have the implementation of the getMBeanInfo() method. The implementation returns a collection of metadata objects back to the agent that describe each element of the resource's management interface.

The DynamicUser implementation is shown in Listing 4.8.

LISTING 4.8   DynamicUser.java

```java
package book.jmx.examples;

import javax.management.*;
import java.util.Iterator;

public class DynamicUser
        extends NotificationBroadcasterSupport
        implements DynamicMBean {


  // mgmt attribute name constants
  final static String ID      = "ID";
  final static String NAME    = "Name";
  final static String ADDRESS = "Address";
  final static String NUMBERS = "PhoneNumbers";
  final static String PASSWD  = "Password";


  // mgmt operation name constants
  final static String PRINT_INFO  = "printInfo";
  final static String ADD_NUMBER  = "addPhoneNumber";
```

LISTING 4.8 continued

```java
final static String REMOVE_NUMBER = "removePhoneNumber";


// fields for attribute values
private long id          = System.currentTimeMillis();
private String name      = "";
private String address   = "";
private String passwd    = null;
private String[] numbers = new String[3];


// getAttribute implementation

public Object getAttribute(String attribute) throws
                          AttributeNotFoundException,
                          MBeanException,
                          ReflectionException {

  if (attribute == null || attribute.equals(""))
    throw new IllegalArgumentException(
        "null or empty attribute name"
    );

  // map the named attributes to fields
  if (attribute.equals(NAME))
    return name;

  if (attribute.equals(ADDRESS))
    return address;

  if (attribute.equals(NUMBERS))
    return numbers;

  if (attribute.equals(ID))
    return new Long(id);

  throw new AttributeNotFoundException(
    "Attribute " + attribute + " not found."
  );
}


// getAttributes implementation

public AttributeList getAttributes(String[] attributes) {
```

4

DYNAMIC
MBEANS

LISTING 4.8 continued

```
  if (attributes == null)
    throw new IllegalArgumentException("null array");

  AttributeList list = new AttributeList();

  for (int i = 0; i < attributes.length; ++i) {
    try {
      list.add(new Attribute(
          attributes[i], getAttribute(attributes[i])
      ));
    }
    catch (JMException ignored) {
      // if the attribute could not be retrieved, skip it
    }
  }

  return list;
}


// setAttribute implementation

public void setAttribute(Attribute attribute) throws
                         AttributeNotFoundException,
                         InvalidAttributeValueException,
                         MBeanException,
                         ReflectionException {

  if (attribute == null) throw new
    AttributeNotFoundException("null attribute");

  // map attributes to fields
  try {
    if (attribute.getName().equals(NAME))
      this.name = (String)attribute.getValue();

    else if (attribute.getName().equals(ADDRESS))
      this.address = (String)attribute.getValue();

    else if (attribute.getName().equals(NUMBERS))
      this.numbers = (String[])attribute.getValue();

    else if (attribute.getName().equals(PASSWD))
```

LISTING 4.8   continued

```java
      this.passwd = (String)attribute.getValue();

    else
      throw new AttributeNotFoundException(
        "attribute "+attribute.getName()+" not found."
      );
  }
  catch (ClassCastException e) {
    throw new InvalidAttributeValueException(
      "Invalid attribute type " +
      attribute.getValue().getClass().getName()
    );
  }
}


// setAttributes implementation

public AttributeList setAttributes(AttributeList list) {

  if (list == null)
    throw new IllegalArgumentException("null list");

  AttributeList results = new AttributeList();
  Iterator it          = list.iterator();

  while (it.hasNext()) {
    try {
      Attribute attr = (Attribute)it.next();
      setAttribute(attr);
      results.add(attr);
    }
    catch (JMException ignored) {
      // if unable to set the attribute, skip it
    }
  }

  return results;
}


// invoke implementation

public Object invoke(String actionName,
```

LISTING 4.8   continued

```
                              Object[] params,
                              String[] signature)
                   throws MBeanException,
                          ReflectionException {

    if (actionName == null || actionName.equals(""))
      throw new IllegalArgumentException("no operation");

    // map operation names to methods
    if (actionName.equals(PRINT_INFO))
      return printInfo();

    else if (actionName.equals(ADD_NUMBER)) {
      addPhoneNumber((String)params[0]);
      return null;
    }

    else if (actionName.equals(REMOVE_NUMBER)) {
      removePhoneNumber(((Integer)params[0]).intValue());
      return null;
    }

    else
      throw new UnsupportedOperationException (
        "unknown operation " + actionName
      );
}


// getMBeanInfo implementation

public MBeanInfo getMBeanInfo() {

  // Is attribute readable and/or writable
  final boolean READABLE  = true;
  final boolean WRITABLE  = true;

  // Is attribute getter in boolean isAttribute()
  // form?
  final boolean IS_GETTER = true;

  // MBean class and description
  String className    = getClass().getName();
  String description  =
```

LISTING 4.8   continued

```
    "User resource with dynamic management interface";

    // metadata for 'ID' attribute.
    MBeanAttributeInfo id   = new MBeanAttributeInfo(
      ID,                                    // name
      long.class.getName(),                  // type
      "Unique identifier of user.",          // description
      READABLE, !WRITABLE, !IS_GETTER        // access
    );

    // metadata for 'Name' attribute.
    MBeanAttributeInfo name = new MBeanAttributeInfo(
      NAME,                                  // name
      String.class.getName(),                // type
      "User's name.",                        // description
      READABLE, WRITABLE, !IS_GETTER         // access
    );

    // metadata for 'Address' attribute.
    MBeanAttributeInfo address = new MBeanAttributeInfo(
      ADDRESS,                               // name
      String.class.getName(),                // type
      "User's address.",                     // description
      READABLE, WRITABLE, !IS_GETTER         // access
    );

    // metadata for 'PhoneNumbers' attribute.
    MBeanAttributeInfo numbers = new MBeanAttributeInfo(
      NUMBERS,                               // name
      String[].class.getName(),              // type
      "User's phone numbers.",               // description
      READABLE, WRITABLE, !IS_GETTER         // access
    );

    // metadata for 'Password' attribute.
    MBeanAttributeInfo passwd  = new MBeanAttributeInfo(
      PASSWD,                                // name
      String.class.getName(),                // type
      "User's password.",                    // description
      !READABLE, WRITABLE, !IS_GETTER        // access
    );


    // metadata for 'printInfo' operation
```

4

**DYNAMIC
MBEANS**

LISTING 4.8   continued

```
MBeanOperationInfo printInfo = new MBeanOperationInfo(
  PRINT_INFO,                            // name
  "String representation of the user.", // description
  null,                                  // signature
  String.class.getName(),                // return type
  MBeanOperationInfo.INFO                // impact
);

// metadata for 'addPhoneNumber' operation.
MBeanOperationInfo addPhoneNumber =
  new MBeanOperationInfo(
    ADD_NUMBER,                          // name
    "Adds phone number for the user.",  // description

    new MBeanParameterInfo[] {           // signature
      new MBeanParameterInfo(
        "number",
        String.class.getName(),
        "The number to add."
      )
    },

    void.class.getName(),                // return type
    MBeanOperationInfo.ACTION            // impact
);

// metadata for 'removePhoneNumber' operation.
MBeanOperationInfo removePhoneNumber =
  new MBeanOperationInfo(
    REMOVE_NUMBER,                       // name
    "Removes phone number from user.",  // description

    new MBeanParameterInfo[] {           // signature
      new MBeanParameterInfo(
        "index",
        int.class.getName(),
        "The index number."
      )
    },

    void.class.getName(),                // return type
    MBeanOperationInfo.ACTION            // impact
);

// mbean constructors
```

LISTING 4.8   continued

```
MBeanConstructorInfo defaultConstructor =
  new MBeanConstructorInfo(
    "Default Constructor",
    "Creates a new user instance.", null
  );

// attribute, constructor and operation lists
MBeanAttributeInfo[] attributes =
  new MBeanAttributeInfo[] {
    id, name, address, numbers, passwd
  };

MBeanConstructorInfo[] constructors =
  new MBeanConstructorInfo[] {
    defaultConstructor
  };

MBeanOperationInfo[] operations =
  new MBeanOperationInfo[] {
    printInfo, addPhoneNumber, removePhoneNumber
  };

// return the MBeanInfo
return new MBeanInfo(
  className, description, attributes,
  constructors, operations, null
);
}

// management operation implementations
public String printInfo() {
  return
    "User: " + name +"\n"+
    "Address: " + address +"\n"+
    "Phone #: " + numbers[0] +"\n"+
    "Phone #: " + numbers[1] +"\n"+
    "Phone #: " + numbers[2] +"\n";
}

public void addPhoneNumber(String number) {
  for (int i = 0; i < numbers.length; ++i)
    if (numbers[i] == null) {
      numbers[i] = number;
      break;
```

4

DYNAMIC MBEANS

LISTING 4.8   continued

```
      }
  }

  public void removePhoneNumber(int index) {
    if (index < 0 || index >= numbers.length)
      return;

    numbers[index] = null;
  }

}
```

Because the management operations and attributes of the DynamicUser MBean are identical to the UserMBean, you can use the same management application to access both managed resources. You can test this by taking the UserClient class you built in Chapter 3 and run it against an MBean server instance that has a DynamicUser instance registered to it. The DynamicUser instance should be bound to the same object name reference "example:name=user" that was used for the UserMBean.

You will need to modify the UserClient class to register DynamicUser class instead of the User. The change to UserClient class is shown in the Listing 4.9.

LISTING 4.9   UserClient.java

```
...

try {
    // register the MBean
    ObjectName name = new ObjectName("example:name=user");
    server.registerMBean(new DynamicUser(), name);

    // Invoke the printInfo operation on an
    // uninitialized MBean instance.
    Object result = server.invoke(
                        name,            // MBean name
                        "printInfo",     // operation name
                        null,            // no parameters
                        null             // void signature
                    );

...
```

When you compile and run the modified `UserClient` that uses the `DynamicUser` component, you should see the exact same results on the console that you saw with the `UserMBean`.

To compile the `DynamicUser.java` and the modified `UserClient.java` execute the command:

```
C:\Examples> javac -d . -classpath jmx-1_0_1-ri_bin\jmx\lib\jmxri.jar;
➡jmx-1_0_1-ri_bin\jmx\lib\jmxtools.jar DynamicUser.java UserClient.java
```

To run the application, enter the command:

```
C:\Examples> java -classpath .;jmx-1_0_1-ri_bin\jmx\lib\jmxri.jar
➡ book.jmx.examples.UserClient
```

You should see the following output:

Non-initialized User object:

```
User:
Address:
Phone #: null
Phone #: null
Phone #: null
Initialized User object:
User: John
Address: Strawberry Street
Phone #: 555-1232
Phone #: null
Phone #: null
```

The difference in the agent between the standard and Dynamic MBean is how the management interface metadata is retrieved. For the Standard MBeans, it was collected by the agent using introspection, whereas for the Dynamic MBeans, the agent invokes the `getMBeanInfo()` method to retrieve the metadata. The agent abstracts the MBean type, standard or dynamic, from the management application by requiring all invocations to propagate through its `invoke()`, `setAttribute()`, and `getAttribute()` methods. What is exposed to the management application is the `MBeanServer` interface that provides the methods to access and discover the management interface.

The metadata description available to the client is either built by the agent or provided by the managed resource explicitly. This, added to the fact that the client is never given a direct Java reference to the managed resource, but instead uses the *object name* reference, leads to a decoupled invocation mechanism. There is no MBean specific, statically typed interface that the management application needs to rely on to access the managed resource. The next section will give you a simplified example on how to switch component implementations between Standard and Dynamic MBean on a live MBean server.

Hot Deploying Resources

You have built two separate implementations of a resource that have an identical management interface. This means that, from the point of view of the management application, these implementations are interchangeable. You have also learned that the JMX architecture decouples the management applications from the managed resources, and seen how the operation invocations are detyped in the MBean server `invoke()` method.

These features of the JMX-based management architecture allow you to implement a managed resource that you can change or update at runtime. This is often called *hot deployment*, a feature you can find in many server-based software applications. It means that a new component can be brought into the server or an existing one can be updated without having to restart the whole server. With JMX this is easy to do. Because the management applications do not have any direct Java references to the managed resources you can switch the component implementations without the client necessarily noticing anything.

To demonstrate this, you will build a `Recycler` application that will allow you to switch the implementation of an MBean on-the-fly. You will use the `DynamicUser` MBean built in Listings 4.8 and the `BroadcastingUser` MBean that you built in Chapter 3. The `Recycler` component will bind one of the two implementations to the MBean server under the `object name` `"example:name=user"`.

The `Recycler` component itself is an MBean, and exposes a `recycle()` management operation to the client. You can use the `recycle()` operation to switch the implementation between a Standard MBean and Dynamic MBean version. The management interface of the `RecyclerMBean` is as follows:

```
package book.jmx.examples;

import javax.management.*;

public interface RecyclerMBean {

  public String recycle();

}
```

The `recycle()` operation will switch the implementation bound to object name `"example:name=user"` in the MBean server. The `RecyclerMBean` will also register and start an HTTP adaptor, so that you can manipulate the components easily via your Web browser. The code for the `Recycler` implementation is shown in Listing 4.10.

LISTING 4.10   Recycler.java

```java
package book.jmx.examples;

import javax.management.*;
import java.util.List;

public class Recycler implements RecyclerMBean {

  private String component   = "Standard User";
  private MBeanServer server = null;

  public String recycle() {

    // Find an agent from this JVM. Null argument will
    // return a list of all MBeanServer instances.
    List list = MBeanServerFactory.findMBeanServer(null);
    server = (MBeanServer)list.iterator().next();

    try {

      // switch implementations between a standard and
      // dynamic mbeans
      if (component.equals("Standard User")) {
        server.unregisterMBean(
          new ObjectName("example:name=User")
        );

        server.registerMBean(
          new DynamicUser(),
          new ObjectName("example:name=User")
        );

        component = "Dynamic User";
      }

      else {
        server.unregisterMBean(
          new ObjectName("example:name=User")
        );

        server.registerMBean(
          new BroadcastingUser(),
          new ObjectName("example:name=User")
        );
```

LISTING 4.10 continued

```
            component = "Standard User";
        }
    }
    catch (JMException e) {
        e.printStackTrace();
    }

    return "Implementation changed to " + component;
}

public static void main(String[] args) {

    MBeanServer server =
        MBeanServerFactory.createMBeanServer();

    ObjectName name    = null;

    try {
        name =  new ObjectName("example:name=recycler");
        server.registerMBean(new Recycler(), name);

        name = new ObjectName("example:name=User");
        server.registerMBean(new BroadcastingUser(), name);

        name = new ObjectName("adaptor:protocol=HTTP");
        com.tivoli.jmx.http_pa.Listener adaptor =
            new com.tivoli.jmx.http_pa.Listener();

        adaptor.startListener();
        server.registerMBean(adaptor, name);
    }
    catch (java.io.IOException e) {
        e.printStackTrace();
    }
    catch (JMException e) {
        e.printStackTrace();
    }
}
}
```

To compile and run the Recycler example, execute these commands (using Tivoli JMX):

```
C:\Examples> javac -d . -classpath .;tmx4j\base\lib\jmxx.jar;tmx4j\base\
➥lib\jmxc.jar;tmx4j\base\lib\log.jar;
➥tmx4j\ext\lib\jmxext.jar Recycler.java RecyclerMBean.java

C:\Examples> java -classpath .;tmx4j\base\lib\jmxx.jar;
➥tmx4j\base\lib\jmxc.jar;
➥tmx4j\base\lib\log.jar;tmx4j\ext\lib\jmxext.jar
➥book.jmx.examples.Recycler
```

When you successfully run the application, the following line will be printed on the console:

```
The HTTP Adaptor started on port number 6969
```

Point your browser to http://localhost:6969 and enter *:* in the Find an MBean query page to get a list of registered MBeans. Select the Recycler MBean by clicking link "example:name=recycler". Execute the recycle() operation to switch the User implementation between the Dynamic MBean and Standard MBean.

Notice that the BroadcastingUser exposes management notifications as part of its management interface. You can see the difference on the HTTP adaptor Web pages in Figures 4.2, 4.3, and 4.4 where the notifications are listed. Another difference worth noticing is that the DynamicUser MBean shows the descriptions for its management operations. These were added as part of the MBeanOperationInfo metadata classes. The ability to access and *extend* the metadata attached to each element of the management interface is an interesting possibility that you will utilize in the later chapters.

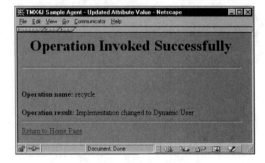

FIGURE 4.2

The results of the recycle operation.

4

DYNAMIC
MBEANS

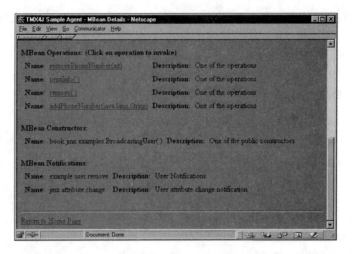

FIGURE 4.3

Management view of the BroadcastingUser *MBean.*

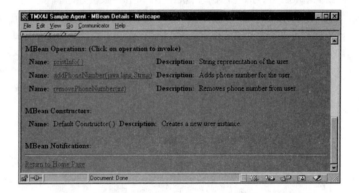

FIGURE 4.4

Management view of the DynamicUser *MBean.*

There are some features that are lacking in the Recycler example. For example, the change of the implementation will not store the state of the MBean. If you have edited the attribute values, they will be lost. To avoid this, you need to persist the MBean's state to the disk, to a database, or some other persistent storage. In Chapter 5, you will look at the Model MBeans and how they implement the MBean persistence.

The other restriction with the `Recycler` example is that both components need to be available for the JVM classloader at start-up time. In practice, when you need to hot deploy components, whether you are updating an existing one or adding new ones, you will need to dynamically add the new classes to the class loader. The JMX provides this possibility with a standard agent service called M-Let service. This allows you to add new components dynamically and load them from across the network. You will see the M-Let service in Chapter 7, "Standard Agent Services," where all the standard agent services are covered.

Summary

As you have seen with the examples, Dynamic MBeans allow the manageable resources to define their management interfaces at runtime, instead of using the statically typed Java interfaces that you needed to implement with Standard MBeans. The agent does not rely on introspection to find the management interface but, instead, directly calls the `getMBeanInfo()` method of the `DynamicMBean` interface to discover the management interface and to invoke operations and to get and set attributes. The Dynamic MBean implementation is required to build metadata that explicitly declares all the elements of the management interface.

Because the Dynamic MBeans do not impose a set of naming rules on the resource classes, they are convenient in exposing already existing resources to management. The attribute and operation invocations can easily be mapped to methods using any kind of naming convention.

An important point to remember about Dynamic MBeans is that they allow the late binding of the management interface instead of the early static binding of a Java interface. Another aspect differentiating the Dynamic MBeans from the Standard MBeans is the fact that the developer has an access to the metadata of the MBean. This is not possible with Standard MBeans.

4

Model MBeans

IN THIS CHAPTER

Model MBeans are an extension of the Dynamic MBean. They provide a generic, configurable template for the developer to easily instrument a resource for management. The JMX agent provides a Model MBean implementation that can be configured with the management interface of the instrumented resource and additional behavioral properties for the MBean.

Model MBeans can be easily configured and created by the resource classes on-the-fly when needed. All compliant JMX agent implementations offer at least one Model MBean implementation in the form of specification mandated `RequiredModelMBean` class. All Model MBean metadata classes also implement a `DescriptorAccess` interface that adds the ability to add custom properties to each element of the metadata.

`ModelMBean` Interface

The `ModelMBean` interface (see Listing 5.1) extends the `DynamicMBean` interface, the `PersistentMBean` interface, and the `ModelMBeanNotificationBroadcaster` interface. The `DynamicMBean` interface is familiar from the previous chapter, the `PersistentMBean` (shown in Listing 5.2) adds methods for persisting the MBean's state, and the `ModelMBeanNotificationBroadcaster` interface provides the methods required by a notification broadcaster MBean.

LISTING 5.1   ModelMBean Interface

```
package javax.management.modelmbean;

public interface ModelMBean extends
    DynamicMBean, PersistentMBean, ModelMBeanNotificationBroadcaster {

    public void setModelMBeanInfo(ModelMBeanInfo inModelMBeanInfo)
        throws MBeanException,
            RuntimeOperationsException;

    public void setManagedResource(Object mr, String mr_type)
        throws MBeanException,
            RuntimeOperationsException,
            InstanceNotFoundException,
            InvalidTargetObjectTypeException;

}
```

The `ModelMBean` interface allows you to describe the management interface of the Model MBean using the metadata classes. The metadata for Model MBeans is extended from the corresponding Dynamic MBean classes by introducing descriptor classes. The descriptors are used for adding behavioral properties to each element of the metadata. These behavioral properties can include the persistence policy of an MBean, transactional behavior, attribute caching policy, security policies, and so on.

LISTING 5.2 PersistentMBean Interface

```
package javax.management;

public interface PersistentMBean {

    public void load() throws  MBeanException,
                               RuntimeOperationsException,
                               InstanceNotFoundException;

    public void store() throws MBeanException,
                               RuntimeOperationsException,
                               InstanceNotFoundException;

}
```

Because the Model MBean instances are provided by the agent, the support for behavioral properties depends on the agent implementation. All agents must provide the `RequiredModelMBean` class, but there is no guarantee what behavioral properties are supported by this implementation. In fact, it is more than likely that JMX agents working in different environments, such as J2ME and J2EE, will have differing implementations of the `RequiredModelMBean` class.

All Model MBean implementations are broadcaster MBeans. Model MBeans automatically send attribute change notifications on any changes to management attributes for all interested listeners.

Descriptors

The descriptor objects are used in the Model MBean metadata to add behavioral policies to the managed bean. These policies vary from persistence to caching to transactional properties, depending on the JMX Agent implementation that provides the Model MBean implementation. The JMX specification defines some standard policies that the Model MBean can implement. The Model MBean implementation can also support custom policies that are not defined in the specification.

A descriptor is a collection of key-value pairs. When defining the management interface for an MBean attribute it is possible to add, for example, a descriptor that describes which caching and persistence policies should be implemented for that attribute. The Model MBean implementation will try to adapt to match the required MBean behavior. It is also possible that the behavioral descriptors are changed at run-time, via a management application or by the managed resource itself.

All descriptor objects must implement the `Descriptor` interface. All descriptors are also made available to management applications by exposing `getDescriptor()` and `setDescriptor()` methods in the Model MBean's metadata classes.

Table 5.1 describes the relevant methods of the `Descriptor` interface.

TABLE 5.1   Relevant Methods of the `Descriptor` Interface

Method	Description
`getFieldNames()`	Returns an array of strings that contain all of the field names in the descriptor.
`getFieldValues(String[] names)`	Returns an object array of field values. If the given array of field names is `null`, all the values in the descriptor are returned. If an array of field names is supplied as a parameter, the returned object array will contain only the values for the named fields in the order defined by the `names` argument. If a named field does not exist, a `null` reference is returned in its place.
`getFieldValue(String name)`	Returns the value of a given field. If the field is not found in the descriptor, a `null` reference is returned.
`getFields()`	Returns an array of strings representing the field and value pairs in the descriptor. The format of the strings is as follows: `fieldName1=fieldValue` `fieldName2=fieldValue` If the type of the field class is not `String`, a `toString()` method is called on the object to retrieve a string representation of the value.

TABLE 5.1   continued

Method	Description
setField(*String name, Object value*)	Sets a field in the descriptor to a given value. If the given field already exists in the descriptor, its value is replaced with the new value; otherwise, a new field is added to the descriptor.
setFields(*String[] names, Object[] values*)	Sets all the field name and value pairs in the descriptor.
removeField(*String name*)	Removes the given field from the descriptor.

The metadata classes of MBean constructors, attributes, operations, and notifications implement the DescriptorAccess interface. This interface contains two methods that allow you to retrieve the descriptor objects and set them—getDescriptor() and setDescriptor(). The getDescriptor() method returns a copy of the descriptor of a management interface element. The setDescriptor() allows you to set a new descriptor for the Model MBean. Notice that the setDescriptor() replaces the existing descriptor completely.

Notification Logging Policy

The Model MBean implementation can be configured to log the notifications that are broadcast by setting a notification logging policy. The notification logging policy can be set either at the MBean level or explicitly per notification type. The notification logging is enabled by setting a log field in the MBean or notification descriptors. The details of the log field are given in the section Model MBean Metadata.

Persistence Policy

The MBean descriptor and management attribute descriptors allow the setting of persistence policies for the MBean's attributes. The MBean's attributes can be persisted periodically to a file system, database, LDAP server, or a custom high-performance cache. Persistence policy can be set at the MBean level for all its attributes or set individually per attribute.

The JMX specification defines some persistence policies that can be implemented by the JMX agent. The four predefined persistence policies are OnUpdate, OnTimer, NoMoreOftenThan and Never. On update persistence is performed every time the attribute's value changes. A timer based persistence is performed at given checkpoints. The persistence operations can also be limited to a maximum amount per time interval; for example, once every five seconds at most.

You will also see the different persistence policies discussed in the Model MBean Metadata section where the descriptor fields are discussed in detail.

Notice that the JMX agent is not required to implement persistence. If the agent is designed to run in an environment where persistence is not supported, its Model MBean implementation can ignore any requests to persist the MBean's state.

Value Caching Policy

The attribute and operation descriptors allow caching of management attribute and management operation return values. The descriptor keeps track of the last invocation times and stores the last known attribute values and operation return values. When a request to retrieve an attribute value is made, the value in the descriptor is checked for its currency and can be returned instead of accessing the managed resource directly, as shown in Figure 5.1. This will help reduce the impact of management operations on managed resources.

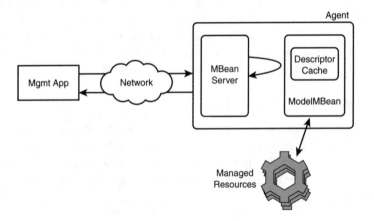

FIGURE 5.1

An attribute value can be returned from a descriptor directly.

The descriptor can also contain default values for attributes and a method mapping to the operations that should be invoked to access the managed resource when the cached value is considered stale.

Export Policy

The Model MBean descriptors allow you to set an export policy on your MBeans. If the JMX agent supports lookup services, for example through JNDI, the MBeans can be located by exporting a serialized object to a lookup service. This allows an MBean a degree of location transparency because the address of the host JMX agent does not have to be known to other agents or management applications beforehand.

Model MBean Metadata

The metadata classes of Model MBeans extend from the metadata classes used with Dynamic MBeans. For each of the metadata class defined in the `javax.management` package, there is an equivalent in the `javax.management.modelmbean` package. The `ModelMBean` interface extends the `DynamicMBean` interface, so it must also implement the `getMBeanInfo()` method. The returned `MBeanInfo` instance of the Model MBean must implement the `ModelMBeanInfo` interface to support the extended metadata provided by the descriptor classes (see Figure 5.2).

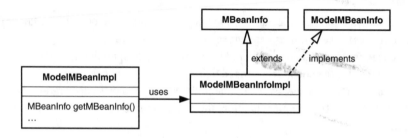

FIGURE 5.2

Class diagram of the `ModelMBeanInfo` *implementation.*

When you invoke the `getMBeanInfo()` method on a Model MBean, you need to cast the returned value to `ModelMBeanInfo` type to access the Model MBean descriptors. This also applies to the other metadata classes that describe the attributes, operations, constructors, and notifications of the management interface. The corresponding Model MBean metadata classes are

- `ModelMBeanAttributeInfo`
- `ModelMBeanOperationInfo`
- `ModelMBeanConstructorInfo`
- `ModelMBeanNotificationInfo`

Each of these classes extend the matching metadata class in the `javax.management` package. In addition, they all implement the `DescriptorAccess` interface (shown in Listing 5.3), which allows the management applications to access the descriptors. You will take a brief look into each of the Model MBean metadata classes next.

LISTING 5.3 DescriptorAccess Interface

```
package javax.management.*;

public interface DescriptorAccess {

    public Descriptor getDescriptor();
    public void setDescriptor(Descriptor descr);

}
```

ModelMBeanInfo

The ModelMBeanInfo interface declares all the methods that are included in the MBeanInfo class. The getAttributes(), getConstructors(), getOperations(), and getNotifications() methods are declared to return the corresponding metadata classes MBeanAttributeInfo, MBeanConstructorInfo, MbeanOperationInfo, and MBeanNotificationInfo, respectively, to match the MBeanInfo class declaration. However, in case of the ModelMBeanInfo implementation, the actual returned object types are the corresponding Model MBean metadata classes.

In addition to the methods identical to the MBeanInfo class declaration, the ModelMBeanInfo interface declares several accessor methods for handling MBean descriptors. These are listed in the next section.

getMBeanDescriptor and setMBeanDescriptor

The getMBeanDescriptor() method returns a descriptor object that contains the behavioral policies that apply to the MBean instance. Accordingly, the setMBeanDescriptor() method sets a new policy descriptor to the MBean. Note that setting a new descriptor completely replaces the previous one in the MBean. Any merging or additions to the existing policies must be processed manually.

The policies set in the MBean descriptor can be overridden by any individual descriptor objects associated with the MBean's attributes, constructors, operations, or notifications.

The additional methods in the ModelMBeanInfo interface you should be aware of are shown in Table 5.2.

TABLE 5.2   Partial List of the Methods of the `ModelMBeanInfo` Interface

Method	Description
`getDescriptors(`*`String type`*`)`	Returns the descriptors defined in the management interface matching to a given type. The type can be
	`mbean`
	`attribute`
	`constructor`
	`operation`
	`notification`
	If the type is a `null` reference, this method returns all the descriptors in the MBean.
`setDescriptors(`*`Descriptor[]descriptors`*`)`	Adds or replaces the descriptors in the array.
	Notice that all descriptors must have at least the `name` and `descriptorType` values.
`getDescriptor(`*`String name,String type`*`)`	Returns a descriptor based on a name and type.
`getMBeanDescriptor()`	Returns the descriptor for the entire MBean. This descriptor contains the default policies for all elements of the management interface. The default values can be overridden by individual management interface elements with descriptors in their own specific metadata classes.
`setMBeanDescriptor(`*`Descriptor`* d`)`	Sets a new descriptor for the MBean. Notice that this is a full replacement of the existing MBean descriptor; no merging is done.

Predefined MBean Descriptor Fields

The JMX specification declares predefined descriptor field names that can be used to configure a Model MBean instance. Note that many predefined descriptor fields are optional and, therefore, may be ignored by the Model MBean implementation. In general, different agents support different sets of descriptor fields in their `RequiredModelMBean` implementation. The documentation for a specific JMX implementation should list the properties that are implemented. As an example, the Sun Reference Implementation supports simple file-based persistence for the MBean, whereas the Tivoli JMX implementation, at the time of this writing, did not support persistent management attributes.

For all descriptors, the `name` and `descriptorType` fields are mandatory. In addition, the field `role` also must be included for the management operation and MBean constructor descriptors.

The MBean descriptor sets policies that are applied to all management attributes and operations in an MBean, such as persistence and value caching. Setting these policies will affect each individual management element, unless it is overridden by associating a specific descriptor for the single attribute or operation. This way, it is easy to set the behavioral properties to all attributes, and then only override the properties for those attributes that require different behaviors from the default.

The following list is not conclusive. The Model MBean implementations are allowed to support any number of custom descriptor fields. The following list contains all the fields described in the JMX specification.

name   The case sensitive name of the MBean. This is a required field for all Model MBeans descriptors.

descriptorType   For descriptors associated with the MBean, this field's value must contain the string "MBean". This is a required field for all Model MBeans descriptors.

displayName   The displayName field can be used to indicate to the management applications to use a string representation other than the MBean's object name in the user interface. This field can be used for localized representation of the MBean name, for example.

persistPolicy   By defining a persistence policy, the management attributes can be persisted by the Model MBean implementation. Defining a persistence policy at the MBean level will affect all the attributes in the MBean. The MBean persistence policy can be overwritten by individual attributes by setting their own policy at the attribute level.

The JMX specification defines four different kinds of persistence policies. Specific Model MBean implementations can provide policies other than mentioned here.

The standardized values for the `persistPolicy` field are as follows:

- Never
- OnUpdate
- OnTimer
- NoMoreOftenThan

The Never policy implies that the attribute values are transient and its state is never persisted. The OnUpdate policy indicates that the Model MBean implementation should persist the state whenever it is updated. The OnTimer policy means that the state of management attributes is persisted based on a time interval. The time interval is set by adding a persistPeriod field to the descriptor. Finally, the NoMoreOftenThan policy tells the Model MBean implementation to persist the state of the management attributes every time they are updated, unless they were already persisted once within a given time limit.

The persistPeriod field is used to set the time interval. The NoMoreOftenThan policy allows you to control the persistence frequency for attributes that may potentially change very often within a short period of time. In such cases, the performance penalty of persisting the attributes on every update can be avoided with the use of NoMoreOftenThan policy.

The persistPolicy field is optional and may not be supported by the JMX implementation.

persistPeriod This field is only valid if the persistPolicy field contains the OnTimer or NoMoreOftenThan policies. If the OnTimer value has been set, this field's value indicates the time interval that is used to persist the state of the management attributes. If the NoMoreOftenThan value has been set, this field's value indicates the minimum time interval between two persistence operations.

The persistPeriod field along with persistPolicy is an optional field for the JMX implementation and, therefore, may not be supported by all agents.

persistLocation The persistLocation field can be used to configure the persistence store for the MBean. This field can contain a directory path where the MBean's state should be persisted; it can contain DataSource reference, table names, and so on. It depends on the JMX implementation which types of persistence locations are supported.

persistName The persistName field can be used in conjunction with the persistLocation field. The persistName field can contain a filename, in case a file based persistence is being used, a column names in the database table that should be used to store the MBean's state, and so on. Again, it depends on the JMX implementation how the value of this descriptor field is interpreted.

log The log field contains a Boolean value. If the value is set to true, all notifications sent by the Model MBean will be logged. This can be used, for example, to log all AttributeChangeNotification objects in the agent to provide a simple audit track for attribute updates.

logFile The logFile field contains the full file path and filename to the log file the JMX agent uses to write the notification logs. This field must be declared when the log field equals true or no logging will be performed.

currencyTimeLimit   The currencyTimeLimit field sets the caching policy for the MBean's attributes. The field value defines, in seconds, how long the attribute value remains current after the last time it was retrieved from the managed resource. If the attribute value stored in the attribute's descriptor is determined to still be current, the managed resource is not invoked to retrieve the value.

The currencyTimeLimit value can be overridden by individual attributes by declaring the field in their corresponding descriptors. The attribute descriptors also allow you to control the operations that are used to retrieve and update the attribute values in managed resource via getMethod and setMethod descriptor fields. The section "Attribute Caching" gives a more detailed description of the use of these fields.

The value 0 in the currencyTimeLimit field means that the attribute retrieval is never cached and an up-to-date value is always returned. Value –1 indicates the attribute value should always be considered valid, and consecutive calls to read the attribute value will always be returned from the cache.

The currencyTimeLimit field is an optional field for Model MBeans. Attribute value caching may not be implemented by the JMX agent.

export   The value of the export field can be a serialized object that is used to export a handle to the MBean. The handle should contain the information necessary for the management applications or other JMX agents to be able to locate and connect to the JMX agent. The indirection provided by the agent or MBean handle allows for location transparency of the agents and MBeans.

visibility   The visibility field allows you to set the level of granularity for the managed beans. This field can act as an indicator to the management applications on how the MBeans should be displayed or grouped in the user interface, or how their importance relates to other MBeans in the same management domain or agent.

The value of this field is an integer ranging from 1 to 4. A visibility value of 1 indicates the most significant, or large granularity, MBeans, whereas a visibility value of 4 indicates the least significant, or small granularity, MBeans.

The visibility field is optional and, therefore, may be ignored by the JMX agent.

presentationString   The presentationString field can be used to associate additional presentation data to the MBean. The content of the presentationString is an XML encoded string that can store information such as how to present and build the user interface for the MBean.

There are no standard DTDs or XML schemas defined for presenting the user interface of an MBean. It is up to the specific protocol adapter and management tool implementations to decide how to interpret the presentation information.

ModelMBeanAttributeInfo

The ModelMBeanAttributeInfo class describes the management attribute of a Model MBean. It extends the MBeanAttributeInfo class and adds the descriptor support by implementing the DescriptorAccess interface (see Figure 5.3).

When associating a descriptor to the Model MBean attribute, the descriptor object must have its descriptorType field set to string value "attribute". The descriptor's name, defined by the name field, must match the name of the attribute defined in the MBeanFeatureInfo class, which is the ancestor class to ModelMBeanAttributeInfo. Note that the descriptor name and the management attribute names are case sensitive.

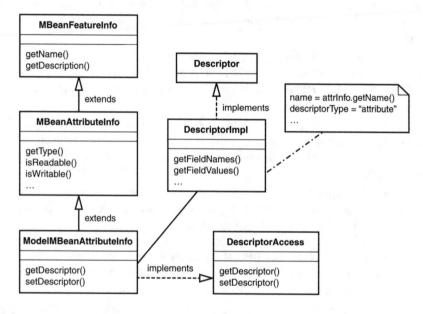

FIGURE 5.3
Class structure of the ModelMBeanAttributeInfo.

Predefined Management Attribute Descriptor Fields

The JMX specification defines descriptor field names for the management attributes that may be supported by the agent's Model MBean implementation. The specification allows customized field names as well, so, depending on the JMX agent implementation, other field names may also be supported. The following field names are standardized by the specification.

name   The name field must contain the name of the attribute with which the descriptor is associated. The name value is case sensitive. The name of the attribute can be retrieved by calling the getName() method of the ModelMBeanAttributeInfo class.

This field is required for all valid attribute descriptor objects.

descriptorType   For descriptors associated with management attributes, this field's value must contain the string value "attribute".

This field is required for all valid attribute descriptor objects.

value   The value field in the descriptor represents the attribute's current value. If attribute caching is enabled, the value object of this field is returned. If the cached attribute value has gone stale, the managed resource is accessed to retrieve an up-to-date value. The retrieved value is stored into the value field in the descriptor. The value caching and descriptor field interactions are covered later in the "Attribute Caching" section.

default   The attribute descriptor allows you to set a default value for the management attribute. The value of the default field is returned if the value field has not been set and the attribute has not been associated with an operation that would retrieve the value from the managed resource.

displayName   The displayName field can be used to indicate to the management applications to use a string representation other than the attribute's programmatic name in the user interface. This field can be used for localized representation of the attribute name, for example.

getMethod   The getMethod field is used to associate a read operation to the attribute's value. When the agent retrieves the attribute value, and the value is not cached or the cached value has gone stale, the managed resource is accessed to retrieve an up-to-date value. The method used for retrieving the value can be mapped to a management operation declared by the getMethod field of the attribute's descriptor. The value of this field must contain the name field of the management operation used for value retrieval. When a value is retrieved, it is stored in this descriptor's value field.

setMethod   The setMethod field associates the corresponding write operation for the attribute's value. As with getMethod, this field's value must contain the name of the management operation that is used to write an attribute's value to the managed resource. When a new attribute value is being written, it is also stored to the descriptors value field.

protocolMap   The value of this field must be another Descriptor object that contains a name-value map useful for protocol adaptors. This field allows the management attribute to be associated with a protocol specific identifier or schema.

persistPolicy   The Model MBean persistence can be defined at the attribute level. Any persistence policy set in the descriptor of a ModelMBeanAttributeInfo object will automatically override the persistence policies set at the Model MBean level. The JMX specification defines four different kinds of persistence policies. Specific Model MBean implementations may provide policies other than those mentioned here.

The standardized values for the `persistPolicy` field are as follows:

- `Never`
- `OnUpdate`
- `OnTimer`
- `NoMoreOftenThan`

The `Never` policy implies that the attribute's value is transient and its state is never persisted. The `OnUpdate` policy indicates that the Model MBean implementation should persist the state whenever it is updated. The `OnTimer` policy means that the attribute's state is persisted based on a time interval. The time interval is set by adding a `persistPeriod` field to the descriptor. Finally, the `NoMoreOftenThan` policy tells the Model MBean implementation to persist the attribute's state every time it is updated, unless the last update was persisted within a given time limit. The time limit is set by adding a `persistPeriod` field to the descriptor. The `NoMoreOftenThan` policy allows you to control the persistence frequency for attributes that may potentially change very often within a short time frame. In such cases, the performance penalty of the attribute's persistence can become an issue and can be avoided with the use of this policy.

persistPeriod This field is only valid if the `persistPolicy` field contains the `OnTimer` or `NoMoreOftenThan` policies. If the `OnTimer` policy has been set, this field's value indicates the time interval that is used to persist the attribute's state. If the `NoMoreOftenThan` policy has been set, this field's value indicates the minimum time interval between two persistence operations.

currencyTimeLimit The `currencyTimeLimit` field indicates to the Model MBean implementation how long the attribute's value can be cached before it should be considered stale. The value of this field defines the number of seconds the `value` field is considered valid. If the time limit set in this field has passed since the last update of the `value` field, the `value` is considered stale and is retrieved from the managed resource on the next request.

If the value of the `currencyTimeLimit` field is set to 0, the retrieval of the attribute's value is directed to the managed resource on every request. A value of –1 indicates to the Model MBean that the attribute's value is never stale.

lastUpdatedTimeStamp The `lastUpdatedTimeStamp` field is set every time the `value` field is updated. This is used in accordance with the `currencyTimeLimit` field to determine whether the value field is valid or stale.

iterable The iterable field can contain a Boolean value that indicates if the contents of the `value` field is an enumerable object.

visibility   The visibility field allows you to set the level of granularity for your management attributes. This field can act as an indicator to the management applications on how the attributes should be displayed or grouped in the user interface, or how their importance relates to other attributes in the MBean.

The value of this field is an integer ranging from 1 to 4. A visibility value of 1 indicates the most significant management attributes, whereas a visibility value of 4 indicates the least significant management attribute.

presentationString   The presentationString field can be used to associate additional presentation data to this attribute. The content of the presentationString is an XML encoded string that can store information such as how to present and access the management attribute and how to render the user interface.

ModelMBeanOperationInfo

The ModelMBeanOperationInfo class describes the management operations of a Model MBean. As with other Model MBean metadata classes, it too extends from its corresponding MBeanOperationInfo class. In addition, the ModelMBeanOperationInfo class implements the DescriptorAccess interface to add the support of descriptors to associate behavioral properties to management operations (see Figure 5.4).

The descriptors associated with Model MBean operations must contain a descriptorType field with the string "operation" as its value. In addition, the role field in the Model MBean operation descriptor must contain one of the following three strings:

```
"operation"
"getter"
"setter"
```

The role field is used to indicate the operations role, whether it is a management operation or used to access the MBean attributes.

The third required descriptor field is the name field, which must contain the name of the management operation with which the descriptor is associated. The management operation's name is defined in the MBeanFeatureInfo class and is accessible through the getName() method.

Predefined Management Operation Descriptor Fields

The predefined descriptor field names for Model MBean operations are listed next. Again, the specification defines these names in an effort to increase the portability of the managed resources from one JMX implementation to another, but the required Model MBean implementation offered by the JMX agent is allowed to support other descriptor fields as well.

name   The name field must contain the name of the operation the descriptor is associated with. Also, note that the value is case sensitive. You can find the name of a management operation by calling the getName() method of the ModelMBeanOperationInfo class. This field is mandatory on all descriptors.

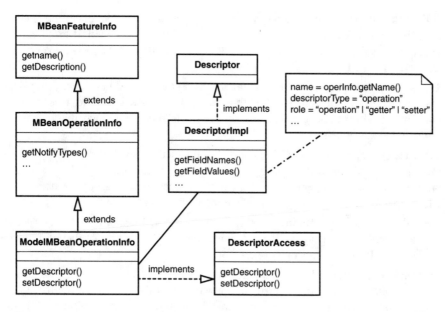

FIGURE 5.4

Class diagram of the ModelMBeanOperationInfo.

descriptorType   The descriptorType field must always contain the string "operation" for descriptors associated with Model MBean operation metadata. This field is mandatory on all descriptors.

displayName   The displayName field can be used to indicate to the management applications to use a string representation other than the operation's programmatic name in the user interface. This field can be used for localized representation of the operation name, for example.

lastReturnedValue   As with the attribute values, the operation return values can also be cached in the Model MBean operation descriptor. The lastReturnedValue field contains the return value of the last invocation of the Model MBean's management operation. The period of time the cached return value remains valid depends on the currencyTimeLimit field value in the same descriptor.

currencyTimeLimit   The currencyTimeLimit is the time period in seconds that the cached return value of the management operation is valid. If the return value caching is enabled and the time limit has not been exceeded, the management operation is not invoked on the managed resource. The validity of the cached return value is checked against the time stamp stored in the lastReturnedTimeStamp field.

If the value of the `currencyTimeLimit` field is `0`, the management operation is always invoked on the managed resource and the return value is not cached. If the `currencyTimeLimit` field has a `-1` value, the return value stored in `lastReturnedValue` is always returned.

lastReturnedTimeStamp   The `lastReturnedTimeStamp` field is updated every time the management operation is invoked on the managed resource. This field is used with `currencyTimeLimit` and `lastReturnedValue` fields to determine whether the cached return value has gone stale.

visibility   The `visibility` field allows you to set the level of granularity for your management operations. The management applications can use this field as an indicator on how to display the operations in their user interface, how to group the operations, which operations are accessed more often than others, and so on.

The value of this field is an integer ranging from 1 to 4. A visibility value of 1 indicates the most significant management operations, whereas the visibility value of 4 indicates the least significant management operation.

presentationString   The `presentationString` field can be used to associate additional presentation data to this attribute. The content of the `presentationString` is an XML encoded string that can store information on how to present and access the management operation, its attributes, and return type. The management application can use the information stored in the XML to decide how to render the user interface.

ModelMBeanNotificationInfo

The `ModelMBeanNotificationInfo` describes the notifications emitted by a Model MBean. As with the previously discussed metadata classes, the `ModelMBeanNotificationInfo` class also extends its corresponding `MBeanNotificationInfo` class (see Figure 5.5).

The mandatory `name` field in the notification descriptor must contain the name of the notification class available via the superclass `getName()` method. The `descriptorType` field must contain the string value `"notification"`.

The predefined descriptor field names for Model MBean notifications are as follows:

name   The name field must contain the name of the notification class. This field is mandatory on all descriptors.

descriptorType   The `descriptorType` field must always contain the string `"notification"` for descriptors associated with Model MBean notification metadata. This field is mandatory on all descriptors.

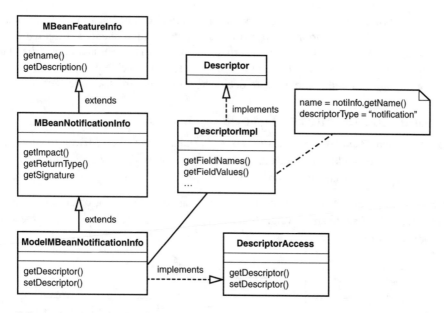

FIGURE 5.5

Class diagram of the `ModelMBeanNotificationInfo`.

severity   The `severity` field can be used to describe the different levels of severity assigned to the notification. The specification defines seven levels of severity:

0—Unknown, Indeterminate

1—Non recoverable

2—Critical, Failure

3—Major, Severe

4—Minor, Marginal, or Error

5—Warning

6—Normal, Cleared, or Informative

The value of the `severity` field is an integer in the range of 0 to 6.

messageId   The `messageId` field allows additional identifier to be added to the notification.

log   This is a Boolean value that can be used to indicate whether the notification should be logged. The `log` field set in a notification descriptor can override the log setting in the MBean descriptor.

logFile   `logFile` is the filename where log entries should be recorded. This descriptor field overrides the MBean-wide log setting.

presentationString The presentationString field can be used to associate additional presentation data to the notification. The content of the presentationString is an XML encoded string that can store information on how to present and access the management operation, its attributes, and return type. The management application can use the information stored in the XML to decide how to render the user interface.

ModelMBeanConstructorInfo

The ModelMBeanConstructorInfo class describes the constructor of an MBean. It extends the MBeanConstructorInfo class and adds the descriptor support by implementing the DescriptorAccess interface (see Figure 5.6).

When associating a descriptor to the constructor metadata, the descriptor object must have its descriptorType field set to string value "operation". The role field must contain the string value "constructor".

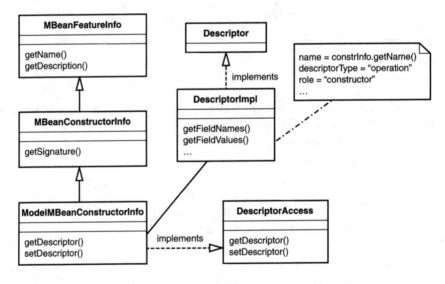

FIGURE 5.6

Class diagram of the ModelMBeanConstructorInfo.

In addition to the `name`, `descriptorType`, and `role` fields, the constructor descriptor can contain the `displayName`, `class`, `visibility`, and `presentationString` fields. The `class` field must contain the fully-qualified name of the class where the constructor is defined. The `name` field must contain the name returned by the `MBeanConstructorInfo.getName()` method. The semantics of the `displayName`, `visibility`, and `presentationString` fields are equal to those defined for Model MBean operation descriptors.

Attribute Caching

The metadata for Model MBean attributes allows you to set a caching policy for attributes and operation return values. One of the properties defined in the descriptor of a management attribute is the management operation that can be invoked to either retrieve the attribute's value or set the attribute value in the resource. This is achieved by declaring the `getMethod` and `setMethod` fields in the attribute's descriptor.

It is also possible to not set any methods as a management attribute's accessors. In practice, this means that all of the attribute's state is kept in the Model MBean instance. Both the `set` and `get` operations access only the attribute's descriptor and never directly invoke any methods on the managed resource. The value of the attribute is stored in the descriptor and can be persisted if the Model MBean implementation supports attribute persistence. The sequence of calls is shown in Figure 5.7.

This attribute behavior allows the management of resources that have no knowledge of the management attributes. It is possible to extend existing resources with new management attributes. It also allows managed resources that are unable to maintain their own state, *transient* resources, to delegate the state management to their Model MBean. The state will be held in the descriptors and managed by the agent.

For managed resources that do maintain their own state, the `getMethod` and `setMethod` fields in the attribute descriptors can be used to map the attribute invocations to operations that access the managed resource.

The following attribute descriptor fields act a part in the attribute value caching in Model MBeans.

```
value
default
getMethod
setMethod
currencyTimeLimit
lastUpdatedTimeStamp
```

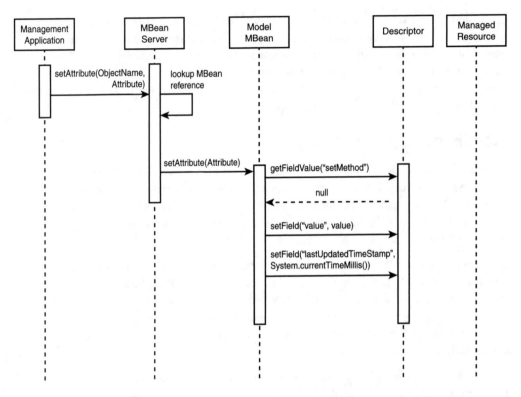

FIGURE 5.7

Management attribute with no setMethod *field will store its state in the attribute descriptor.*

The value field is used by the agent to store the current value of an attribute. This field is updated whenever a new attribute value is written. If the setMethod field in the attribute descriptor has been set, the corresponding method in the managed resource is called. If no setMethod value has been defined, the attribute state is stored in the descriptor and the value field is updated directly. After the value field has been updated, the lastUpdatedTimeStamp field in the descriptor is reset with the current time. The sequence of descriptor field updates with setMethod is shown in Figure 5.8.

The getAttribute() operation in a Model MBean works in a similar fashion as setAttribute(). If the caching of management attributes is enabled, the descriptor for the attribute is accessed with each getAttribute() call to check the validity of cached values.

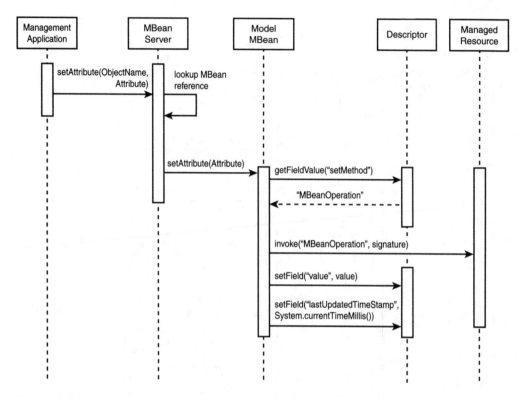

FIGURE 5.8

Management attribute with setMethod *mapping.*

If the value field for an attribute is not declared in its descriptor, the existence of getMethod field is checked. If the getMethod declaration is found in the descriptor, the management operation declared in the getMethod field will be invoked. The return value of the operation invocation will be taken as the attribute's value. If getMethod field was not declared in the descriptor, and value field was not available, the descriptor is checked for default field. If the default field is found, its value is returned as the attribute's value.

When the attribute's value is retrieved via the operation declared in the getMethod field, the return value is stored in the value field. If value caching has been enabled by setting a non-zero value to the currencyTimeLimit field in the descriptor, the validity of the attribute value is checked each time getAttribute() is called and before the getMethod operation of the managed resource is invoked. The sequence of calls to retrieve a management attribute that has a cache lifetime of five seconds is shown in Figure 5.9.

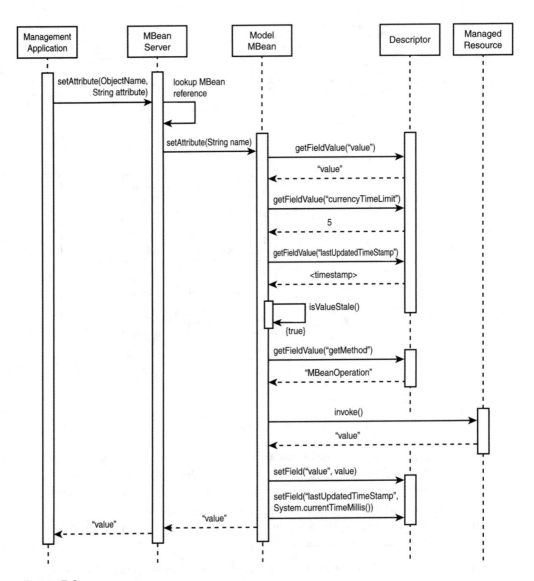

FIGURE 5.9

Retrieval of management attribute where descriptor cache has gone stale after five seconds.

The value cache validity is checked by comparing the values of `lastUpdatedTimeStamp` field and `currencyTimeLimit` field. If `currencyTimeLimit` field is set to -1, the contents of the `value` field are always valid. If the `currencyTimeLimit` is set to 0, the value caching is disabled. Any positive integer stored as a value of the `currencyTimeLimit` descriptor field is interpreted as the number of seconds the attribute value stored in the value field should be considered valid. If the cached value is valid, the `getMethod` operation of the managed resource will not be invoked.

Model MBean Example

The next example will use a Model MBean to add management features to an existing class. The example shows how an existing class, `Printer`, can be managed using the generic management template provided by the Model MBean.

The `Printer` class itself is not aware of its manageability. It could implement methods that control the printer through a parallel or USB port for general printing functions, but it doesn't really contain the kind of management information that is required for a specific management task.

The `Printer` class in Listing 5.4 has only one method for demonstrating purposes called `isActive()`. It always returns a Boolean value `true` and prints a message to the console indicating it has been called. It will serve as a mock-up of an object that represents a printer. The more interesting part of this example is that you can add management domain-specific attributes to the Model MBean without affecting the original class. For this example, you will add a management attribute `RoomName` to show the name or number of the office the printer is located in and the attribute `Active`, which indicates if the printer is currently online waiting for printing tasks to be queued.

Adding a room name to the `Printer` class might be too specific and not really relevant to a class that implements basic printer functionality itself. You could subclass the printer and create a `MyOfficePrinter` class and have it implement a corresponding Standard MBean interface. However, you do not have to declare and implement new classes or interfaces at all with a Model MBean. You can configure the Model MBean with the relevant management information and keep the `Printer` class untouched. You will separate the management implementation from the resource class and only provide a reference of the printer resource to the Model MBean.

Listing 5.5 shows a Model MBean creation and configuration for the `Printer` resource. The Model MBean will be configured with a management attribute `RoomName` that is stored by the agent in the attribute's descriptor. The `Active` attribute has to access the `Printer` resource to retrieve the status of the printer. You will map the getter method of the `Active` attribute to an `isActive()` management operation. You will cache the state of the `Active` attribute to remain in the descriptor cache for 10 seconds, so that each query for the printer's state does not have to access the printer itself.

LISTING 5.4   Printer.java

```java
package book.jmx.examples;

public class Printer {

  public boolean isActive() {
    System.out.println("isActive() called");
    return true;
  }

}
```

LISTING 5.5   ModelExample.java

```java
package book.jmx.examples;

import javax.management.*;
import javax.management.modelmbean.*;

public class ModelExample {

    final static boolean READABLE = true;
    final static boolean WRITABLE = true;
    final static boolean BOOLEAN  = true;

    public static void main(String[] args) {

      MBeanServer server =
          MBeanServerFactory.createMBeanServer();


      // build 'RoomName' read-write attribute
      Descriptor descr1 = new DescriptorSupport();
      descr1.setField("name", "Room");
      descr1.setField("descriptorType", "attribute");
      descr1.setField("displayName", "Room Number");
      descr1.setField("default", "D325");

      ModelMBeanAttributeInfo roomNameInfo =
          new ModelMBeanAttributeInfo(
            "Room",                     // attribute name
            String.class.getName(),     // attribute type
            "Room name or number.",     // description
            READABLE, WRITABLE, !BOOLEAN,  // read write
```

LISTING 5.5   continued

```
            descr1                              // descriptor
        );


    // build 'Active' read-only attribute
    Descriptor descr2 = new DescriptorSupport();
    descr2.setField("name", "Active");
    descr2.setField("descriptorType", "attribute");
    descr2.setField("getMethod", "isActive");
    descr2.setField("currencyTimeLimit", "10");

    ModelMBeanAttributeInfo activeInfo =
        new ModelMBeanAttributeInfo(
          "Active",
          boolean.class.getName(),
          "Printer state.",
          READABLE, !WRITABLE, !BOOLEAN,
          descr2
        );

    // build 'isActive' getter operation
    Descriptor descr3 = new DescriptorSupport();
    descr3.setField("name", "isActive");
    descr3.setField("descriptorType", "operation");
    descr3.setField("role", "getter");

    ModelMBeanOperationInfo isActiveInfo =
        new ModelMBeanOperationInfo(
          "isActive",                      // name & description
          "Checks if the printer is currently active.",
          null,                            // signature
          boolean.class.getName(),         // return type
          MBeanOperationInfo.INFO,         // impact
          descr3                           // descriptor
        );

    // MBean descriptor
    Descriptor descr4 = new DescriptorSupport();
    descr4.setField("name", "Printer");
    descr4.setField("descriptorType", "mbean");

    // create ModelMBeanInfo
    ModelMBeanInfo info = new ModelMBeanInfoSupport(
      RequiredModelMBean.class.getName(),  // class name
```

5

MODEL MBEANS

LISTING 5.5   continued

```
        "Printer",                                // description
        new ModelMBeanAttributeInfo[] {           // attributes
            roomNameInfo,
            activeInfo
        },
        null,                                     // constructors
        new ModelMBeanOperationInfo[] {           // operations
            isActiveInfo
        },
        null,                                     // notifications
        descr4                                    // descriptor
    );

    try {
      // create and configure model mbean
      RequiredModelMBean model = new RequiredModelMBean();
      model.setManagedResource(new Printer(), "ObjectReference");
      model.setModelMBeanInfo(info);
      server.registerMBean(model, new ObjectName("example:name=model"));

      // create the adaptor
      com.tivoli.jmx.http_pa.Listener adaptor =
          new com.tivoli.jmx.http_pa.Listener();

      server.registerMBean(adaptor,
          new ObjectName("adaptor:protocol=HTTP"));

      adaptor.startListener();
    }
    catch (Exception e) {
      e.printStackTrace();
    }

  }

}
```

To compile and run the example, execute the following commands (using the Tivoli JMX implementation):

```
C:\Examples> javac -d . -classpath tmx4j\base\lib\jmxx.jar;
➡ tmx4j\base\lib\jmxc.jar;tmx4j\base\lib\log.jar;tmx4j\ext\lib\jmxext.jar
➡ Printer.java ModelExample.java
```

```
C:\Examples> java -classpath .;tmx4j\base\lib\jmxx.jar;
➥tmx4j\base\lib\jmxc.jar;tmx4j\base\lib\log.jar;
➥tmx4j\ext\lib\jmxext.jar book.jmx.examples.ModelExample
```

If you now browse the management view created by the HTTP adaptor (http://local-host:6969) and query for the example:name=model MBean, you should see a Web page, as shown in Figure 5.10.

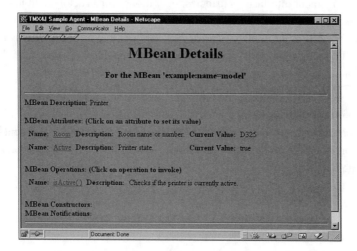

FIGURE 5.10

Management view of the Printer *resource.*

Notice that you now have a management attribute RoomName, even though the Printer resource itself is not aware of it. You also expose the Active attribute that you cache at the JMX agent, more specifically in the descriptor of the Model MBean. When you select and reload the management view of the MBean and the Active attribute, you will notice that approximately every 10 seconds, the Printer resource is actually accessed to retrieve an up-to-date value of the Active attribute. You will know when the resource is accessed when you see the following message printed on the console

```
The HTTP Adaptor started on port number 6969
isActive() called
isActive() called
isActive() called
```

Invoking the isActive() management operation explicitly will always access the Printer resource and return the current status.

Summary

Model MBeans provide a generic template for creating the management implementation for resources. You can easily separate the management implementation from the resource implementation, which often leads to a cleaner design of two separate problem domains.

Model MBeans allow you to extend the metadata to include behavioral properties in all the elements of the management interface—attributes, operations, constructors, and notifications. The behavioral properties can include caching properties, security properties, transactional properties, persistence properties, presentation properties, and so on. The JMX specification defines some common field names that can be used to provide some degree of interoperability between JMX agent implementations.

All JMX agents must provide at least one implementation of the Model MBean in the `javax.management.modelmbean.RequiredModelMBean` class. The functionality of the `RequiredModelMBean` may vary depending on the run-time environment the agent has been designed for. Some of the implementation details of Model MBeans will be discussed in Chapter 8, "Extended Services."

MBean Server

IN THIS CHAPTER

In this chapter, you will look at the MBean server classes in detail and cover the relevant methods of the interfaces and classes required to interact with the MBean server. You will look at the invocations and how they are handled in the MBean server, go through the methods of the `MBeanServer` interface, and cover the `MBeanServerFactory` class, `MBeanRegistration` interface, `ObjectName` class, and the `MBeanServerDelegateMBean`. At the end of this chapter, you will also learn how to build queries for MBeans.

The MBean server is a core component of the JMX agent layer. As the examples in the previous chapters have shown, the MBean server is responsible for decoupling the management applications from the managed resources. The MBean server achieves this by abstracting the managed resources behind a management interface and object name references.

The MBean server acts as a registry to the MBeans and contains the metadata describing the management interface of each MBean. MBeans are always accessed through the methods of the `MBeanServer` interface. The `MBeanServer` interface declares the methods for setting and getting the management attributes and invoking the management operations of an MBean. MBeans are always referenced via their object names instead of direct references to the resources themselves. This is essential for isolating the management applications from the resources and is the main responsibility of the MBean server.

In addition, you have seen that the MBean type, whether a Standard or a Dynamic MBean, is abstracted from the management tools. A management application using the services of an MBean server is not aware of the managed resource is implemented. Regardless of the MBean type, the MBean server exposes the same metadata structures to the management application. If Standard MBeans are used, the agent uses the Java introspection to build the metadata based on the method naming conventions discussed in Chapter 3, "Standard MBeans." In the case of the Dynamic MBean, the agent discovers the management interface by invoking the `getMBeanInfo()` method of the `DynamicMBean` interface.

Invocation Mechanism

In the previous chapters, you invoked methods of managed resources through an HTTP protocol adaptor. You also programmatically manipulated the MBeans via the `MBeanServer` interface. When using the HTTP protocol adaptors, you either had to choose the MBean by selecting it from a list of object names, or by entering a query on the Web page, which returned a list of matching object names representing the MBeans. With programmatic invocations, you created an `ObjectName` instance and used it with each invocation of management operation.

The `MBeanServer` interface declares the methods required to manipulate MBeans. When the MBean registers itself to the MBean server, the server stores a Java object reference of the resource and maps it to the `ObjectName` reference. This layer of indirection guarantees that the management applications do not rely on the interface of the managed resource directly, but only on the management interface exposed by the agent. For the isolation of application and resource to work, all communication between the two must travel through the JMX agent. This is guaranteed as long as the `ObjectName` references are the only way for the client to access the MBean. The MBean server will delegate the invocation to the correct resource instance based on its internal mapping of object names to resource references.

NOTE

The management applications never directly reference the managed resources. All communication between the application and the managed resource must go through the JMX agent layer.

If you recall the `DynamicMBean` interface from Chapter 4, "Dynamic MBeans," you may remember that the interface mainly consists of almost exact matches of the `invoke()`, `setAttribute()`, and `getAttribute()` methods of the `MBeanServer` interface. The difference between the method declarations is the `ObjectName` argument the MBean server requires the clients to include in the invocation.

When the invocation gets to the MBean server, it looks up the resource reference for the corresponding `ObjectName` and delegates the call from the server to the MBean's `DynamicMBean` interface. The methods of the `DynamicMBean` interface match those in the `MBeanServer` with the exception of `ObjectName` reference, which is not required. If the MBean server needs to invoke methods of a Standard MBean, the server looks up the correct resource reference and uses introspection to find and invoke the corresponding method on the Standard MBean.

The Figure 6.1 illustrates this sequence of calls from the client to the MBean server.

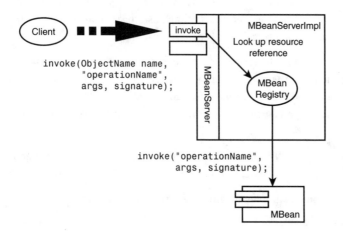

FIGURE 6.1

The management application accesses the MBeans using `ObjectName` reference.

Because the Standard MBeans require introspection to be used, they do not perform as well as Dynamic MBeans under a heavy load of invocations. Usually, however, the performance difference between Standard and Dynamic MBeans is not relevant to the managed component.

Also notice that when notifications are being broadcast from MBeans, it is the MBean server's responsibility to map the `Notification` instance's `source` field from a direct Java object reference to an `ObjectName` reference. This ensures that the receiver of the notification will also reference the source via its object name instead of directly.

ObjectName class

The `ObjectName` class represents a reference to the MBean component in the agent. An `ObjectName` is unique within an MBean server and is used by the management applications and other MBeans to invoke operations and manipulate MBean components registered to the server.

The `ObjectName` consists of two parts—the domain name and an unordered list of property-value pairs. The string representation of an `ObjectName` must follow the following syntax:

```
[DomainName]:property=value[,property=value]*
```

The `DomainName` part of the `ObjectName` is optional. If no domain name is specified, the agent assigns a default domain name to the object. You can define the default domain name by passing it as an argument to the `createMBeanServer()` or `newMBeanServer()` method in the `MBeanServerFactory` class. You can retrieve the default domain name from the MBean server via the `getDefaultDomain()` method call.

The domain name is case sensitive. Its structure and semantic is application dependent. However, the domain name string is not allowed to use any of the special characters that are used as object name separators or wild cards by the JMX implementation. Such characters include the colon (:), comma (,), equals sign (=), asterisk (*), and question mark (?). The latter two are used to compose patterns of `ObjectName` instances.

The property list part of the `ObjectName` string representation can contain any number of property-value pairs. Unique properties can be freely assigned and do not have to match the management attributes exposed by the MBean in its management interface. The property list part must contain at least one property-value pair. If more than one property-value pair is used, the order is not significant.

The canonical name of an MBean is a string representation of the `ObjectName` instance where the properties are sorted in a lexical order.

The following are some examples of properly formed object names:

```
Connector:transport=RMI
:name=ExportService,type=Service
Connector:*
```

MBeanServerFactory Class

The MBeanServerFactory class allows you to create instances of MBeanServer implementations. The MBeanServerFactory class consists of six methods:

```
public static MBeanServer createMBeanServer();
public static MBeanServer createMBeanServer(String domain);
public static MBeanServer newMBeanServer();
public static MBeanServer newMBeanServer(String domain);
public static ArrayList findMBeanServer(String AgentId);
public static void releaseMBeanServer(MBeanServer mbeanServer);
```

You have already seen the createMBeanServer() method used in several examples. This method creates an MBean server implementation and returns it to the caller. It also adds the created MBean server reference to an internal data structure that allows you to find the server instance later via the findMBeanServer() method call.

The createMBeanServer() method uses a default domain name specified by the JMX implementation for MBeans that do not include a domain name as part of their registration. It is possible to override the default domain name with an overloaded version of the createMBeanServer(), which allows you to specify your own default domain name.

The newMBeanServer() method works much the same as the createMBeanServer() method. The difference is that the server instances created with the newMBeanServer() call are not stored for later retrieval. Therefore, the instances cannot be found by the findMBeanServer() method call. Also, these server instances may be garbage collected as soon as no live references are kept to them.

The releaseMBeanServer() method allows you to remove any internal references kept by the JMX implementation for the given MBeanServer instance. This allows the MBean server to be garbage collected by a JVM if no other references to it exist.

Finally, the findMBeanServer() method is used to find any existing and registered MBeanServer instances in the JVM. You can either search for all instances by providing a null reference as parameter to the method call, or you can find a specific instance of an MBeanServer by providing an AgentID as parameter to the method call. The AgentID identifier can be retrieved from all MBean server instances via the MBeanServerDelegateMBean. A MBeanServerDelegateMBean is automatically registered with each compliant MBean server instance. A more detailed look at this MBean and what other information can be retrieved via its management interface will be discussed a little later in the "MbeanServerDelegate" section called.

Those were all the methods of the MBeanServerFactory class. Using this factory class, you can create, find, and release MBeanServer instances. Next, take a look at what the MBeanServer interface itself holds in store for you.

MBeanServer Interface

As mentioned at the beginning of the chapter, the MBean server is the core component of the JMX agent layer. The management applications interact with the MBean server through the MBeanServer interface that all the MBean server instances implement. Among the responsibilities of the MBean server are the registration and unregistration of the MBean components and access to management operations and attributes of an MBean. In addition, the MBean server provides the means for decoupling the management applications from the resources, as was discussed earlier. Also, the management operation invocations in the MBean server are detyped through the invoke() method. Because the management clients do not rely on statically typed Java interfaces to invoke the management operations, you can freely let the interfaces evolve without having to change the existing clients. This can become helpful where the maintenance of components is concerned.

You have already used many of the methods in the MBeanServer interface. Next you will go through the relevant methods of the interface to refresh what you have already learned and fill in some new details. Remember that all the communication between the management applications and the MBeans go through this interface, so you should become familiar with it.

invoke()

The invoke() method is interesting in that it plays a vital part in decoupling the management clients from the managed resources. As discussed in Chapter 2, "Architecture," and earlier in this chapter, the decoupling of the management applications from the resource is one of the key design points of the JMX-based architecture. In the signature of the invoke() method, this design becomes evident to the application developer. You will notice that the MBeans are always referenced via the ObjectName reference—never directly.

The complete signature of the invoke() method of the MBeanServer interface is as follows:

```
public Object invoke(ObjectName name, String operationName,
                     Object[] params, String[] signature)
              throws InstanceNotFoundException, MBeanException,
                     ReflectionException
```

The indirection provided by the object name references allows you to change the component implementation without affecting the existing clients. It is not necessary to detach the client-server communication while components are being updated. If the component is momentarily unavailable, the MBean server could suspend the invocation or redirect it to another MBean. If the MBeans are synchronizing their state, through a database for example, they can implement a simple failover functionality this way.

Another significant point to notice in the invoke() method declaration is how the management operation invocation is detyped and does not rely on a statically typed Java interface that the resource implements. All operation invocations are carried through the invoke() method, which contains the name and signature of the operation you want to invoke. This means that in addition to switching the implementation "behind the scenes" from the client, it is possible for the management interface of a component to evolve—to add a new management attributes and operations. Due to the detyped invocation, this evolution of the component's management interface can occur without affecting existing clients. A new management application can take advantage of the recently added management operation, but the existing clients will continue to work as long as the management interface for the operations they require does not change.

The exception types included in the invoke() method declaration are as follows:

- InstanceNotFoundException   Thrown when the MBean server cannot find a registered MBean for the given object name
- MbeanException   Can be used by the managed resource to wrap application-specific exceptions
- ReflectionException   Thrown when the actual invocation operation from the MBean server to the managed resource fails

The invoke() method returns an object reference that represents the return value of the management operation. Notice that implicit type conversion between primary return types of a Standard MBean interface to corresponding object types is performed by the agent.

createMBean

The createMBean() method is overloaded with four different versions in the MBeanServer interface. The different versions of the createMBean() method allow you to create an MBean instance in the agent with a given ObjectName reference, optionally with an explicit constructor signature if the default constructor cannot be used, and an explicit class loader.

The following are declarations of the createMBean() methods in the MBeanServer interface. The exceptions have been left out for the sake of brevity.

```
public ObjectInstance createMBean(String className,
                                  ObjectName name);

public ObjectInstance createMBean(String className,
                                  ObjectName name,
                                  Object[] params,
                                  String[] signature);
```

```
public ObjectInstance createMBean(String className,
                                  ObjectName name,
                                  ObjectName loaderName);

public ObjectInstance createMBean(String className,
                                  ObjectName name,
                                  ObjectName loaderName,
                                  Object[] params,
                                  String[] signature);
```

The first overloaded version of the createMBean() method instantiates the given class using the default constructor and attempts to register the object as an MBean to the server. If successful, it binds the MBean to a given ObjectName reference.

The second overloaded version of the createMBean() method allows you to define the signature of the constructor that the agent uses to instantiate the MBean component. You can specify the constructor by providing an array of objects that contain the values of the constructor call and an array of String objects that contain the fully qualified classnames of the value objects. The agent can determine the signature of the constructor from the String array with classnames and pass the objects as values to the instantiation call.

The last two overloaded versions of the createMBean() method are identical to the first two with an additional ObjectName reference to a class loader. The loaderName parameter can be used to explicitly define a class loader that should be used to load the MBean component.

The createMBean() method call declares five common exception types to indicate error conditions in either the MBean object initialization or in the MBean registration phase. The ReflectionException can be thrown if the class cannot be loaded with the default class loader or with the explicitly declared class loader. A ReflectionException is also thrown if there were any other exceptions thrown while trying to invoke the MBean's constructor, for example, if the MBean did not declare a public, no-args constructor. You can retrieve the original exception via the getTargetException() method of the ReflectionException class.

The InstanceAlreadyExistsException can be thrown from the createMBean() method call if the ObjectName reference is already in use and mapped to another MBean component. The MBeanRegistrationException can be thrown if the MBean component implements the MBeanRegistration interface and throws an exception in its preRegister() method. You will see the details of the MBeanRegistration interface in the section of the same name later in this chapter.

Also, the MBeanRegistrationException class exposes the original exception class via the getTargetException() method.

The MBeanException wraps any application exceptions that can be thrown from the implementation of the MBean's constructor. The NotCompliantMBeanException is thrown if the classname supplied is not a compliant MBean. This can occur if the agent is unable to find the corresponding Standard MBean interface or the DynamicMBean interface in the class hierarchy.

In addition to these exceptions described, the InstanceNotFoundException object can be thrown by the two createMBean() methods that require an ObjectName reference to the class loader to load the MBean component. In case the ObjectName reference is not found in the agent, the InstanceNotFoundException can be thrown.

Notice that the functionality of the createMBean() invocation is roughly the equivalent of calling the instantiate() and then registerMBean() methods on the server. However, because the createMBean() method does not expose or require direct references to resource objects but works with the ObjectName references, it is better suited for management applications trying to create and register new MBean components remotely. You will see the details of both the instantiate() and registerMBean() methods a bit later in this chapter in the "RegisterMBean and UnregisterMBean" section.

addNotificationListener and removeNotificationListener

Recall from Chapter 3 the discussion of the JMX notification mechanism. It requires that all MBeans wanting to broadcast management notifications must implement the NotificationBroadcaster interface. This interface includes the addNotificationListener() and removeNotificationListener() methods that are almost identical to the ones declared in the MBeanServer interface. Again, the difference is in the MBeanServer interface where the ObjectName reference is required as a first argument for both method implementations. As with the invoke() method, the addNotificationListener() and removeNotificationListener() methods look up the corresponding MBean reference based on the supplied ObjectName and delegate the method invocation to the registered MBean.

```
public void addNotificationListener(ObjectName name,
                            NotificationListener listener,
                            NotificationFilter filter,
                            Object handback)
                 throws InstanceNotFoundException;

public void addNotificationListener(ObjectName name,
                            ObjectName listener,
                            NotificationFilter filter,
                            Object handback)
                 throws InstanceNotFoundException;
```

```
public void removeNotificationListener(
                          ObjectName name,
                          NotificationListener listener)
            throws InstanceNotFoundException,
              ListenerNotFoundException;

public void removeNotificationListener(
                          ObjectName name,
                          ObjectName listener)
            throws InstanceNotFoundException,
              ListenerNotFoundException;
```

The second variation of both the addNotificationListener() and
removeNotificationListener() methods allows you to register another MBean directly
as a listener to the broadcaster MBean. This will become especially useful when dealing with
remote notifications.

getAttribute and setAttribute

The getAttribute() and setAttribute()methods also have their corresponding equivalents
in the DynamicMBean interface. In the case of the Standard MBean instrumentation, the agent
attempts to invoke a correct accessor method by introspecting the MBean class and building
the invocation based on the Standard MBean naming conventions.

registerMBean and unregisterMBean

The registerMBean() call allows you to register a pre-existing object as an MBean to the server.
Notice that if the ObjectName argument is null, the MBean may provide an ObjectName itself by
implementing the MBeanRegistration interface. You will see how this works in practice when
the interface is covered in detail.

The following is the declaration of registerMBean() and unregisterMBean() methods:

```
public ObjectInstance registerMBean(Object object,
                          ObjectName name)
              throws InstanceAlreadyExistsException,
                MBeanRegistrationException,
                NotCompliantMBeanException;

public void unregisterMBean(ObjectName name)
              throws InstanceNotFoundException,
                MBeanRegistrationException;
```

The MBean may cancel the registration by throwing an exception from its preRegister() method of an MBeanRegistration interface. In that case, the exception will be wrapped in the MBeanRegistrationException instance and can be retrieved through the getTargetException() method. In a similar fashion, the unregistering of an MBean can be prevented by an exception thrown from the preDeregister() method of the MBeanRegistration interface. Also, notice that the agent does attempt to verify that the class being registered is a valid MBean. If a validation error occurs, a NotCompliantMBeanException is thrown by the registerMBean() method.

Because the registerMBean() method takes a reference to a pre-existing Java object as an argument, it often does not make sense to use this method from a remote location. Because the distribution layer for the JMX is not yet defined, some JMX connectors may choose to not allow this method to be accessed remotely at all. Remember that you can always use the createMBean() methods instead.

queryMBeans and queryNames

The queryMBeans() and queryNames() methods allow you to query the server for MBean object instances or object names. The query can be built by defining a name pattern as an ObjectName argument or by providing a query expression to the server. The queries are explained in detail at the end of this chapter.

```
public Set queryMBeans(ObjectName name, QueryExp query);

public Set queryNames(ObjectName name, QueryExp query);
```

Both methods return either a set of ObjectInstance objects or ObjectName objects that represent the matching MBeans for the given query or object name pattern.

Other MBeanServer Methods

The getDefaultDomain() method returns the default domain string used by the agent. If the MBean is registered with an object name that does not contain the domain part, the return value of this method is used as a default domain value.

The getMBeanCount() method returns the number of MBeans registered to the MBean server.

The getMBeanInfo() method returns the metadata of a given MBean. The management applications can use the returned MBeanInfo object to discover the management operations, attributes, and notifications of the MBean.

The isInstanceOf() method allows you to test if a given MBean is an instance of a class type. The classname is given as an argument to this method.

The isRegistered() method allows you to test whether an MBean registered to a given object name already exists in the MBean server.

MBeanRegistration Interface

The MBean life cycle can be defined from the moment it is registered to the MBean server to the moment it is unregistered from the MBean server. During this time, the MBean component is accessible to the management tools and other MBean components through its object name reference.

The JMX API defines an MBeanRegistration interface that can be used to receive callbacks in the MBean implementation of the life cycle events. The MBeanRegistration defines four methods that the MBean server is required to invoke on any MBean implementing the MBeanRegistration interface.

```
public ObjectName preRegister(
                    MBeanServer server,
                    ObjectName name
              ) throws java.lang.Exception;

public void postRegister(Boolean registrationDone);

public void preDeregister() throws java.lang.Exception;

public void postDeregister();
```

The preRegister() and postRegister()methods are called by the agent just before the MBean is registered to the MBean server and right after the registration. The preDeregister() and postDeregister() methods are similarly called right before the MBean is unregistered from the agent and right after it has successfully been unregistered from the agent.

preRegister and postRegister

The preRegister() method has two parameters—a MBeanServer reference and an ObjectName reference. The MBeanServer reference is a reference to the MBean server to which the MBean is being registered. If the MBean requires interaction with the server, for example to use services of other MBeans, this reference should be stored by the MBean component.

The object name reference is the name that was given as a parameter with the registerMBean() or createMBean() method call on the MBean server. Notice that the return type of the preRegister() method is an ObjectName type. If a null pointer is passed as an object name when the MBean is being registered, the MBean is free to supply its own ObjectName instance to the agent.

It is also possible to cancel the registration of the MBean by throwing an exception from the preRegister() method. If any exceptions from the method are thrown, the agent will not register the MBean to the server. In this case, the agent will create an MBeanRegistrationException that wraps the original exception and propagates it to the original caller.

The preRegister() method is useful for initializing the resources the MBean may need. It is also possible for the MBean to investigate the MBean server if it supports the required services and has them available. It is also possible to cancel the registration of an MBean in the preRegister() method.

The sequence of calls invoked when the MBean is being registered and implements the MBeanRegistration interface is shown in Figure 6.2.

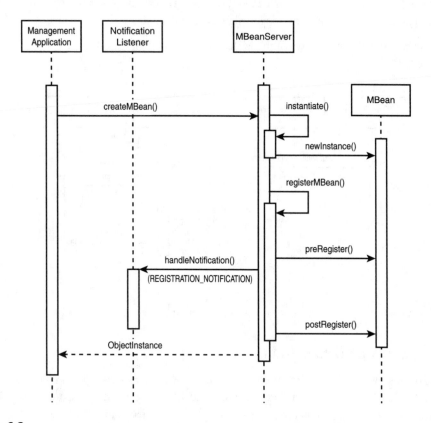

FIGURE 6.2

Sequence of MBeanRegistration *interface callbacks on MBean registration.*

preDeregister and postDeregister

The preDeregister() method should be used to clean up any resources the MBean may have acquired before it is unregistered from the server. If there is an exception thrown from invocation of the preDeregister() method, it is caught by the agent and wrapped into an MBeanRegistrationException instance before it's propagated to the caller. The postDeregister() method callback is made by the agent after the MBean has been unregistered from the MBean server. This method can be used for any additional cleanup operations that are required after the MBean is no longer registered to the agent.

The sequence of calls invoked when the MBean is being unregistered from the server is shown in Figure 6.3.

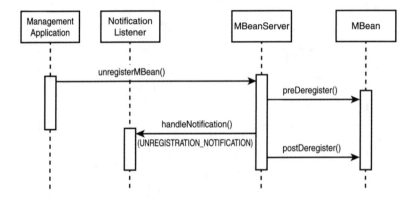

FIGURE 6.3

Sequence of MBeanRegistration *interface callbacks on MBean unregistration.*

MBeanServerDelegate

Each MBean server instance is required to register an MBeanServerDelegateMBean instance when it is created. The server delegate is available to all management applications and other MBeans. The server delegate is always registered with the object name JMImplementation:type=MBeanServerDelegate.

The MBeanServerDelegateMBean exposes information about the server implementation and provides notification of MBean registration and unregistration events. Among the information you may query the server delegate for is the agent ID, specification version the server implements, vendor name, server version, and product name.

The operations of the MBeanServerDelegateMBean are listed in Table 6.1.

TABLE 6.1   Management Operations of the `MBeanServerDelegate` MBean

Operation	Description
getImplementationName()	Returns the name of the JMX implementation, in other words the product name, such as JMX RI or Tivoli JMX Agent.
getImplementationVendor()	Returns the name of the vendor of the product, such as Sun Microsystems or Tivoli Systems Inc.
getImplementationVersion()	Returns a string containing the version of the product.
getSpecificationName()	Returns the full specification name the product implements.
getSpecificationVendor()	Returns the vendor of the specification.
getSpecificationVersion()	Returns the version of the specification the product implements.
getMBeanServerID()	This is an identifier for the agent. The specification does not explicitly define the scope of the ID, so you may have to check with your vendor's implementation. A common implementation is an ID that is unique within the host machine.

In addition, the `MBeanServerDelegateMBean` is a broadcaster MBean and implements the `addNotificationListener()` and `removeNotificationListener()` methods. Management applications and other MBeans can invoke these methods to register their interest to receive MBean server notifications, such as registration and unregistration events.

The `MBeanServerDelegateMBean` emits notifications on every `registerMBean()` and `unregisterMBean()` method invocation executed on the server. The notification class that is sent by the server delegate is an `MBeanServerNotification` class. It extends the `Notification` class by adding a `getMBeanName()` method that returns the `ObjectName` reference of the MBean that has been registered or unregistered. The notification types of the `MBeanServerNotification` events are defined in the class as the two constants `REGISTRATION_NOTIFICATION` and `UNREGISTRATION_NOTIFICATION`.

Queries

The JMX specification defines a query mechanism that can be used for querying the MBean server for a set of MBeans. The queries can be based on an object name pattern or the management attribute values of MBeans.

The two methods on the `MBeanServer` interface used for queries are the `queryMBeans()` and `queryNames()` methods. Both methods require an `ObjectName` for their first parameter. The `ObjectName` for these methods represents the scope of the query. Any query expression passed as the second parameter will be applied only to those MBeans whose object name matches the pattern given as scope.

Scope of Queries

The scope is defined by creating an object name that matches a pattern of MBean names in the agent. For example, all MBeans in the `Connector` management domain can be matched by creating the following object name:

```
Connector:*
```

Any query executed with this scope will only be applied to the MBeans registered under the specific domain. Setting the query scope to `null` indicates that all MBeans in the server will be within the scope of the query. This is the equivalent of setting the scope to `*:*`.

The domain part of the object name can also use the `'?'` sign for defining patterns that match a single character. For example, an object name pattern

```
Domain?:*
```

will match management domain names such as `DomainA`, `DomainB`, and so on.

The key property list part of the object name can also use the asterisk (`*`) wildcard to create a name pattern. Notice, however, that only complete property key-value pairs are considered. For example, you cannot use the wildcard to match a specific property value. You can use the wildcard to require that the scope of the query contains only MBeans whose object names have a specific property value set. For example,

```
Service:type=automatic,*
Service:type=*          // NOT VALID !!
```

The first scope will match all MBeans in the `Service` domain that have a `type` property with value `automatic` set. However, the second scope is not valid because no pattern matching is performed on the property values.

Building Queries

The JMX specification does not define a specific query language for the MBean server queries. Instead, the queries are built programmatically with the help of a `Query` class. The `Query` class contains a set of static methods that return query expressions based on the given parameters. These query expressions are represented by the `QueryExp` interface that both the `queryMBeans()` and `queryNames()` methods use.

The `Query` class contains methods for query expressions, such as greater than, less than, equals, and so on. These query expressions can be combined with relational query expressions and, or, not, and so on. In addition, there are query expressions for string values such as `"starts With"`, `"ends With"`, and `"contains"` string. These types of queries are represented in the JMX API with a `QueryExp` interface. The `Query` class returns instances of this interface when you use the query expression methods.

For values used in the queries, another interface, `ValueExp`, is declared in the JMX API. Again, you get the implementations of the value expressions by using the factory methods in the `Query` class.

For example, to build a simple string matching query on a management attribute `Name`, you could write the following query generation code:

```
AttributeValueExp attribute = Query.attr("Name");
StringValueExp name = Query.value("John");
QueryExp query = Query.match(attribute, name);
```

In this example, both `AttributeValueExp` and `StringValueExp` classes implement the `ValueExp` interface. The `match` method requires these two classes as parameters and returns an instance of the `QueryExp` interface representing the query where the attribute `Name` matches the string `John`. The query expression can then be invoked on the server:

```
Set resultSet = server.queryNames(new ObjectName("*:*"), query);
```

The returned collection would contain the `ObjectName` references to all MBeans that have a `Name` management attribute containing the string value `"John"`.

Table 6.2 lists some the methods of the `Query` class.

TABLE 6.2   Query Class Methods

Method	Description

`and(QueryExp a, QueryExp b)`
`or(QueryExp a, QueryExp b)`
`not(QueryExp q)`
	These methods build queries that use the relational operations on the given query expressions.

`anySubString(AttributeValueExp attr,` `StringValueExp string)`	These methods work on string type management attributes
	The `anySubString` checks whether the given string expression is a substring of the attribute value.
`finalSubString(AttributeValueExp attr,` `StringValueExp string)`	The `finalSubString` checks whether the given string expression is a suffix of the attribute value.

TABLE 6.2 Continued

Method	Description
`initialSubString(AttributeValueExp attr, StringValueExp string)`	The `initialSubString` checks whether the given string expression is a prefix of the attribute value.
`match(AttributeValueExp attr, StringValueExp string)`	The match method tests the equality of the string value expressions and the attribute string value. The match allows wildcards * and ? to be used, character sets [Aa] and character ranges [A-Z].
`between(ValueExp a, ValueExp b, ValueExp c)` `in(ValueExp a, ValueExp[] set)`	The between method builds a query expression where the first value has to be within the boundaries specified by the latter two value expressions. All value expressions must be numeric values. The in method builds a query expression that tests whether the given value expression is part of the set given as a `ValueExp` array.
`plus(ValueExp a, ValueExp b)` `minus(ValueExp a, ValueExp b)` `times(ValueExp a, ValueExp b)` `div(ValueExp a, ValueExp b)`	These methods perform an arithmetic operation to the given value expression and return a new value expression that represents the result of the operation. All value expressions must be numeric values.
`eq(ValueExp a, ValueExp b)` `geq(ValueExp a, ValueExp b)` `gt(ValueExp a, ValueExp b)` `leq(ValueExp a, ValueExp b)` `It(ValueExp a, ValueExp b`	These methods return a query expression that represents equality between twp value expressions, greater than or equal to, greater than, less than or equal to, and less than comparisons between the value expressions.
`attr(String s)`	Creates an attribute value expression for the given attribute name.

TABLE 6.2 Continued

Method	Description
value()	Creates a value expression for the given numeric or string value. The value() method is overloaded to accept most primary types, subclasses of Number, or a string as argument.

Listing 6.2 shows an example code of some simple queries that can be executed on the MBean server.

LISTING 6.2 Queries.java

```java
package book.jmx.examples;

import java.util.*;
import javax.management.*;

public class Queries {

  public static void main(String[] args) throws Exception {
    MBeanServer server = MBeanServerFactory.createMBeanServer();

    ObjectName john = new ObjectName("DomainA:name=john");
    ObjectName mike = new ObjectName("DomainA:name=mike");
    ObjectName xena = new ObjectName("DomainA:name=xena");

    server.createMBean("book.jmx.examples.User", john);
    server.createMBean("book.jmx.examples.User", mike);
    server.createMBean("book.jmx.examples.User", xena);

    server.setAttribute(john, new Attribute("Name", "John"));
    server.setAttribute(mike, new Attribute("Name", "Mike"));
    server.setAttribute(xena, new Attribute("Name", "Xena"));

    server.setAttribute(john,
        new Attribute("Address", "King's Road 11"));
    server.setAttribute(mike,
        new Attribute("Address", "Strawberry St. 5"));
    server.setAttribute(xena,
        new Attribute("Address", "Strawberry St. 12"));
```

LISTING 6.2   Continued

```
    testQueries(server);
  }

  static void testQueries(MBeanServer server) throws Exception {

    QueryExp exp =
        Query.match(Query.attr("Name"), Query.value("John"));

    ObjectName scope = new ObjectName("DomainA:*");
    Set set       = server.queryNames(scope, exp);
    Iterator it  = set.iterator();

    System.out.println("MBeans with attribute Name = 'John'\n");

    while (it.hasNext()) {
      System.out.println(it.next());
    }

    scope = new ObjectName("DomainA:*");
    exp   = Query.initialSubString(Query.attr("Address"),
                                    Query.value("Strawberry"));

    set   = server.queryNames(scope, exp);
    it    = set.iterator();

    System.out.println(
        "\nMBeans with Address startsWith 'Strawberry'\n");

    while (it.hasNext()) {
      System.out.println(it.next());
    }
  }

}
```

When you compile and run the queries example, you should see the following output on your console.

```
C:\Examples> javac -d . -classpath jmx\lib\jmxri.jar Queries.java

C:\Examples> java -classpath .;jmx\lib\jmxri.jar book.jmx.examples.Queries

MBeans with attribute Name = 'John'
```

```
DomainA:name=john

MBeans with Address startsWith 'Strawberry'

DomainA:name=mike
DomainA:name=xena

C:\Examples>
```

Summary

The MBean server is central part of the JMX management architecture. Primarily, the MBean server acts as a registry to the MBeans. It also decouples the management applications from the resource class implementations. As discussed in this chapter, the management applications never directly reference the MBean classes but use object name references to access the managed resources.

For the decoupling to work, the communication between the management applications and the MBeans must always go through the JMX MBean server. The MBeanServer interface exposes the methods for creating and registering MBeans, invoking management operations, accessing the management attributes of an MBean, and executing queries on the server.

Also keep in mind that no statically typed Java interfaces are exposed to the management clients. The clients can discover the management interface, the operations, attributes, and notifications via the metadata information exposed by the agent for each MBean. This also allows the management interfaces to evolve over time without affecting the existing management applications. New management operations and attributes can be added to the resources transparently to the clients. This eases maintenance in the long term, because distribution of updated interfaces is not required for existing clients.

Standard Agent Services

IN THIS CHAPTER

The agent layer of the JMX architecture is formed by the MBean server and a set of agent services that are registered to the MBean server. The agent services are MBeans themselves and are handled by the MBean server in a manner similar to any managed resource. This allows the configuration of the agent based on the requirements of each management system, and also makes parts of the agent itself manageable through the JMX instrumentation layer.

The JMX specification does not set any specific requirements for MBeans that are registered as agent services. However, the specification does define four separate services that can be considered standard and can be expected to be available on every compliant JMX implementation. The standard agent services are as follows:

M-Let Service

Timer Service

Monitoring Service

Relation Service

The services are shown in Figure 7.1. In this chapter, you will go through each standard agent service and look at examples using them.

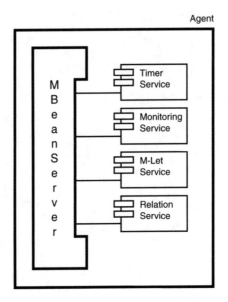

FIGURE 7.1

The standard services of the agent layer.

> **NOTE**
>
> The standard agent services are mandatory services implemented by all compliant JMX implementations.

Recall from Chapter 2, "Architecture," that the MBean server itself does not differentiate between agent service MBeans and regular managed resource MBeans. That is to say, the distinction is purely on the architectural level and not on the code implementation level. When agent service MBeans are registered to the MBean server, they are handled the same way as any other MBean.

M-Let Service

The M-Let service is a mechanism defined by the JMX specification to dynamically load new Java classes to the MBean server. The new classes can be loaded from a local machine or they can be downloaded from a remote host accessible from the network. In addition, the M-Let service allows the configuration of the application to be moved onto a remote server, thus allowing a centralized location of the configuration of an application or server.

In the next pages, you will see how the M-Let service is used to write a network-enabled application that will load all of its MBean components from a remote host.

The M-Let service itself is, as are all other standard agent services, an MBean. The `MLetMBean` exposes a management interface that allows you to add new Java classes to the agent or load an M-Let text file. You will take a closer look at the management interface of the M-Let service in the next section.

MLetMBean

The `MLetMBean` interface exposes the relevant operations of the M-Let service for management. You can add new classes to the agent by providing an URL of a Java archive or an M-Let text file, which allows you to automate both the loading of new classes and the registration of the MBeans to the agent.

First, let's go through the most relevant operations of the `MLet` MBean. The `addURL()` operation enables the addition of new classes to the agent. The `getMBeansFromURL()` operation allows the loading of the M-Let text file to instantiate and register the MBean components to the server. In addition, the `MLetMBean` interface exposes operations for finding resources in addition to class files via the `getResource()`, `getResources()`, and `getResourceAsStream()` methods and listing the URLs that have been added to the `MLet` class via the `getURLs()` operation.

MLET Tag

The getMBeansFromURL() operation allows you to read an M-Let text file from a given URL. The M-Let text file is a collection of MLET tags that describe MBean components. With the MLET tags, it is possible to describe a set of MBeans that should be loaded from the network and registered to the MBean server.

The MLET tag is very similar in format to a regular XML document tag. However, be aware that although the M-Let text file looks very close to an XML file, it in fact is not. The agent implementation is not required to be able to parse XML files, so the only format of the M-Let text file that is guaranteed to work is the tag described here. Any additional features, such as the XML style <!— and —> comment tags, are not within the scope of the JMX specification and may not be supported.

The definition of the MLET tag is as follows.

```
<MLET  CODE = class  |  OBJECT = serfile
       ARCHIVE = "archivelist"
       [CODEBASE = codebaseURL]
       [NAME = MBeanName]
       [VERSION = version]
>

       [arglist]

</MLET>
```

The MLET tag allows the declaration of the MBean class, the Java archive (JAR) it can be located in, and optionally define from where the Java archive can be loaded. It is also possible to set the object name that should be used to register the MBean to the MBean server.

Each of the attributes of the MLET tag is described in detail in the list that follows.

CODE The CODE attribute specifies the fully-qualified classname of the MBean to instantiate and register to the agent. The class specified by this attribute must be available in one of the Java archive files listed with the ARCHIVE attribute.

Either CODE or the OBJECT attribute must be present in the MLET tag.

OBJECT The OBJECT attribute can be used in place of the CODE attribute to point to a serialized instance of an MBean. The file containing the serialized representation of the MBean must be contained in one of the archives specified by the ARCHIVE attribute. If the Java archive contains a directory hierarchy, the correct path to the serialized file must be specified in full.

Either CODE or the OBJECT attribute must be present in the MLET tag.

ARCHIVE   The ARCHIVE attribute lists one or more Java archive files that are added to the MLet's class loader. One of the archives listed with this attribute must contain the class or .ser file specified with the CODE or OBJECT attribute, respectively.

If more than one Java archive is listed with the ARCHIVE attribute, they must be separated by a comma (,) character. The entire list must be enclosed in double quotation marks. The additional Java archives can contain support classes required by the MBean implementation.

For example,

```
<MLET CODE=com.mycompany.Foo
     ARCHIVE="MyComponents.jar,AcmeComponents.jar">
</MLET>
```

The Java archives specified with the ARCHIVE attribute must be found in the URL specified with the CODEBASE attribute. If no CODEBASE is specified within the MLET tag, the default code base is used. The default code base is set to the URL where the M-Let text file was loaded.

The ARCHIVE attribute is mandatory in the MLET tag.

CODEBASE   The CODEBASE attribute defines an URL from which the Java archives specified with the ARCHIVE attribute can be loaded. Notice that the code base does not have to point to the same location as the URL for the M-Let text file.

If the CODEBASE attribute is not defined in the MLET tag, the M-Let service uses the URL of the M-Let text file as its base. In this case, all the Java archives in the ARCHIVE attribute must be found in the same location as the M-Let text file.

The CODEBASE attribute is optional in the MLET tag.

NAME   The NAME attribute specifies the object name with which the loaded MBean is registered when the M-Let service adds the component to the agent. The object name is given in a string form. The string form must be a valid object name as was described in Chapter 6, "MBean Server."

The NAME attribute is optional in the MLET tag.

VERSION   The VERSION attribute can be used to specify a version of an MBean and its associated Java archives. The VERSION attribute can be used by the M-Let service to determine whether the archives already loaded to the server should be updated.

Notice that the current 1.0 version of the Sun Reference Implementation does not make use of the VERSION attribute.

The VERSION attribute is optional in the MLET tag.

arglist   The arglist defines a list of arguments passed to the MBean's constructor. The M-Let service attempts to find a constructor that has a matching signature to the contents of the arglist. If such constructor is found, it is invoked when the MBean is instantiated in the agent.

The `arglist` consists of one or more `ARG` tags. The `ARG` tag has two attributes, `TYPE` and `VALUE`, and can be defined as follows:

```
<ARG TYPE=argumentType VALUE=argumentValue>
```

The `TYPE` attribute consists of the fully-qualified classname of the argument type, and the `VALUE` attribute consists of a string representation of the argument value.

Notice that because the argument values are restricted to types that can have a string representation, not every kind of constructor can be invoked through the M-Let file. Generally, arguments with `String` type or the primitive types, and their corresponding classes, work with the M-Let service implementation. You may need to check with your JMX implementation for which argument types are supported with the M-Let service.

The `arglist` is an optional element inside the `MLET` tag. If no `arglist` is specified, a default no-args constructor is invoked.

Hot Deployment Revisited

In Chapter 4, "Dynamic MBeans," you saw how the different implementations of the User resource could be switched behind the scenes, away from the management applications. You saw that, with the decoupled JMX architecture and its invocation mechanism, it was possible to change the resource implementation on-the-fly, without having to shut down the server or detach the client communication.

One restriction with the example in Chapter 4 was that the classes you recycled needed to be available in the JVM at startup time. In a real life scenario, this is rarely the case, because you will want to update parts of your application with new components or introduce updated versions of the existing ones. The only way to bring new classes to the application, in this case to the JMX agent, is to dynamically load them to the JVM.

The JMX agent provides this capability via the M-Let service. With the M-Let service, you can add new classes to the agent dynamically. You can also use the M-Let file to locate and load MBeans from a remote host and register them to the MBean server.

You will now revisit the Recycler example from Chapter 4 to re-implement the `Recycler` MBean to load the User resource implementations dynamically using the M-Let service. You will also use the M-Let file to load the `Recycler` MBean, leaving only the creation of the MBean server and the registration of the M-Let service to the core application. The core of the application that is responsible for the loading of the other application components is often called the *bootstrap* application.

The general design of the application is shown in Figure 7.2.

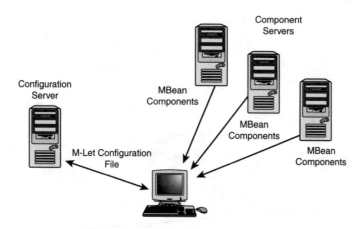

FIGURE 7.2

M-Let based application design.

With the design shown in Figure 7.2, you can build a central configuration and component management where the administrator can configure and update components in one location. The JMX-enabled application using M-Lets can then update and reconfigure themselves from dedicated servers without requiring administrator interaction on each host machine (see Figure 7.3). For each node, only the bootstrap is required, which creates the MBean server and registers the M-Let service. The bootstrap is capable of loading the list of MBean components for the application and each individual component from their respective host machines. This greatly reduces the amount of work on the administrator's part and provides a simple yet powerful mechanism of distributing software updates to the clients.

Now, take a look at the new and improved `Recycler` implementation. The signature of the `recycle()` management operation has changed slightly. It will now require two parameters—a classname string and a Java archive URL string. In addition, the recycle() method have declares `MalformedURLException` to be thrown if there is a problem converting the URL string to an actual `URL` object.

The updated `recycle()` management operation allows you to supply the classname you want to bind to the object name `"example:name=User"`. The URL parameter is used for providing the Java archive location in the network where the class is located. You can now load any implementation from the network to be added as the User resource.

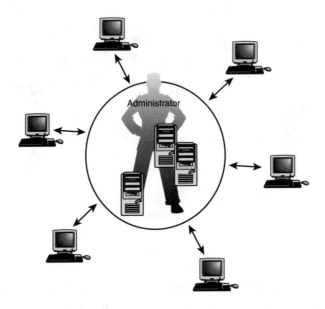

FIGURE 7.3
Centralized management of JMX-enabled software.

The management interface of the new `Recycler` component is shown in Listing 7.1.

LISTING 7.1   `RecyclerMBean.java`

```
package book.jmx.examples;

import java.net.*;

public interface RecyclerMBean {

   public String recycle(String clazz, String url)
      throws MalformedURLException;

}
```

The `Recycler` implementation has changed a bit more from what you saw in Chapter 4. The given URL will be added to the `MLet` instance via the `addURL()` method. If a User MBean already exists in the server, it is unregistered and replaced by the loaded component.

There are a couple of things you should notice here. First, the `MLet` instance is used to load the new component at runtime. Therefore, the new classes need not be available when the application is started.

Second, a new MLet instance is created for each loaded component. There is a very specific reason for this. In Java, there is no explicit way to tell a class loader to unload one of its classes. The unloading of a class only occurs when no live references to the class loader exist any longer and it is garbage collected. Therefore, if you want to load an updated version of one of the existing classes you need to create a new class loader for it. This can be done quite easily via M-Lets, as you can see in Listing 7.2. A new MLet instance is created for each loaded component and it is explicitly referenced in the instantiate() call to indicate to the MBean server which class loader should be used to load the class. Because a Java class identity is formed by its fully-qualified name and its defining class loader, an updated version of the class can be loaded to the same JVM in this manner. The newly registered MBean class is associated with its own class loader.

The mechanism just described allows you to reload new, updated versions of the classes to the server. In the example, the old resource is replaced with the new class instances. However, it would also be possible to register the new resource instance with a different object name and have two different versions of the same class servicing the clients.

The revised implementation of the Recycler MBean is shown in Listing 7.2.

LISTING 7.2   Recycler.java

```java
package book.jmx.examples;

import javax.management.*;
import javax.management.loading.*;
import java.net.*;

public class Recycler
  implements RecyclerMBean, MBeanRegistration {

  protected String component  = "Standard User";
  private MBeanServer server = null;


  // retrieve the server reference
  public ObjectName preRegister(MBeanServer server,
                                ObjectName name) {

    this.server = server;
    return name;
  }

  // recycle implementation

  public String recycle(String clazz, String url)
```

7

STANDARD AGENT
SERVICES

LISTING 7.2   continued

```java
        throws MalformedURLException {

    ObjectName user = null;
    URL jarURL      = new URL(url);

    try {

        user = new ObjectName("example:name=User");

        // create new MLet class loader
        ObjectName loader = new ObjectName(
            "Loader:class=" + clazz +
            ",timestamp="   + System.currentTimeMillis()
        );

        MLet mlet = new MLet();
        mlet.addURL(jarURL);

        // unregister the old implementation
        if (server.isRegistered(user))
            server.unregisterMBean(user);

        // register the loaded mbean
        server.registerMBean(mlet, loader);
        Object mbean = server.instantiate(clazz, loader);
        server.registerMBean(mbean, user);

        component = clazz;
    }
    catch (JMException e) {
        e.printStackTrace();
    }

    return "Implementation changed to " + component;
}


public void postRegister(Boolean b) {}
public void preDeregister() throws Exception {}
public void postDeregister() {}

}
```

As was mentioned earlier, the example application will also load the MBean components from the network. To achieve this, you will need a minimal application bootstrap called `NetworkApp`. It creates an MBean server, registers the M-Let service, and loads the M-Let text file from the network. This sequence is shown in Figure 7.4.

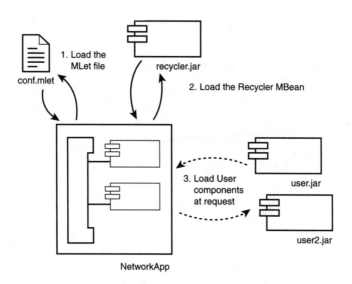

FIGURE 7.4
Sequence of operations of the bootstrap application.

The `NetworkApp` is not specific to the `Recycler` example. You can use it to load any application. The `NetworkApp` class could be used as a bootstrap for any application, from something as simple as the `Recycler` example to something as complicated as an entire J2EE application server.

The `NetworkApp` code is shown in Listing 7.3.

LISTING 7.3   `NetworkApp.java`

```java
package book.jmx.examples;

import javax.management.*;
import javax.management.loading.*;
import java.io.*;
import java.net.*;

public class NetworkApp {

  public static void main(String[] args) {

    // create the MBean server
```

LISTING 7.3   continued

```java
MBeanServer server =
    MBeanServerFactory.createMBeanServer();

ObjectName name = null;

try {

  // instantiate and register the M-Let service
  name = new ObjectName("service:name=MLet");
  server.registerMBean(new MLet(), name);

  // load M-Let text file
  server.invoke(name, "getMBeansFromURL",
    new Object[] {
        new URL("http://myconfigserver/conf.mlet")
    },
    new String[] {
        URL.class.getName()
    }
  );

  // create and register HTTP adaptor
  com.sun.jdmk.comm.HtmlAdaptorServer adaptor =
      new com.sun.jdmk.comm.HtmlAdaptorServer();

  server.registerMBean(adaptor,
      new ObjectName("adaptor:protocol=HTTP"));

  adaptor.start();
}
catch (JMException e) {
  e.printStackTrace();
}
}

}
```

Creating the MBean server, registering the M-Let service, and loading the M-Let file takes less than ten lines of code. This is a very small footprint bootstrap code capable of loading a complex application. All that is required from the software is to use a component-based design, in this case, MBeans.

The last thing you need to write is the M-Let file and compile and package the components. The M-Let file is loaded from the URL shown in Listing 7.3, `http://myconfigserver/conf.mlet`. You should replace the URL to match the setup of your system. If you want to read the M-Let file from a local file system, you can write the URL using the `file:` identifier, for example, `file://C:/Examples/conf.mlet`.

The configuration shown in Listing 7.4 is quite simple, as it only loads the `Recycler` MBean.

LISTING 7.4   `conf.mlet`

```
<MLET
    CODE=book.jmx.examples.Recycler
    ARCHIVE=recycler.jar
    CODEBASE=http://mycomponentserver
    NAME=example:name=recycler>
</MLET>
```

The final step is to compile and package the components. The packages are regular Java archives and do not require any special meta information in manifest files. If you have compiled the previous examples to your working directory, the classes should be under `book/jmx/examples` directory. From the work directory, you can then execute the following commands:

```
C:\Examples> javac -d . -classpath .;jmx-1_0_1-ri_bin\jmx\lib\jmxri.jar;
➥jmx-1_0_1-ri_bin\jmx\lib\jmxtools.jar NetworkApp.java Recycler.java
➥ RecyclerMBean.java

C:\Examples> jar -cvf user.jar book/jmx/examples/User.class
➥ book/jmx/examples/UserMBean.class
C:\Examples> jar -cvf user2.jar
➥ book/jmx/examples/BroadcastingUser.class
➥ book/jmx/examples/BroadcastingUserMBean.class
C:\Examples> jar -cvf user3.jar book/jmx/examples/DynamicUser.class

C:\Examples> jar -cvf recycler.jar book/jmx/examples/Recycler.class
➥ book/jmx/examples/RecyclerMBean.class
C:\Examples>java -classpath .;jmx-1_0_1-ri_bin\jmx\lib\jmxri.jar;
➥jmx-1_0_1-ri_bin\jmx\lib\jmxtools.jar book.jmx.examples.NetworkApp
```

This should give you four packaged components—`user.jar`, `user2.jar`, `user3.jar`, and `recycler.jar`. The user archives contain the Standard User MBean, the broadcasting User MBean and a Dynamic User MBean, respectively.

Drop the Java archives to a Web server, if you have one available, or set one up on your local machine. Edit the `conf.mlet` file to point to the correct URL in the `CODEBASE` attributes and edit the `NetworkApp` to load the `conf.mlet` file from the correct location.

You can also load the components from the local file system by using the `file:` protocol identifier in the URL. See the Java API documentation for detailed information on how to convert the instances of `File` class to URL form using the `toURL()` method.

After you have packaged the components and started the `NetworkApp` application, you can browse the agent using the HTTP adaptor, as shown in Figure 7.5. In the `Recycle` MBean, try to load another implementation of the user resource to replace the one packaged in `user.jar`.

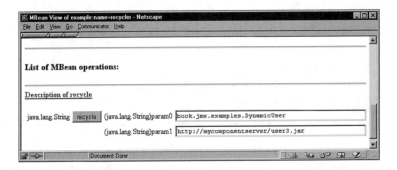

FIGURE 7.5
View of the recycle operation (Sun HTTP Adaptor).

You can now switch between different implementations of the User MBean. You can also update the existing classes with new versions and dynamically load them to the system.

Timer Service

As part of the standard agent services, the JMX specification defines a Timer service. The Timer service is based on the JMX notification mechanism and can be used to schedule notifications to occur at a given date and time or at defined intervals. The JMX Timer service is a similar service to the *cron* service on Unix and Linux systems, and the *Task Scheduler Service* on Windows NT systems. The Timer service offers similar functionality to these operating system services in the Java management domain.

The Timer service classes can be found in the `javax.management.timer` package. The service consists of one interface and two classes:

```
TimerMBean
Timer
TimerNotification
```

The `TimerMBean` is the management interface of the Timer service. The management interface contains methods for starting and stopping the service and adding and removing scheduled notifications to the service. Having the Timer service implemented as an MBean allows you to set up and configure a scheduler service using the same tools and methods you would use to manage any other MBean.

The `TimerNotification` class is a specialization of the JMX `Notification` class and is used for all notifications from the Timer service. The notification type is specified by the application when a new timed event is scheduled.

Timer MBean

The Timer MBean is a broadcaster MBean, so it implements the `NotificationBroadcaster` interface. To receive notifications from the timer, the notification consumer must implement the `NotificationListener` interface and register itself to the timer via `addNotificationListener()` method. This is the normal registration procedure for all management event consumers that were discussed in Chapter 3, "Standard MBeans."

As part of its management interface, the Timer MBean exposes methods to schedule notifications to the service. The scheduled notifications can be sent only once or can be repeated within a given interval. The repeated notifications can define a maximum number of occurrences they are sent or can be sent indefinitely. To schedule a notification, you must use the `addNotification()` method. The `TimerMBean` management interface exposes three overloaded versions of the `addNotification()` method that are shown here.

```
public Integer addNotification(String type, String message,
        Object userData, Date date);

public Integer addNotification(String type, String message,
        Object userData, Date date, long period);

public Integer addNotification(String type, String message,
        Object userData, Date date, long period, long occurrences);
```

The `type` argument is the notification type available for the notification filter and listener via the `getType()` method of the `Notification` class. Similarly, the `message` and `userData` arguments are used to initialize the `Notification` objects sent from the Timer service.

The `date` argument is the scheduled time point when the notification is sent. If the notifications are repeated, the date represents the time of the first notification being sent in the sequence. For repeated notifications, the `period` argument must be used that represents the interval between notifications in milliseconds. If the repeated notifications should not continue indefinitely, use the `occurrences` argument. If the number of occurrences is greater than zero, only the defined number of notifications will be sent. For indefinite numbers of notifications, the occurrences should be zero or `null`, and period should be any non-zero value.

The returned integer from the addNotification() call is an identifier for the scheduled notification or notifications. The identifier is attached to all TimerNotification objects sent by the Timer service. The identifier is available via the getNotificationID() method of the TimerNotification class. The identifier is unique in the Timer MBean instance and will remain the same no matter how many occurrences the scheduled event contains.

The next example shows a Timer service MBean registered to the agent, and another MBean, TimerReceiver, registered for receiving a scheduled notification from the service. The notification is set to go off five seconds after it has been added to the Timer service. The code is shown in Listings 7.5, 7.6, and 7.7.

LISTING 7.5   TimerAgent.java

```
package book.jmx.examples;

import javax.management.*;
import javax.management.timer.*;
import java.util.Date;
import java.util.List;

public class TimerAgent {

    private MBeanServer server   = null;
    private ObjectName timer     = null;
    private ObjectName receiver  = null;

    public void run() {

        // Find an agent from this JVM. Null argument will
        // return a list of all MBeanServer instances.
        List list = MBeanServerFactory.findMBeanServer(null);
        server = (MBeanServer)list.iterator().next();

        try {

            // register the timer and receiver mbeans
            timer    = new ObjectName("service:name=timer");
            receiver = new ObjectName("example:name=listener," +
                                      "source=timer");

            server.registerMBean(new Timer(), timer);
            server.registerMBean(new TimerReceiver(), receiver);

            // start the timer service
            server.invoke(timer, "start", null, null);

            // add scheduled notification to five seconds
```

LISTING 7.5   continued

```java
    // past the registration
    Date date = new Date(System.currentTimeMillis() +
        Timer.ONE_SECOND * 5);

    Integer id = (Integer)server.invoke(
      timer,                           // MBean
      "addNotification",               // operation

      new Object[] {                   // arguments:
        "timer.notification",          // type
        "Scheduled notification.",     // message
        null,                          // user data
        date
      },

      new String[] {                   // signature
        String.class.getName(),
        String.class.getName(),
        Object.class.getName(),
        Date.class.getName()
      }
    );

    // add listener to the timer
    NotificationFilter filter = new TimerFilter(id);
    server.addNotificationListener(
              timer, receiver, filter, null);
  }
  catch (JMException e) {
      e.printStackTrace();
  }
}


//
// Notification filter implementation.
//
class TimerFilter implements NotificationFilter {

  private Integer id = null;

  TimerFilter(Integer id) {
    this.id = id;
```

LISTING 7.5   continued

```
    }

    public boolean isNotificationEnabled(Notification n) {

      if (n.getType().equals("timer.notification")) {
        TimerNotification notif = (TimerNotification)n;

        if (notif.getNotificationID().equals(id))
          return true;
      }

      return false;
    }
  }


  //
  // Main method for the client. This will instantiate
  // an agent in the JVM.
  //
  public static void main(String[] args) {

    MBeanServer server =
        MBeanServerFactory.createMBeanServer();

    new TimerAgent().run();
  }
}
```

LISTING 7.6   TimerReceiver.java

```
package book.jmx.examples;

import javax.management.*;
import javax.management.timer.*;

public class TimerReceiver
    implements TimerReceiverMBean, NotificationListener {

    public void handleNotification(Notification n, Object hb) {
        System.out.println(n.getMessage());
    }
}
```

LISTING 7.7   TimerReceiverMBean.java

```
package book.jmx.examples;

import javax.management.*;
import javax.management.timer.*;

public interface TimerReceiverMBean {

}
```

Compile the three classes:

```
C:\Examples> javac -d . -classpath jmx-1_0_1-ri_bin\jmx\lib\jmxri.jar
➥ TimerAgent.java TimerReceiver.java TimerReceiverMBean.java
C:\Examples> java -classpath .;jmx-1_0_1-ri_bin\jmx\lib\jmxri.jar
➥ book.jmx.examples.TimerAgent
```

When you run the example, you should see a message printed on the console about five seconds after the startup.

```
Scheduled notification.
```

If you try to schedule notifications to a date that is earlier than the current date of the Timer service, the service will try to update the scheduled notifications until the current time is reached. If the scheduled notifications have a period set to them, the Timer service will add the time period to the submitted date until it has reached the current date in the service. When the next scheduled notification is set at the current date or past it, the rest of the scheduled notifications will be processed as usual.

If the scheduled notifications had the occurrences argument set with the period, the Timer service adds only the number of periods allowed by the occurrences argument to the submitted date. If the submitted date will reach the current date or past that, the notification occurrences that are left for the scheduled event will be processed as usual. If, however, the addition of the maximum number of occurrences will not reach the current date in the Timer service, an IllegalArgumentException is thrown. The exception indicates that all the occurrences of the scheduled notifications are scheduled for a date earlier than the current date and cannot be sent.

Part I

TABLE 7.1   Operations of the Timer Service

Operation	Description
start()	Starts the Timer service.
	If the SendPastNotifications attribute has been set to true, any notifications that occurred during the time the service was not running will be sent as soon as the start() is called.
stop()	Stops the Timer service and disables all scheduled notifications until the service is started again.
	If the SendPastNotifications attribute has been set to true, the notifications that occur during the time the service is stopped will be sent as soon as the service is started again.
getSendPast Notifications()	Allows the manipulation of the SendPastNotifications attribute.
setSendPast Notifications()	This attribute indicates whether the notifications scheduled to be sent while the service has been stopped should be sent when it is started again.
getAllNotification IDs()	Returns all the notification identifiers that have been registered to the timer service.
	The returned object is a vector of Integer objects. If there are no registered notifications in the timer service, an empty vector is returned.
getNotificationIDs (*String type*)	Returns all the notification identifiers that have been registered with the given notification type.
	The returned object is a vector of Integer objects. If no matching identifiers are found, an empty vector is returned.
getNbOccurences()	Returns the number of notifications scheduled in the timer service.
isActive()	Returns a Boolean value indicating whether the Timer service is currently active. The Timer service is activated via the start() operation.
isEmpty()	Returns a Boolean indicating whether the scheduled notification queue is empty.
removeAllNotification (*String type*)	Removes all scheduled notifications from the Timer service.
Remove Notifications	Removes all notifications based on the notification type (dot separated string).
removeNotification (*Integer id*)	Removes a notification from the Timer service based on the identifier.

In addition to the operations listed in Table 7.1, the Timer service exposes operations for reading the values of individual scheduled notifications based on their identifier. You can retrieve the number of occurrences left for the notification with getNbOccurences() operation, retrieve the period value with getPeriod() operation, and read the date when the notification is scheduled to be sent with the getDate() operation. Notice, that these values are not modifiable after you have scheduled the notification to the Timer service. If you need to change the period or number of occurrences of start date, you need to remove the old notification and schedule a new one with a different identifier.

Monitoring Service

The Monitoring service in the JMX agent layer defines a set of MBeans that can be used to monitor the attributes of managed resources. The Monitoring service implements three different types of monitor MBeans. You can utilize these MBeans to provide notifications that indicate attribute changes in the observed MBean. The monitor notifications differ from the usual attribute change notifications in that you can provide a threshold and granularity period to the notifications. In the case of the attribute change notifications, the broadcaster MBean will send an event with every change of the attribute. This can become a burden to the system if the attribute is changed frequently and also can bog down the receiver if it must manage too many notifications from the emitting MBean.

With the Monitoring service, you can configure the notifications to only occur at a given granularity period, for example, every three seconds. You can also set the threshold for the attribute value being monitored. In the case that the value has not changed during the granularity period, or the change has been a minor one not requiring a notification, the notification with the redundant information will not be sent.

The JMX Monitoring service provides three different types of monitor implementations:

> Counter monitor
>
> Gauge monitor
>
> String monitor

The counter monitor can be used to track attribute values that act like counters. This means that the value being monitored is integer type, is always greater than or equal to zero, and is only incremented. The gauge monitor can be used to monitor attribute values that are either integer or floating point types and arbitrarily either increase or decrease. The string monitor can be used to monitor attributes of the String type and notify the interested listeners whether the observed attribute value matches an expected string value or differs from it.

All the three monitors are based on a common abstract superclass, Monitor, which contains the implementation for functionality shared with the different monitor types. All the notifications sent by the monitors are instances of the MonitorNotification class. The MonitorNotification class extends the JMX Notification class to provide some additional information for the monitoring events.

Because all the monitors are implemented as MBeans themselves, they can be dynamically configured at runtime The monitors can also be temporarily stopped and restarted through their management interfaces.

Let's look at each of the relevant classes in the Monitoring service next.

Monitor

The Monitor class is an abstract superclass for all concrete monitor classes. Table 7.2 lists the most relevant methods of the Monitor class.

TABLE 7.2 Partial List of the Methods of the Monitor Class

Operation	Description
start()	Starts the attribute monitoring. Notice that an explicit call to the start() operation is required to initially activate the service.
stop()	Stops the monitor. The stop() operation can be called at any time by an management application or another MBean. Unregistering the monitor MBean from the MBeanServer will implicitly stop the monitor.
isActive()	Returns a Boolean value true if the monitor has been started.
getObservedObject() setObservedObject()	Read-write access to the ObservedObject attribute.
getObservedAttribute() setObservedAttribute()	Read-write access to the ObservedAttribute attribute. The observed attribute is a management attribute of an observed MBean set via the setObservedObject() operation.
getGranularityPeriod() setGranularityPeriod()	Read-write access to the GranularityPeriod attribute. The granularity period is set in milliseconds and indicates how often the observed attribute is being checked when monitoring has been activated.

MonitorNotification

The MonitorNotification class extends the Notification class with methods to access both the observed object and the observed attribute. In addition, you can retrieve the derived gauge value from the notification and the threshold value that caused the notification to be triggered.

The MonitorNotification class defines constants used for the notification type for the three different types of monitors supported by all JMX implementations. The notification types are shown in the Table 7.3.

TABLE 7.3   Notification Types Defined in the *MonitorNotification* Class

Notification Type	*Description*
THRESHOLD_VALUE_EXCEEDED	This notification type is reserved for the counter monitors. It indicates that the counter value has increased over the threshold that triggers the notification.
THRESHOLD_HIGH_VALUE_EXCEEDED	This notification type is reserved for the gauge monitors. It indicates the monitored value has reached or increased over the high value threshold and triggered an event.
THRESHOLD_LOW_VALUE_EXCEEDED	This notification type is reserved for the gauge monitors. It indicates that the monitored value has decreased to or below the low value threshold and triggered an event.
STRING_TO_COMPARE_VALUE_MATCHED	This notification type is reserved for the string monitors. It indicates that the monitored string attribute matches the string-to-compare value.
STRING_TO_COMPARE_VALUE_DIFFERED	This notification type is reserved for the string monitors. It indicates that the monitored string attribute differs from the string-to-compare value.

Counter Monitor

The counter monitor observes the attributes that are integer types and behave like counters. The integer types in the Java language are instances of the Short, Long, Byte, and Integer classes. The runtime type of the management attribute being observed by the counter monitor must be either one of the aforementioned types or their corresponding primitive types.

The counter behavior is defined by the JMX specification to have an integer value that is always greater than or equal to zero. Also, the counters can only be incremented—never decreased. It is possible for the counters to roll over at a certain value.

The counter monitor uses threshold value to determine when a notification should be sent to the interested listeners. When the observed attribute's value increases to match or exceed the threshold, a notification is sent. The offset is added to the threshold as many times as it is necessary for the threshold value to become greater than the current observed attribute value. However, only one notification is ever sent, no matter how many times the offset must be added to the threshold value. The behavior of a counter monitor is shown in the Figure 7.6.

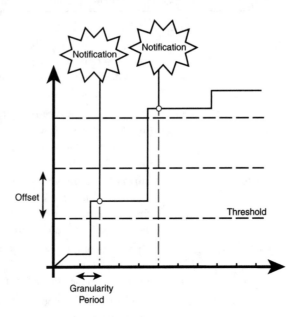

FIGURE 7.6

Notifications sent by a counter monitor.

For counters that roll over at a given point, it is necessary to set a *modulus* value. The modulus value is set to the value point where the observed counter attribute rolls over. When the threshold is increased, it is checked against the modulus value and, if the increased threshold value is greater than the modulus, the threshold is rolled over and set back to its original value before any offset increments.

The *derived gauge* is the value derived from the observation of an attribute. The derived gauge can be either the exact value of the observed attribute at a given time or a difference value between two consecutive observations. The type of the derived gauge is determined by the difference mode of the counter monitor.

Notice that the notifications from the counter monitor to the listeners must be explicitly enabled via a `setNotify()` method call.

Table 7.4 lists the relevant operations of a `CounterMonitorMBean` interface.

TABLE 7.4   Partial List of CounterMonitor MBean Operations

Operation	Description
`getDerivedGauge()`	Returns the derived gauge that is either the current value of the observed attribute or the difference between two consecutive samples, depending on the difference mode.
`getDifferenceMode()` `setDifferenceMode()`	Sets the difference mode in the counter monitor. If difference mode is `true`, the derived gauge will return the difference between two consecutive observed attribute values. If difference mode is `false`, the current value of the attribute is returned with the `getDerivedGauge()` operation.
`getModulus()` `setModulus()`	Access to the `Modulus` attribute. The modulus should be set if the counter value can roll over. In that case the maximum value for the counter should be set as the modulus value in order for the threshold value to roll over with the counter value.
`getNotify()` `setNotify()`	Enables monitor event notification.
`getOffset()` `setOffset()`	Access to the `Offset` attribute of the counter monitor. The offset is the value added to the threshold whenever the counter value exceeds it. The offset is added as many times as is necessary for the threshold value to exceed the counter value again.
`getThreshold()` `setThreshold()`	Access to the `Threshold` attribute. The threshold indicates the value that will cause a monitor notification to be sent when the counter value exceeds it.

Gauge Monitor

A gauge monitor is a monitor for integer and floating point types that fluctuate between given high and low thresholds. You can use the gauge monitor to monitor values such as memory consumption or thread count that can either increase or decrease and often oscillate around the threshold emitting the notification.

The GaugeMonitor class extends the abstract Monitor class by introducing HighThreshold and LowThreshold attributes. These attributes are used for setting the limits, which trigger monitor notifications. If the observed attribute either increases to or over the high threshold value or decreases to or below a low threshold value, a MonitorNotification instance is sent to all the interested listeners (see Figure 7.7).

The notifications sent by the gauge monitor when a high or low threshold boundary has been crossed will have either a THRESHOLD_HIGH_VALUE_EXCEEDED or THRESHOLD_LOW_VALUE_EXCEEDED as their notification type. Both of the constant values are declared in the MonitorNotification class. Also, as with the CounterMonitor class, the notifications must be explicitly enabled via setNofityHigh() and setNotifyLow() methods. In a gauge monitor, you can separately enable either the high threshold notifications, low threshold notifications, or both.

The gauge monitor implements a so-called *hysteresis* mechanism, which means that the notification is sent only once—when the high or low threshold is crossed for the first time. As a result, a fluctuating value around the threshold will not cause repeated notifications to be sent to the listeners. Another notification triggered by the same threshold boundary will only be sent if the value has crossed the other end of the hysteresis interval between the current and the previously triggered notification.

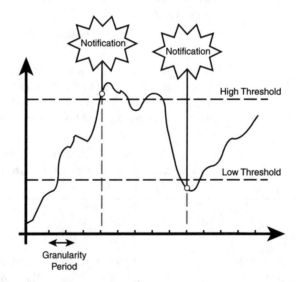

FIGURE 7.7

The notifications sent by a gauge monitor.

Table 7.5 lists the most relevant methods of the gauge monitor class.

TABLE 7.5 Descriptions of the Relevant Operations of the Gauge Monitor Management Interface

Operation	Description
getDerivedGauge()	Returns the last observed value of the attribute. The DerivedGauge can be either the last observed value or the difference between the last two observations depending on the DifferenceMode of the gauge monitor.
getDerivedGaugeTimeStamp()	Returns the time stamp of last attribute value observation.
getDifferenceMode() setDifferenceMode()	Read-Write access to the DifferenceMode attribute. If DifferenceMode is set to true, the DerivedGauge attribute's value is a difference between the last two consecutive observations. Otherwise, DerivedGauge attribute contains the value of the last observation.
getHighThreshold() getLowThreshold()	Returns the values of the HighThreshold and LowThreshold attributes of the gauge monitor. The high and low threshold values comprise of the hysteresis interval.
setNotifyHigh(*boolean value*) setNotifyLow(*boolean value*)	Enables the notifications triggered by the gauge crossing either the high threshold or low threshold values.
setThresholds(*Number high*, *Number low*)	Sets the high and low threshold values. Both the high and low values must be of the same type and must match the type of the observed attribute.
start() stop()	Starts and stops the monitor

Gauge Monitor Example

One useful application of the gauge monitor is to observe the resource use of the application, for example, a server. It is often important for the administrator to be notified when the server is using up a lot of the machine resources so the administrator can alleviate the problem by balancing the load.

You will next see an example of a gauge monitor that observes the number of threads in the JVM. You will build a simple Standard MBean that provides you with the management attribute that contains the thread count and then monitors that attribute and prints a warning when the high threshold of the gauge monitor is exceeded.

The thread monitor MBean implementation is fairly simple. You define a management interface with one read-only attribute, `ThreadCount`. The management interface declaration and the MBean implementation are shown in Listings 7.8 and 7.9.

LISTING 7.8   ThreadMonitorMBean.java

```
package book.jmx.examples;


public interface ThreadMonitorMBean {

    int getThreadCount();
}
```

LISTING 7.9   ThreadMonitor.java

```
package book.jmx.examples;


public class ThreadMonitor implements ThreadMonitorMBean {

    ThreadGroup root = null;

    public ThreadMonitor() {

        ThreadGroup group =
            Thread.currentThread().getThreadGroup();

        while (group.getParent() != null)
          group = group.getParent();

        root = group;
    }

    public int getThreadCount() {
      return root.activeCount();
    }

}
```

In the `ThreadMonitorClient` class, you create the MBean server, register the thread monitor MBean to it, and then create and configure the gauge monitor. You set the observed attribute via the `setObservedAttribute()` method and set the granularity period of the observations to five seconds via the `setGranularityPeriod()` method.

The gauge monitor is configured to send a notification when the high threshold of the monitor is crossed. To better demonstrate the example, the high threshold is set to a relatively low value of thirty threads and the low threshold to twenty threads. This means that the notification is sent when the `ThreadCount` first exceeds the thirty thread limit. Another notification will not be sent before the thread count decreases below twenty threads. Because the thread count is likely to fluctuate in a real-life scenario, this prevents the administrator from being spammed with a constant stream of warnings.

After the monitor has been configured, it is registered to the MBean server and started. You then register a listener to the monitor that will print out a warning whenever the high threshold notification is triggered. The threshold is tested by creating 35 sleeper threads in the JVM.

When you run the `ThreadMonitorClient` application, you should see the following message being printed to the console about five seconds after startup.

```
Warning, Thread count exceeds 30
Current Thread count = 40
```

The high threshold value is retrieved from the `MonitorNotification` class via the `getTrigger()` method and the actual observed count via the `getDerivedGauge()` method. The source for the `ThreadMonitorClient` is shown in Listing 7.10.

LISTING 7.10   `ThreadMonitorClient.java`

```java
package book.jmx.examples;

import javax.management.*;
import javax.management.monitor.*;
import java.util.List;

public class ThreadMonitorClient {

  private MBeanServer server   = null;
  private ObjectName threads   = null;
  private ObjectName monitor   = null;

  public void run() {

    // Find an agent from this JVM. Null argument will
    // return a list of all MBeanServer instances.
```

LISTING 7.10   continued

```
List list = MBeanServerFactory.findMBeanServer(null);
server     = (MBeanServer)list.iterator().next();

try {
  // register the MBean reporting thread count
  threads = new ObjectName("Observable:type=Threads");
  server.registerMBean(new ThreadMonitor(), threads);

  // configure the monitor
  GaugeMonitor threadMon = new GaugeMonitor();
  threadMon.setObservedObject(threads);
  threadMon.setObservedAttribute("ThreadCount");
  threadMon.setGranularityPeriod(5 * 1000);
  threadMon.setNotifyHigh(true);

  threadMon.setThresholds(
      new Integer(30), new Integer(20)
  );

  // register the monitor
  monitor = new ObjectName("Monitor:type=Threads");
  server.registerMBean(threadMon, monitor);
  threadMon.start();

  server.addNotificationListener(
      monitor, new MonitorListener(), null, monitor
  );

  // test the monitor by creating 35 extra threads
  for (int i = 0; i < 35; ++i) {
    Thread thread = new Thread(new Runnable() {

        public void run() {
            try {
                Thread.sleep(10000);
            }
            catch (Exception ignored) {}
        }
    });

    thread.start();
  }

} catch (JMException e) {
```

LISTING 7.10 continued

```java
        e.printStackTrace();
    }
}


// notification listener implementation

class MonitorListener implements NotificationListener {

    public void handleNotification(Notification n,
                                    Object handback) {

        MonitorNotification notif = (MonitorNotification)n;

        if (notif.getType().equals
         (MonitorNotification.THRESHOLD_HIGH_VALUE_EXCEEDED)
        ) {

            System.out.println(
                "Warning, Thread count exceeds " +
                notif.getTrigger()
            );

            System.out.println(
                "Current Thread count = " +
                notif.getDerivedGauge()
            );
        }
    }
}


//
// Main method for the client. This will instantiate
// an agent in the JVM.
//
public static void main(String[] args) {

    MBeanServer server =
        MBeanServerFactory.createMBeanServer();

    new ThreadMonitorClient().run();
}
}
```

To compile and run the thread monitor example, execute the following commands on the console:

```
C:\Examples> javac -d . -classpath .;jmx-1_0_1-ri_bin\jmx\lib\jmxri.jar
➥ ThreadMonitor.java ThreadMonitorMBean.java ThreadMonitorClient.java

C:\Examples> java -classpath .;jmx-1_0_1-ri_bin\jmx\lib\jmxri.jar
➥ book.jmx.examples.ThreadMonitorClient
```

StringMonitor

The third and last of the monitor types is the string monitor. The string monitor enables the monitoring of management attributes that are of the Java `String` type. It is possible to configure the string monitor to trigger a notification either when the observed string attribute matches that of the compared string or when the observed string attribute differs from the compared string.

The configuration of the string monitor is achieved via the `NotifyDiffer` and `NotifyMatch` attributes. Setting the `NotifyDiffer` to `true` will enable notifications whenever the observed string attribute differs from the `StringToCompare` attribute. Similarly, setting the `NotifyMatch` attribute to `true` enables notifications to be sent whenever the observed string matches the `StringToCompare` attribute. Setting both `NotifyDiffer` and `NotifyMatch` attributes to `true` will cause notifications to be sent whenever the observed attribute's condition changes.

Table 7.6 lists the relevant methods of the string monitor MBean.

TABLE 7.6   Operations of the `StringMonitorMBean` Interface

Method	Description
`getDerivedGauge()`	Returns the value of the observed string attribute. In the case of the string monitor, there is no difference mode. The returned string is always the value of the observed attribute.
`getDerivedGaugeTimeStamp()`	Returns the time stamp of the last observation used for setting the derived gauge.
`getStringToCompare()` `setStringToCompare()`	Read-Write access to the `StringToCompare` management attribute. The string is used with comparison to the observed attribute.
`getNotifyDiffer()` `setNotifyDiffer()`	Read-Write access to the `NotifyDiffer` management attribute. Setting this attribute to `true` will trigger notifications whenever the value of the observed attribute differs from the value of the `StringToCompare` attribute.

TABLE 7.6   continued

Method	Description
getNotifyMatch() setNotifyMatch()	Read-Write access to the NotifyMatch management attribute. Setting this attribute to true will trigger notifications whenever the value of the observed attribute differs from the value of the StringToCompare attribute.

Relation Service

As a fourth standard service, the JMX specification defines a Relation service for MBeans. The Relation service can be used for defining relations between MBeans, defining roles to MBeans, and associating MBean instances in different roles as part of the relations.

The Relation service maintains consistency of the relations. Consequently, if an MBean belonging to a relation is unregistered and the relation no longer can be considered consistent, the relations are removed from the service. Notice, however, that the relation service never directly manipulates any MBeans associated with the relations. Instead, the relation service emits notifications on changes in the relation instances, such as creation, updates, and removal of relations.

The Relation service consists of metadata information that is used to describe the relation types and the roles participating in the relation. In addition, as with all other standard services, the relation service itself provides a management interface that allows the manipulation of the relations. You will next go through the relevant classes of the relation service and finish with an example demonstrating the use of this service.

Relation Service Metadata

The Relation service uses two different metadata classes to describe the relation types and role information of relation instances. Each MBean that is associated with a relation through the Relation service participates in a described role of that relation instance. The roles are described with RoleInfo objects and composed of RoleType objects that act as templates for the kinds of relations that can be registered to the Relation service.

RoleInfo
The RoleInfo class of the JMX specification describes the roles of a relation. The RoleInfo class consists of the name of the role, the multiplicity of the role in a given relation, the class-name of the MBean participating in the role, and a description of the role. The multiplicity of the role is expressed as a range between a minimum and maximum number of MBeans that can participate in that role.

To create role information for a role named `"Monitor"`, the following code can be used:

```
RoleInfo monitorInfo = new RoleInfo(
    "Monitor",                              // role name
    "javax.management.monitor.GaugeMonitor",// class name
    true, true,                             // isReadable, isWritable
    0, RoleInfo.ROLE_CARDINALITY_INFINITY,  // cardinality [0..*]
    "Describes a Monitor role."             // description
);
```

The previous code snippet describes a role that consists of zero or more instances of JMX GaugeMonitor MBean instances.

Similarly, to describe a role for an observable MBean that can be observed by a gauge monitor MBean, the following role info could be created:

```
RoleInfo observableInfo = new RoleInfo(
    "Observable",                           // role name
    "book.jmx.examples.ThreadMonitor",      // class name
    true, true,                             // isReadable, isWritable
    1, 1,                                   // cardinality [1..1]
    "Describes an observed MBean role."     // description
);
```

RelationType

Where `RoleInfo` class describes the metadata of MBean roles in a relation, the `RelationType` interface is used for describing the metadata of the relation instances. The relation types are collections of role information objects. A `RelationType` instance describes a relation in terms of what roles can participate in the relation and what consistency rules must be followed for the relation to be valid. The relation type also contains the name of the relation template that is used as an identifier.

To create a relation type metadata for a `Relation` instance that represents the relation between an observed MBean and the monitor MBeans, you can create a relation template and call it `"ObservedMBean"`. The `"ObservedMBean"` relation consists of two roles, `"Observable"` and `"Monitor"` where one observable component may have zero or more monitors. Using the `RelationTypeSupport` class, you can create this relation type using the following snippet of code:

```
RelationTypeSupport relationType = new RelationTypeSupport(
    "ObservedMBean",
    new RoleInfo[] { observableInfo, monitorInfo }
);
```

The previous code creates a relation type template that expects the participating components to meet the consistency requirements set in the role information metadata objects.

Relation Service MBean

The Relation service provides a management interface that allows both the manipulation of relations and queries to relations to be made. Table 7.7 offers a brief overview of the relevant operations of the Relation service.

TABLE 7.7 Relevant Operations of the Relation Service

Method	Description
createRelationType() addRelationType()	createRelationType() method allows registering a new relation type to the service without implementing the RelationType interface directly. This is a so-called internal relation type.
	addRelationType() method requires an implementation of the RelationType interface as an argument. This is a so-called external relation type. The benefit of using external relation types comes from the possibility of creating predefined, static types.
createRelation() addRelation()	The createRelation() method creates a new relation instance to the relation service. The relation instance is associated with a unique ID string and must provide the name of one of the registered relation types in the relation service.
	The addRelation() method can be used to create a so-called external relation. The addRelation() method takes an object name of an MBean as an argument. This MBean must implement the Relation interface.
getPurgeFlag() setPurgeFlag() purgeRelations()	The PurgeFlag attribute indicates whether the relation service should immediately purge relations that are no longer valid when an MBean is unregistered. The purgeRelations() method allows the explicit purging of non-valid relations if the purge flag is not used.

In addition to the methods listed in Table 7.7, Relation service MBeans expose several methods for querying the service for information on the relations. It is possible to query for relation-associated MBeans via the findAssociatedMBeans() method, look for referencing relation instances via the findReferencingRelations() method, and so on. You will see an example of how to use the query methods in Listing 7.10.

RelationNotification

The relation service broadcasts events on create, update, and remove operations on the relation instances. The notifications are instances of the `RelationNotification` object, which extends the JMX `Notification` class.

The `RelationNotification` class adds methods for retrieving more specific information on the operation that occurred on the relation instance. In the case of a role update notification, you can access the new and old role values. For all Relation service notifications, the affected relation type and the relation ID is sent with the notification.

Role and RoleList

To associate an MBean with a role in the Relation service, the `Role` class is used. The `Role` object requires a role name, which must be one of the names defined in the role information objects, and a list of role values. The role value list is an array of object names that represent the MBeans associated with the named role. The role list is given as a specific `RoleList` list object.

Relation Example

To wrap up all the code snippets shown in the previous pages and the discussion on the Relation service, the next example builds a simple application that creates a relation between an observed MBean and a monitoring MBean.

In the example, you define two role information objects that are identical to the `"Observable"` and `"Monitor"` role information discussed earlier. You form a one-to-many relation between the `ThreadMonitor` MBean from the gauge monitor example and the monitoring MBean. In addition to creating the metadata objects for role information and relation type, you add a listener to the relation service that is interested in the relation removal events. When a relation is removed, the code lists the object names of all referenced MBeans based on the relation ID that is retrieved from the Relation service notification. As you may remember, the relation service itself never manipulates the MBeans directly, so it is up to the application developer to decide how to handle the MBeans that are no longer part of the relation.

Because the example uses a one-to-many relation between the observable MBean and the monitoring MBean, unregistering the monitoring MBean will not trigger a removal notification from the relation service. However, when the observed MBean is unregistered, the relation is no longer valid and a notification of a relation removal is sent. The notification is set immediately because the purge relations flag has been set.

The source code for the relation example is shown in Listing 7.11.

LISTING 7.11   RelationAgent.java

```java
package book.jmx.examples;

import java.util.*;
import javax.management.*;
import javax.management.monitor.*;
import javax.management.relation.*;

public class RelationAgent {

  public static void main(String[] args) {
    try {

    MBeanServer server = MBeanServerFactory.createMBeanServer();

    // create the "observable" MBean
    ThreadMonitor threads = new ThreadMonitor();
    server.registerMBean(threads, new ObjectName("Example:name=Threads"));

    // create the "observer"
    GaugeMonitor mon      = new GaugeMonitor();
    mon.setObservedObject(new ObjectName(":name=Threads"));
    mon.setObservedAttribute("ThreadCount");
    mon.setGranularityPeriod(5 * 1000);
    mon.setNotifyHigh(true);
    mon.setThresholds(new Integer(30), new Integer(20));

    server.registerMBean(mon, new ObjectName("Monitor:target=Threads"));
    mon.start();

    // create relation service, purgeRelations=true
    ObjectName relationService = new ObjectName("Service:name=Relation");
    RelationService service = new RelationService(true);

    service.addNotificationListener(new RelationListener(), null, null);
    server.registerMBean(service, relationService);

    // "monitor" role meta data
    RoleInfo monitorInfo = new RoleInfo(
        "Monitor",                                // role name
        "javax.management.monitor.GaugeMonitor",// class name
        true, true,                               // isReadable, isWritable
```

LISTING 7.11   continued

```
    0, RoleInfo.ROLE_CARDINALITY_INFINITY,  // multiplicity [0..*]
    "Describes a Monitor role."             // description
);


// "observable" role meta data
RoleInfo observableInfo = new RoleInfo(
    "Observable",                           // role name
    "book.jmx.examples.ThreadMonitor",      // class name
    true, true,                             // isReadable, isWritable
    1, 1,                                   // multiplicity [1..1]
    "Describes an observed MBean role."     // description
);


// relation type template
RelationTypeSupport relationType = new RelationTypeSupport(
    "ObservedMBean",
    new RoleInfo[] { observableInfo, monitorInfo }
);


// add relation type to the service
server.invoke(relationService, "addRelationType",
    new Object[] { relationType },
    new String[] { RelationType.class.getName() }
);


// associate MBean to role
ArrayList list = new ArrayList();
list.add(new ObjectName("Monitor:target=Threads"));
Role monitor = new Role("Monitor", list);


// associate MBean to role
list = new ArrayList();
list.add(new ObjectName("Example:name=Threads"));
Role target = new Role("Observable", list);

RoleList roleList = new RoleList();
roleList.add(monitor);
roleList.add(target);


// create the relation
server.invoke(relationService, "createRelation",
    new Object[] { "MyRelationID", "ObservedMBean", roleList },
    new String[] {
        String.class.getName(),
        String.class.getName(),
```

LISTING 7.11   continued

```
            RoleList.class.getName()
    }
);

// create the adaptor instance
com.sun.jdmk.comm.HtmlAdaptorServer adaptor =
    new com.sun.jdmk.comm.HtmlAdaptorServer();

server.registerMBean(adaptor,
    new ObjectName("adaptor:protocol=HTTP"));

adaptor.start();

} catch (JMException e) {
  e.printStackTrace();
} catch (ClassNotFoundException e) {
  e.printStackTrace();
}

}

static class RelationListener implements NotificationListener {

  public void handleNotification(Notification n, Object hb) {

    if (n instanceof RelationNotification) {
      RelationNotification notif = (RelationNotification)n;

      System.out.println(notif.getRelationId());
      System.out.println(notif.getType());
      System.out.println(notif.getMessage());

      if (notif.getType().equals(
          RelationNotification.RELATION_BASIC_REMOVAL)
      ) {
        try {
          String ID = notif.getRelationId();
          ObjectName relationService = new ObjectName(
              "Service:name=Relation"
          );

          MBeanServer server =
              (MBeanServer)MBeanServerFactory.findMBeanServer(null).get(0);

          Map map = (Map)server.invoke(
```

LISTING 7.11   continued

```
                relationService,
                "getReferencedMBeans",
                new Object[] { ID },
                new String[] { String.class.getName() }
            );

            Iterator it = map.keySet().iterator();

            while(it.hasNext()) {
              System.out.println("MBeans referenced by the relation:");
              System.out.println(it.next());
            }
          } catch (JMException e) {
            e.printStackTrace();
          }
        }
      }
    }
  }

}
```

To compile and run this, execute the following commands. The commands assume that you have already compiled the earlier thread monitor example in the current working directory.

```
C:\Examples> javac -d . -classpath .;jmx-1_0_1-ri_bin\jmx\lib\jmxri.jar;
➥jmx-1_0_1-ri_bin\jmx\lib\jmxtools.jar RelationAgent.java

C:\Examples> java -classpath .;jmx-1_0_1-ri_bin\jmx\lib\jmxri.jar;
➥jmx-1_0_1-ri_bin\jmx\lib\jmxtools.jar book.jmx.examples.RelationAgent
```

When you start the agent, you should see a notification printed on the console informing of the creation of a relation with ID string "MyRelationID".

```
MyRelationID
jmx.relation.creation.basic
Creation of relation MyRelationID
```

You can now point your browser to http://localhost:8082 and see if the relation behavior acts as expected when you unregister the observed MBean or the monitoring MBean.

Summary

The JMX specification defines four standard agent services that can be used to extend the functionality of the basic agent level. All four standard services are mandatory and therefore are implemented by all compliant JMX agents. Each agent service also exposes a management interface allowing standard management of the JMX agent level itself.

The M-Let service can be used to dynamically load new components to the MBean server. This is particularly useful for applications that require updates and maintenance while providing availability to the clients. The Timer service can be used to schedule notifications for tasks that need to be run once or at regular intervals in the system. Monitoring service defines three different types of monitor MBeans that can be used to monitor the state of management attributes of MBeans. Finally, the Relation service allows you to define relations between MBean components and react to changes in case of MBean dependencies.

JMX in the J2EE Platform

PART
II

THIS PART

XMBean: Model MBean Implementation

IN THIS CHAPTER

In this chapter, you will build an implementation of a Model MBean. You will create an implementation that can handle the basic attribute caching, a simple file-based persistence, and can read and create its management interface from an XML file.

When using Dynamic and Model MBeans the metadata creation of the management interface is left up to the MBean developer. Because this can create quite a bit of extra work, the implementation you build will allow you to create generic builder implementations that can generate the metadata for you. The Model MBean implementation in this chapter will use an XML file to define the management interface but the implementation is easily extended to support other means for building the MBean interface.

The basic attribute method mapping and persistence implementation will allow you to have a consistent Model MBean implementation across several JMX implementations. Remember that the JMX specification does not require either functionality in the mandatory `RequiredModelMBean` class, so for MBeans that require them it is safer to use your own Model MBean implementation.

`ModelMBean` Interface Implementation

The `ModelMBean` interface itself extends three other interfaces defined in the JMX API—the `DynamicMBean` interface, `PersistentMBean` interface, and the `ModelMBeanNotificationBroadcaster` interface (see Figure 8.1)

The `DynamicMBean` interface declares the methods for getting and setting the MBean's attributes and invoking its operations. The `PersistentMBean` interface adds the `store()` and `load()` callbacks to indicate when the MBean should persist or load its state. The `ModelMBeanNotificationBroadcaster` interface adds methods for adding and removing notification listeners and sending notifications to interested listeners.

The `ModelMBean` interface itself declares two additional methods—`setManagedResource()` and `setModelMBeanInfo()`. In total, you need to implement 19 methods to create a Model MBean implementation (both `sendAttributeChangeNotification()` and `sendNotification()` methods require two overloaded versions to be implemented):

- `addAttributeChangeNotificationListener`
- `addNotificationListener`
- `getAttribute`
- `getAttributes`
- `getMBeanInfo`
- `getNotificationInfo`
- `invoke`

- load

- sendAttributeChangeNotification (×2)

- sendNotification (×2)

- setAttribute

- setAttributes

- setManagedResource

- setModelMBeanInfo

- store

- removeAttributeChangeNotificationListener

- removeNotificationListener

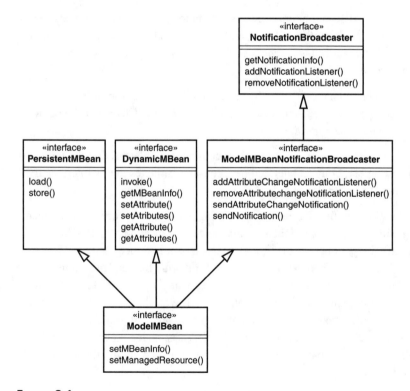

FIGURE 8.1

ModelMBean *class diagram.*

As you can see, it is quite a bit of work to do. However, remember that the Model MBeans are used as generic, configurable MBean templates to the resource classes, so you only need to build this implementation once and then you will be able to reuse it in most MBean server environments.

The `setManagedResource()` implementation allows you to specify the type of the reference it passes to the Model MBean implementation. The type is a logical name representing what kind of a resource the Model MBean is representing. For example, it can be a string representing an Inter-ORB Reference (IOR), RMI Reference, an EJBHandle, JNDI name, or a regular Java object reference. Different Model MBean implementations can accept different reference types. If the Model MBean implementation does not recognize the type string supplied by the resource, it will throw an `InvalidTargetObjectTypeException` from the `setManagedResource()` method.

You will implement a Model MBean that only accepts a common Java object reference type as its resource. However, the implementation is left open for extension by verifying the resource type string in a protected `isSupportedResourceType()` method that the subclasses can extend to accept additional reference types.

The Model MBean implementation class you will implement is called `XMBean`. It implements the `ModelMBean` interface, the `MBeanRegistration` interface (covered in Chapter 6, "MBean Server"), and an `XMBeanConstants` interface.

The `XMBeanConstants` interface declares a set of useful constant variables used in the implementation, shown in Listing 8.1. You can later add new constant variables to this interface if you decide to extend the `XMBean` implementation.

The `XMBean` class declaration and fields are shown in Listing 8.2. The reference to the MBean server is stored along with the reference to the resource object instance the Model MBean is representing, the resource's type (`ObjectReference`), management interface metadata, and the MBean's object name. In addition, there are integer fields for storing the sequence numbers for MBean notifications, and an instance of a `NotificationBroadcasterSupport` class that you will use to delegate all the notification related invocations to. The attribute and operation map fields will contain a map of the management operations and attributes indexed by their names. The values of the map will contain references to the helper classes, `XMBeanAttribute`, and `XMBeanOperation` (see Figure 8.2), that handle the logic for setting and getting the attribute values and invoking operations.

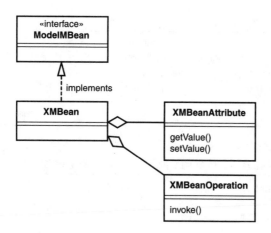

FIGURE 8.2

Class structure of the XMBean implementation.

LISTING 8.1   XMBeanConstants.java

```java
package book.jmx.examples;

public interface XMBeanConstants {

    // resource types
    final static String OBJECT_REF = "ObjectReference";

    // notification types
    final static String GENERIC_MODELMBEAN_NOTIFICATION =
        "jmx.modelmbean.generic";

    // MBean descriptor field names
    final static String VALUE = "value";
    final static String GET_METHOD = "getMethod";
    final static String SET_METHOD = "setMethod";
    final static String PERSIST_POLICY = "persistPolicy";
    final static String PERSIST_PERIOD = "persistPeriod";
    final static String PERSIST_NAME = "persistName";
    final static String PERSIST_LOCATION = "persistLocation";
    final static String CURRENCY_TIME_LIMIT = "currencyTimeLimit";
    final static String LAST_UPDATED_TIME_STAMP = "lastUpdatedTimeStamp";
    final static String EXPORT = "export";

    final static String XML_DEFINITION_URL = "xml.definition.url";

    // persistence policies
```

LISTING 8.1   continued

```
    final static String ON_UPDATE = "OnUpdate";
    final static String NO_MORE_OFTEN_THAN = "NoMoreOftenThan";
    final static String NEVER = "Never";
    final static String ON_TIMER = "OnTimer";


}
```

LISTING 8.2   XMBean.java (Class Declaration and Object Fields)

```
package book.jmx.examples;

import java.net.*;
import java.io.*;
import java.util.*;
import java.lang.reflect.*;
import javax.management.*;
import javax.management.modelmbean.*;
import javax.management.loading.*;


public class XMBean implements ModelMBean, MBeanRegistration,
    XMBeanConstants {

  protected MBeanServer server = null;

  // managed resource, resource type, model mbean metadata
  // and object name reference
  protected Object resource         = null;
  protected String resourceType     = null;
  protected ModelMBeanInfo metadata = null;
  protected ObjectName name         = null;

  // sequence numbers for notifications
  protected long notifierSequence     = 0;
  protected long attrNotifierSequence = 0;

  // support for generic notification listeners
  private NotificationBroadcasterSupport notifier =
      new NotificationBroadcasterSupport();

  // maps mbean attribute and operation names to
  // corresponding XMBeanAttribute and XMBeanOperation objects
  protected Map attributeMap         = new HashMap();
  protected Map operationMap         = new HashMap();

  // Continue...
```

Next are the `setModelMBeanInfo()` and `setManagedResource()` method implementations. The `setModelMBeanInfo()` implementation stores the supplied management interface metadata to the metadata field of the class. The `setManagedResource()` implementation checks the supported resource types via the `isSupportedResourceType()` call before storing the managed resource reference and the type string (see Listing 8.3).

LISTING 8.3   `XMBean.java` (`ModelMBean` Interface Implementation)

```
// XMBean continued...

// ModelMbean interface

public void setModelMBeanInfo(ModelMBeanInfo metadata)
    throws MBeanException, RuntimeOperationsException {

  if (metadata == null) {
    throw new IllegalArgumentException(
        "The Model MBeanInfo cannot be null."
    );
  }

  this.metadata = metadata;
}

public void setManagedResource(Object ref, String resourceType)
    throws MBeanException,
           InstanceNotFoundException,
           InvalidTargetObjectTypeException {

  if (ref == null) {
    throw new IllegalArgumentException(
        "Resource reference cannot be null."
    );
  }

  // check that is a supported resource type
  if (!isSupportedResourceType(resourceType)) {
    throw new InvalidTargetObjectTypeException(
        "Unsupported resource type: " + resourceType
    );
  }

  this.resource = ref;
  this.resourceType = resourceType;
}
```

Listing 8.3   continued

```
protected boolean isSupportedResourceType(
    String resourceType) {

  if (resourceType == null)                return false;
  if (resourceType.equals(OBJECT_REF))  return true;

  return false;
}
```

Now, let's look at how to build the map of management attributes and operations from the metadata.

MBeanRegistration Interface

Recall that you declared the MBeanRegistration interface to be implemented by the XMBean class. The XMBean implementation uses the MBeanRegistration interface to retrieve a reference to the MBean server, to store its object name, and to build a map of both management attributes and operations based on the metadata configured for the Model MBean.

You will use the attribute and operation maps to associate special helper classes for each attribute and operation. The helper classes will implement the logic that handles, for example, the attribute value caching and persistence callbacks to ModelMBean.store(). Both XMBeanAttribute and XMBeanOperation classes can also be extended to implement more sophisticated logic that should be executed with each invocation: security checks, logging, transaction demarcation and so on. Each map will have an attribute name or operation name and signature as its key and an XMBeanAttribute or XMBeanOperation instance as its value.

The implementation of MBeanRegistration interface is shown in Listing 8.4. The preRegister() method of the interface is the only one with an implementation in it. The operation and attribute maps are created with the private methods createAttributeMap() and createOperationMap(). The XMBeanAttribute and XMBeanOperation classes are discussed in detail in the next section.

Listing 8.4   XMBean.java (MBeanRegistration Implementation)

```
// XMBean continued...
// MBeanRegistration interface

public ObjectName preRegister(MBeanServer server,
                            ObjectName name)
                            throws Exception {
```

LISTING 8.4   continued

```
    // store the server reference and name
    this.server = server;
    this.name   = name;

    // create attribute and operation maps
    attributeMap = createAttributeMap(metadata.getAttributes());
    operationMap = createOperationMap(metadata.getOperations());

    return name;
}

public void postRegister(Boolean registrationSuccessful) {}
public void preDeregister() throws Exception {}
public void postDeregister() {}

private Map createAttributeMap(MBeanAttributeInfo[] attributes)
    throws MBeanException  {

  Map attrMap = new HashMap();

  for (int i = 0; i < attributes.length; ++i) {
    String name = attributes[i].getName();

    ModelMBeanAttributeInfo info =
        (ModelMBeanAttributeInfo)attributes[i];

    attrMap.put(name, new XMBeanAttribute(this, info));
  }

  return attrMap;
}

private Map createOperationMap(MBeanOperationInfo[] operations)
    throws MBeanException {

  Map operMap = new HashMap();

  for (int i = 0; i < operations.length; ++i) {
    String name = operations[i].getName();
    MBeanParameterInfo[] params = operations[i].getSignature();

    // create signature
    for (int j = 0; j < params.length; ++j)
      name += params[j].getType();
```

LISTING 8.4   continued

```
    ModelMBeanOperationInfo info =
        (ModelMBeanOperationInfo)operations[i];

    operMap.put(name, new XMBeanOperation(this, info));
    }

    return operMap;
}
```

DynamicMBean Interface

Model MBeans are extensions of the Dynamic MBeans, so they too implement the
`DynamicMBean` interface. As you learned in Chapter 4, "Dynamic MBeans," the `DynamicMBean`
interface consists of the following six methods:

- `getMBeanInfo`
- `getAttribute`
- `getAttributes`
- `invoke`
- `setAttribute`
- `setAttributes`

Also, recall from Chapter 5, "Model MBeans," that the Model MBeans can be configured with
the descriptor objects to include behavioral properties, such as persistence policy and `setter`
and `getter` method mapping.

invoke

The implementation of the `invoke()` operation is quite straightforward. You look up the corresponding `XMBeanOperation` object based on the operation name and signature and execute
`invoke()` on the `XMBeanOperation` instance. The `XMBeanOperation` implementation will use
reflection on the managed resource object to invoke a matching method. The implementation
of the XMBean `invoke()` method is shown in Listing 8.5. The `XMBeanOperation` class is
shown in Listing 8.6. Notice that the `invoke()` implementation in Listing 8.6 does nothing but
delegate the invocation to the corresponding method in the resource class. This is where you
could add your security implementation and other additional logic you wish to execute before
the actual operation is invoked.

If you wish to extend the implementation to invoke other types of resources, for example an EJB reference, you can also create a new implementation of the XMBeanOperation that handles the required EJB lookups and leaves the security and transaction demarcation to the EJB container. In such case however, it is probably a good idea to abstract the XMBeanOperation as a separate interface and create specific ObjectOperation and EJBOperation implementations. The XMBean implementation can then choose the right implementation to be added to the operation map based on the resource type.

LISTING 8.5   XMBean.java (Invoke Implementation)

```
// XMBean continued...


public Object invoke(String actionName, Object[] params,
                     String[] signature)
    throws MBeanException, ReflectionException {

  String method = actionName;

  // build signature
  if (signature != null) {
    for (int i = 0; i < signature.length; ++i)
      method += signature[i];
  }

  XMBeanOperation operation =
      (XMBeanOperation)operationMap.get(method);

  if (operation == null) {
    throw new ReflectionException(
      new IllegalArgumentException("unknown operation")
    );
  }

  return operation.invoke(params);
}
```

LISTING 8.6   XMBeanOperation.java

```
package book.jmx.examples;

import java.lang.reflect.*;
import javax.management.*;
import javax.management.modelmbean.*;
```

LISTING 8.6   continued

```java
import javax.management.loading.*;

public class XMBeanOperation implements XMBeanConstants {

  // management operation name
  protected String operationName        = null;

  // reference to the resource
  protected Object managedResource       = null;

  // corresponding method on the resource class
  protected Method operationMethod       = null;

  // signature of the resource method
  protected Class[] signature            = null;

  public XMBeanOperation(XMBean mbean,
      ModelMBeanOperationInfo operationInfo) throws MBeanException {

    try {
      this.operationName   = operationInfo.getName();
      this.managedResource = mbean.resource;
      this.signature       = createSignature(operationInfo);
      this.operationMethod = managedResource.getClass().
          getMethod(operationName, signature);
    }
    catch (NoSuchMethodException e) {
      throw new MBeanException(e,
          "Resource method " + operationName + " not found."
      );
    }
  }

  // creates class signature from MBean parameter metadata
  private Class[] createSignature(ModelMBeanOperationInfo info)
      throws MBeanException {

    Class[] paramTypes        = null;
    MBeanParameterInfo[] sign = info.getSignature();

    if (sign != null) {
      paramTypes = new Class[sign.length];

      for (int i = 0; i < paramTypes.length; ++i) {
```

LISTING 8.6   continued

```
      try {
        String type = sign[i].getType();
        paramTypes[i] = DefaultLoaderRepository.loadClass(type);
      }
      catch (ClassNotFoundException e) {
        throw new MBeanException(e,
            "Error loading parameter class " + sign[i].getType()
        );
      }
    }
  }

  return paramTypes;
}


// straight forward resource invocation implementation
public Object invoke(Object[] args) throws ReflectionException {

  if (operationMethod == null) {
    throw new ReflectionException(new Exception(
        "Method " + operationName + " not found.")
    );
  }

  try {
    return operationMethod.invoke(managedResource, args);
  }
  catch (Exception e) {
    throw new ReflectionException(e);
  }
}

}
```

getAttribute and getAttributes

The getAttribute() implementation is built in a similar fashion to invoke(). You delegate the implementation to the corresponding XMBeanAttribute instance that you look up from the attributeMap (see Listing 8.7).

The getValue() (Listing 8.8) method in the XMBeanAttribute implements the logic to retrieve an attribute value. It implements attribute caching based on the currencyTimeLimit and getMethod fields in the attribute's descriptor.

In the getValue() method implementation, a check is first made to ensure that the attribute is allowed to be read. If that is true, the required descriptor fields—value, getMethod, lastUpdatedTimeStamp, and currencyTimeLimit—are retrieved. If getMethod mapping exists, it is invoked if the value in the descriptor is considered stale as determined by a time stamp check. If the value in the descriptor is still valid, it is returned directly.

LISTING 8.7   XMBean.java (getAttribute and getAttributes Implementation)

```
// XMBean continued...

// DynamicMBean interface

public Object getAttribute(String attribute)
    throws AttributeNotFoundException, MBeanException,
    ReflectionException {

  XMBeanAttribute attr =
      (XMBeanAttribute)attributeMap.get(attribute);

  if (attr == null)
    throw new AttributeNotFoundException();

  return attr.getValue();
}


public AttributeList getAttributes(String[] attributes) {

  if (attributes == null)
    throw new IllegalArgumentException("null array");

  AttributeList list = new AttributeList();

  for (int i = 0; i < attributes.length; ++i) {
    try {
      list.add(new Attribute(
          attributes[i], getAttribute(attributes[i])
      ));
    }
    catch (JMException ignored) {
      // if the attribute could not be retrieved, skip it
    }
  }

  return list;
}
```

LISTING 8.8   XMBeanAttribute (getValue Implementation)

```
public Object getValue() throws MBeanException,
    ReflectionException, AttributeNotFoundException {

  ModelMBeanInfo mbeanInfo = (ModelMBeanInfo)mbean.getMBeanInfo();
  ModelMBeanAttributeInfo attrInfo = mbeanInfo.getAttribute(name);

  // see if we're allowed to read this value
  if (!attrInfo.isReadable())
    throw new AttributeNotFoundException("Attribute is not readable");


  Descriptor desc    = attrInfo.getDescriptor();
  Descriptor mmbDesc = mbeanInfo.getMBeanDescriptor();

  // retrieve the relevant values from the attribute's descriptor
  long lastUpdate    = 0;
  long currTimeLimit = -1;
  Object field       = null;
  Object result      = desc.getFieldValue(VALUE);
  Object getMethod   = desc.getFieldValue(GET_METHOD);

  // last update timestamp to check cache validity
  if((field = desc.getFieldValue(LAST_UPDATED_TIME_STAMP))!=null)
    lastUpdate  = Long.parseLong(field.toString());

  // get currencyTimeLimit from MBean descriptor first, overwrite
  // with attribute's descriptor field, if available
  if((field = mmbDesc.getFieldValue(CURRENCY_TIME_LIMIT))!=null)
    currTimeLimit = Long.parseLong(field.toString()) * 1000;
  if((field = desc.getFieldValue(CURRENCY_TIME_LIMIT))!=null)
    currTimeLimit = Long.parseLong(field.toString()) * 1000;

  // if getMethod is specified and cache is stale, invoke it
  if (getMethod != null) {
    long time = System.currentTimeMillis();

    if (time > lastUpdate + currTimeLimit) {

      result = mbean.invoke((String)getMethod, null, null);

      // update descriptor
      desc.setField(VALUE, result);
      desc.setField(LAST_UPDATED_TIME_STAMP, "" + time);
      mbeanInfo.setDescriptor(desc, "attribute");
```

8

XMBEAN: MODEL
MBEAN
IMPLEMENTATION

LISTING 8.8   continued

```
      }
   }

   return result;
}
```

setAttribute and setAttributes

The `setAttribute()` method of the XMBean class also does a look up for the corresponding `XMBeanAttributeInfo` object and invokes its `setValue()` method. The `setValue()` implements the required callbacks to the MBean `invoke()` method if the `setMethod` field has been set in the attributes descriptor and to the MBean `store()` if the `persistPolicy` field is found in the attribute descriptor.

The implementation for the `setAttribute()` and `setAttributes()` methods in the XMBean class is shown in Listing 8.9.

LISTING 8.9   `MBean.java` (setAttribute and setAttributes Implementation)

```
// XMBean continued...

public void setAttribute(Attribute attribute)
    throws AttributeNotFoundException,
    InvalidAttributeValueException, MBeanException,
    ReflectionException {

   String attrName  = attribute.getName();
   Object attrValue = attribute.getValue();

   XMBeanAttribute attr =
       (XMBeanAttribute)attributeMap.get(attrName);

   if (attr == null)
     throw new AttributeNotFoundException();

   try {
     attr.setValue(attrValue);
   }
   catch (InstanceNotFoundException e) {

     // may be thrown by PersistentMBean.store()

     throw new MBeanException(e);
```

LISTING 8.9   continued

```
    }
  }

  public AttributeList setAttributes(AttributeList list) {

    if (list == null)
      throw new IllegalArgumentException("null list");

    AttributeList results = new AttributeList();
    Iterator it            = list.iterator();

    while (it.hasNext()) {
      try {
        Attribute attr = (Attribute)it.next();
        setAttribute(attr);
        results.add(attr);
      }
      catch (JMException ignored) {
        // if unable to set the attribute, skip it
      .}
    }

    return results;
  }
```

In the setValue() implementation (Listing 8.10), first a check is made via the isWritable() method to see if the attribute is declared as writable. If the setMethod field has been set in the attribute descriptor, the corresponding management operation is invoked with the new attribute value as an argument. After the setter operation invocation, the value field and the lastUpdatedTimeStamp are updated. After the attribute descriptors have been updated, the attribute change notification is sent. Last, the persistence policy descriptors are checked to make the proper callbacks to the Model MBean store() method. If the persistence policy has been set to OnUpdate, the store() method is invoked with every setValue() call. If the NoMoreOftenThan policy has been set, the time difference between the previous update and the current one is calculated and checked against the persistPeriod descriptor field. If the difference is greater than the minimum time allowed between store() calls, the store() method of the ModelMBean interface is invoked.

This implementation does not contain the "OnTimer" persistence policy. You can easily add it by checking the policy descriptor in the preRegister() method of the MBeanRegistration interface and register the XMBean instance with a Timer service as a listener of periodic notifications. In the handleNotification method of the listener implementation, invoke the callback to the Model MBean's store() method.

The XMBeanAttribute class is shown completely in the Listing 8.10 with both the getValue() and setValue() implementations.

LISTING 8.10   XMBeanAttribute.java

```java
package book.jmx.examples;

import javax.management.*;
import javax.management.loading.*;
import javax.management.modelmbean.*;
import java.lang.reflect.*;


public class XMBeanAttribute implements XMBeanConstants {

  // mbean reference for invoke and persistence callbacks
  protected XMBean mbean           = null;

  // reference to the resource instance
  protected Object managedResource = null;

  // name of the management attribute
  protected String name            = null;


  public XMBeanAttribute(XMBean mbean,
     ModelMBeanAttributeInfo attrInfo) throws MBeanException {

    this.mbean           = mbean;
    this.managedResource = mbean.resource;
    this.name            = attrInfo.getName();
  }


  public Object getValue() throws MBeanException,
     ReflectionException, AttributeNotFoundException {

    ModelMBeanInfo mbeanInfo = (ModelMBeanInfo)mbean.getMBeanInfo();
    ModelMBeanAttributeInfo attrInfo = mbeanInfo.getAttribute(name);

    // see if we're allowed to read this value
    if (!attrInfo.isReadable())
      throw new AttributeNotFoundException("Attribute is not readable");


    Descriptor desc     = attrInfo.getDescriptor();
```

LISTING 8.10   continued

```
Descriptor mmbDesc = mbeanInfo.getMBeanDescriptor();

// retrieve the relevant values from the attribute's descriptor
long lastUpdate    = 0;
long currTimeLimit = -1;
Object field       = null;
Object result      = desc.getFieldValue(VALUE);
Object getMethod   = desc.getFieldValue(GET_METHOD);

// last update timestamp to check cache validity
if((field = desc.getFieldValue(LAST_UPDATED_TIME_STAMP))!=null)
  lastUpdate  = Long.parseLong(field.toString());

// get currencyTimeLimit from MBean descriptor first, overwrite
// with attribute's descriptor field, if available
if((field = mmbDesc.getFieldValue(CURRENCY_TIME_LIMIT))!=null)
  currTimeLimit = Long.parseLong(field.toString()) * 1000;
if((field = desc.getFieldValue(CURRENCY_TIME_LIMIT))!=null)
  currTimeLimit = Long.parseLong(field.toString()) * 1000;

// if getMethod is specified and cache is stale, invoke it
if (getMethod != null) {
  long time        = System.currentTimeMillis();

  if (time > lastUpdate + currTimeLimit) {

    result = mbean.invoke((String)getMethod, null, null);

    // update descriptor
    desc.setField(VALUE, result);
    desc.setField(LAST_UPDATED_TIME_STAMP, new Long(time));
    mbeanInfo.setDescriptor(desc, "attribute");
  }
}

return result;
}

public boolean setValue(Object value) throws MBeanException,
    ReflectionException, InstanceNotFoundException  {

  ModelMBeanInfo mbeanInfo = (ModelMBeanInfo)mbean.getMBeanInfo();
  ModelMBeanAttributeInfo attrInfo = mbeanInfo.getAttribute(name);

  // check if we're allowed to write this attribute
```

8

LISTING 8.10   continued

```
if (!attrInfo.isWritable())
  throw new RuntimeException("Attribute is not writeable");

Descriptor desc    = attrInfo.getDescriptor();
Descriptor mmbDesc = mbeanInfo.getMBeanDescriptor();

// retrieve the relevant descriptor values
Object setMethod    = desc.getFieldValue(SET_METHOD);
Object oldValue     = desc.getFieldValue(VALUE);
Object newValue     = value;

// if setMethod specified, invoke it
if (setMethod != null) {
  mbean.invoke(
      (String)setMethod,
      new Object[] { value},
      new String[] { attrInfo.getType() }
  );
}


long persistPeriod    = 0;
long lastUpdate       = 0;
Object field          = null;
String persistPolicy = mmbDesc.getFieldValue(PERSIST_POLICY).
                       toString();

if ((field = desc.getFieldValue(PERSIST_POLICY))!=null)
  persistPolicy = field.toString();

if ((field = mmbDesc.getFieldValue(PERSIST_PERIOD))!=null)
  persistPeriod = Long.parseLong(field.toString());

if ((field = desc.getFieldValue(PERSIST_PERIOD))!=null)
  persistPeriod = Long.parseLong(field.toString());

if ((field = desc.getFieldValue(LAST_UPDATED_TIME_STAMP))!=null)
  lastUpdate    = Long.parseLong(field.toString());

// update descriptor
desc.setField(LAST_UPDATED_TIME_STAMP,
    "" + System.currentTimeMillis());
desc.setField(VALUE, value);
mbeanInfo.setDescriptor(desc, "attribute");


// send attribute change notification
```

LISTING 8.10 continued

```
    mbean.sendAttributeChangeNotification(
        new Attribute(name, oldValue),
        new Attribute(name, newValue)
    );

    // persistence
    if (persistPolicy != null) {
      if (persistPolicy.equalsIgnoreCase(ON_UPDATE)) {
        mbean.store();
        return true;
      }
      else if (persistPolicy.equalsIgnoreCase(NO_MORE_OFTEN_THAN)) {
        long interval = System.currentTimeMillis() - lastUpdate;
        if (interval > persistPeriod) {
          mbean.store();
          return true;
        }
        else
          return false;
      }
    }

    return false;
  }

}
```

Persistence

The XMBean class implements a basic file-based persistence. It uses object streams from java.io package to read and write the MBean metadata to a location pointed by the persistLocation and persistName descriptor fields. The implementation is shown in Listing 8.11.

LISTING 8.11 XMBean.java (PersistentMBean Implementation)

```
// XMBean continued...

// PersistentMBean interface

public void load() throws MBeanException,
    InstanceNotFoundException {

  // throw new UnsupportedOperationException();
```

LISTING 8.11   continued

```
  if (metadata == null)
    return;

  Descriptor d = metadata.getMBeanDescriptor();
  String dir  = (String)d.getFieldValue(PERSIST_LOCATION);
  String file = (String)d.getFieldValue(PERSIST_NAME);

  if (file != null) {
    try {
      File f = new File(dir, file);
      FileInputStream fis = new FileInputStream(f);
      ObjectInputStream ois = new ObjectInputStream(fis);

      metadata = (ModelMBeanInfoSupport)ois.readObject();
    }
    catch (Exception e) {
      System.out.println("Error loading MBean state");
    }
  }
}

public void store() throws MBeanException,
    InstanceNotFoundException {

  try {
    Descriptor d = metadata.getMBeanDescriptor();
    String dir  = (String)d.getFieldValue(PERSIST_LOCATION);
    String file = (String)d.getFieldValue(PERSIST_NAME);

    File f = new File(dir, file);
    FileOutputStream fos  = new FileOutputStream(f);
    ObjectOutputStream oos = new ObjectOutputStream(fos);

    oos.writeObject(metadata);
    oos.flush();
    oos.close();
  }
  catch (IOException e) {
    throw new MBeanException(e, "Error in persisting MBean.");
  }
}
```

The persistence implementation serializes the whole contents of the `MBeanInfo` and its associated objects to the file system. This is a heavy handed persistence implementation and probably should not be used with the `OnUpdate` persistence policy. However, it should be quite usable for the `NoMoreOftenThan` or `OnTimer` persistence policies. For more fine-grained persistence you can create different implementations for the `store()` method. For a more modular approach it would be advisable to create a separate interface that abstracts the persistence implementation from the Model MBean. You could then plug in persistence implementations that make use of JDBC or JDO API, or even delegate the persistence to an Entity EJB. Similar approaches to abstracting the metadata generation with a specific interface will be shown in the section "Metadata Generation" later in this chapter.

ModelMBeanNotificationBroadcaster Implementation

The bulk of the methods required to be implemented by a Model MBean implementation is due to the different types of notification broadcaster implementations. Luckily, their implementation is easy with the help of the `NotificationBroadcasterSupport` class. Most methods can be implemented by writing one or few lines of code.

Listing 8.12 shows the complete XMBean implementation. It includes the `DynamicMBean` implementation, `PersistentMBean` implementation, and `ModelMBeanNotificationBroadcaster` implementation. What is still missing is the metadata generation from the XML file. This will be covered in the next section, Metadata Generation.

LISTING 8.12 XMBean.java

```
package book.jmx.examples;

import java.net.*;
import java.io.*;
import java.util.*;
import java.lang.reflect.*;
import javax.management.*;
import javax.management.modelmbean.*;
import javax.management.loading.*;


public class XMBean implements ModelMBean, MBeanRegistration,
    XMBeanConstants {

  protected MBeanServer server = null;
```

LISTING 8.12 continued

```
// sequence numbers for notifications
protected long notifierSequence      = 0;
protected long attrNotifierSequence  = 0;

// support for generic notification listeners
private NotificationBroadcasterSupport notifier =
    new NotificationBroadcasterSupport();

// maps mbean attribute and operation names to
// corresponding XMBeanAttribute and XMBeanOperation
protected Map attributeMap           = new HashMap();
protected Map operationMap           = new HashMap();

// managed resource, resource type, model mbean metadata
// and object name reference
protected Object resource            = null;
protected String resourceType        = null;
protected ModelMBeanInfo metadata    = null;
protected ObjectName name            = null;


// Constructors.

public XMBean() {}

public XMBean(ModelMBeanInfo info) throws MBeanException {
  setModelMBeanInfo(info);
}


// ModelMBean interface

public void setModelMBeanInfo(ModelMBeanInfo metadata)
    throws MBeanException, RuntimeOperationsException {

  if (metadata == null) {
    throw new IllegalArgumentException(
        "The Model MBeanInfo cannot be null."
    );
  }

  this.metadata = metadata;
}

public void setManagedResource(Object ref, String resourceType)
```

LISTING 8.12   continued

```
        throws MBeanException,
            InstanceNotFoundException,
            InvalidTargetObjectTypeException {

    if (ref == null) {
      throw new IllegalArgumentException(
          "Resource reference cannot be null."
      );
    }

    // check that is a supported resource type
    if (!isSupportedResourceType(resourceType)) {
      throw new InvalidTargetObjectTypeException(
          "Unsupported resource type: " + resourceType
      );
    }

    this.resource = ref;
    this.resourceType = resourceType;
  }

  protected boolean isSupportedResourceType(
      String resourceType) {

    if (resourceType == null)              return false;
    if (resourceType.equals(OBJECT_REF))  return true;

    return false;
  }



  // ModelMBeanNotificationBroadcaster interface

  public void addNotificationListener(
      NotificationListener l, NotificationFilter filter,
      Object hback) {

    notifier.addNotificationListener(l, filter, hback);
  }

  public void removeNotificationListener(
      NotificationListener l)
      throws ListenerNotFoundException {

    notifier.removeNotificationListener(l);
```

LISTING 8.12   continued

```java
}

public void addAttributeChangeNotificationListener(
    NotificationListener l, String attributeName,
    Object hback) throws MBeanException {

  AttributeChangeNotificationFilter filter =
      new AttributeChangeNotificationFilter();

  filter.enableAttribute(attributeName);

  notifier.addNotificationListener(l, filter,hback);
}

public void removeAttributeChangeNotificationListener(
    NotificationListener l, String attributeName)
    throws MBeanException, ListenerNotFoundException {

  notifier.removeNotificationListener(l);
}

public void sendNotification(String message)
    throws MBeanException {

  Notification notif = new Notification(
      GENERIC_MODELMBEAN_NOTIFICATION, // type
      this,                            // source
      ++notifierSequence,              // sequence number
      message                          // message
  );

  sendNotification(notif);
}

public void sendNotification(Notification notif)
    throws MBeanException {

  notifier.sendNotification(notif);
}

public void sendAttributeChangeNotification(
    AttributeChangeNotification notif)
    throws MBeanException {
```

LISTING 8.12   continued

```
    notifier.sendNotification(notif);
}

public void sendAttributeChangeNotification(
    Attribute oldValue, Attribute newValue)
    throws MBeanException {

  String attr = oldValue.getName();
  String type = oldValue.getClass().getName();

  AttributeChangeNotification notif =
      new AttributeChangeNotification(
          this,                        // source
          ++attrNotifierSequence,      // seq. #
          System.currentTimeMillis(),  // time stamp
          "" + attr + " changed from " // message
          + oldValue + " to " + newValue,
          attr, type,                  // name & type
          oldValue, newValue           // values
      );

  notifier.sendNotification(notif);
}

public MBeanNotificationInfo[] getNotificationInfo() {

  int size = metadata.getNotifications().length;
  MBeanNotificationInfo[] notifInfo = metadata.getNotifications();

  MBeanNotificationInfo[] modelInfo =
      new MBeanNotificationInfo[size + 2];

  for (int i = 0; i < size ;++i)
    modelInfo[i] = notifInfo[i];

  Descriptor descr1 = new DescriptorSupport();
  descr1.setField("name", "generic");
  descr1.setField("descriptorType", "notification");
  descr1.setField("severity", "5");

  ModelMBeanNotificationInfo generic = new ModelMBeanNotificationInfo(
      new String[] { GENERIC_MODELMBEAN_NOTIFICATION },
      "generic",
      "A generic Model MBean notification.",
```

8

XMBEAN: MODEL
MBEAN
IMPLEMENTATION

LISTING 8.12   continued

```
        descr1
    );

    Descriptor descr2 = new DescriptorSupport();
    descr2.setField("name", AttributeChangeNotification.class.getName());
    descr2.setField("descriptorType", "notification");

    ModelMBeanNotificationInfo attrChange = new ModelMBeanNotificationInfo(
        new String[] { AttributeChangeNotification.ATTRIBUTE_CHANGE },
        AttributeChangeNotification.class.getName(),
        "Notifies a change in attribute's value.",
        descr2
    );

    modelInfo[size-2] = generic;
    modelInfo[size-1] = attrChange;

    return modelInfo;
}


// PersistentMBean interface

public void load() throws MBeanException,
    InstanceNotFoundException {

    throw new UnsupportedOperationException();
}

public void store() throws MBeanException,
    InstanceNotFoundException {

  try {
    Descriptor d = metadata.getMBeanDescriptor();
    String dir  = (String)d.getFieldValue(PERSIST_LOCATION);
    String file = (String)d.getFieldValue(PERSIST_NAME);

    File f = new File(dir, file);
    FileOutputStream fos  = new FileOutputStream(f);
    ObjectOutputStream oos = new ObjectOutputStream(fos);

    oos.writeObject(metadata);
  }
  catch (IOException e) {
    throw new MBeanException(e, "Error in persisting MBean.");
```

LISTING 8.12   continued

```
  }
  //throw new UnsupportedOperationException();
}


// MBeanRegistration interface

public ObjectName preRegister(MBeanServer server,
                              ObjectName name)
                              throws Exception {

  // store the server reference
  this.server = server;
  this.name    = name;

  // create attribute and operation maps
  attributeMap = createAttributeMap(metadata.getAttributes());
  operationMap = createOperationMap(metadata.getOperations());

  return name;
}

private Map createAttributeMap(MBeanAttributeInfo[] attributes)
    throws MBeanException  {

  Map attrMap = new HashMap();

  for (int i = 0; i < attributes.length; ++i) {
    String name = attributes[i].getName();

    ModelMBeanAttributeInfo info =
        (ModelMBeanAttributeInfo)attributes[i];

    attrMap.put(name, new XMBeanAttribute(this, info));
  }

  return attrMap;
}

private Map createOperationMap(MBeanOperationInfo[] operations)
    throws MBeanException {

  Map operMap = new HashMap();

  for (int i = 0; i < operations.length; ++i) {
    String name = operations[i].getName();
```

LISTING 8.12   continued

```
        MBeanParameterInfo[] params = operations[i].getSignature();

        for (int j = 0; j < params.length; ++j)
          name += params[j].getType();

        ModelMBeanOperationInfo info =
            (ModelMBeanOperationInfo)operations[i];

        XMBeanOperation operation = new XMBeanOperation(this, info);
        operMap.put(name, operation);

      }

      return operMap;
    }


    public void postRegister(Boolean registrationSuccessful) {}
    public void preDeregister() throws Exception {}
    public void postDeregister() {}


    // DynamicMBean interface

    public Object getAttribute(String attribute)
        throws AttributeNotFoundException, MBeanException,
        ReflectionException {

      XMBeanAttribute attr =
          (XMBeanAttribute)attributeMap.get(attribute);

      if (attr == null)
        throw new AttributeNotFoundException();

      return attr.getValue();
    }


    public AttributeList getAttributes(String[] attributes) {

      if (attributes == null)
        throw new IllegalArgumentException("null array");

      AttributeList list = new AttributeList();

      for (int i = 0; i < attributes.length; ++i) {
```

LISTING 8.12   continued

```
    try {
      list.add(new Attribute(
          attributes[i], getAttribute(attributes[i])
      ));
    }
    catch (JMException ignored) {
      // if the attribute could not be retrieved, skip it
    }
  }

  return list;
}


public void setAttribute(Attribute attribute)
    throws AttributeNotFoundException,
    InvalidAttributeValueException, MBeanException,
    ReflectionException {

  String attrName  = attribute.getName();
  Object attrValue = attribute.getValue();

  XMBeanAttribute attr =
      (XMBeanAttribute)attributeMap.get(attrName);

  if (attr == null)
    throw new AttributeNotFoundException();

  try {
    attr.setValue(attrValue);
  }
  catch (InstanceNotFoundException e) {

    // may be thrown by PersistentMBean.store()

    throw new MBeanException(e);
  }
}

public AttributeList setAttributes(AttributeList list) {

  if (list == null)
    throw new IllegalArgumentException("null list");

  AttributeList results = new AttributeList();
```

LISTING 8.12   continued

```
    Iterator it          = list.iterator();

    while (it.hasNext()) {
      try {
        Attribute attr = (Attribute)it.next();
        setAttribute(attr);
        results.add(attr);
      }
      catch (JMException ignored) {
        // if unable to set the attribute, skip it
      }
    }

    return results;
  }


  public Object invoke(String actionName, Object[] params,
                       String[] signature)
      throws MBeanException, ReflectionException {

    String method = actionName;

    if (signature != null) {
      for (int i = 0; i < signature.length; ++i)
        method += signature[i];
    }

    XMBeanOperation operation =
        (XMBeanOperation)operationMap.get(method);

    if (operation == null) {
      throw new ReflectionException(
        new IllegalArgumentException("unknown operation")
      );
    }

    return operation.invoke(params);
  }

  public MBeanInfo getMBeanInfo() {
    return (MBeanInfo)metadata;
  }


}
```

At this point you can try and compile the Java files:

XMBean.java, XMBeanAttribute.java, XMBeanOperation.java and
XMBeanConstants.java.

```
C:\Examples> javac -d . -classpath .;jmx-1_0_1-ri_bin\jmx\lib\jmxri.jar
➥ XMBean.java XMBeanAttribute.java XMBeanOperation.java XMBeanConstants.java
```

The end result should be a working Model MBean implementation. However, the most interesting part is still left to implement. In the next section you will modify the classes to include an automated management interface creation from an external XML file.

Metadata Generation

The example implementation in this section will create the management interface from an XML file. You will define a document type definition (DTD) for the XML document instances and see the required code for parsing the XML.

The metadata generation will be abstracted by a MetaDataBuilder interface. You will be able to later extend the XMBean class with different implementations that can parse XML document instances conforming to different DTDs or with implementations that access a database or LDAP directory to retrieve and build the MBean's management interface, as illustrated in Figure 8.3. It is also possible to create builder implementations that use Java introspection on existing classes or interfaces to create the management interface for a Model MBean. This will add convenience to defining the management interface similar to Standard MBeans.

8

XMBEAN: MODEL
MBEAN
IMPLEMENTATION

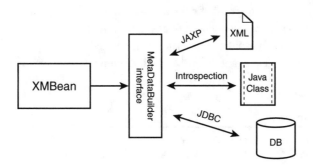

FIGURE 8.3
MetaDataBuilder interface abstracts the generation of metadata object instances.

XML Document Instances and DTD

The XML document instances will contain all the basic elements of the MBean management interface metadata that you have seen so far. You will be able to declare the MBean's management operations, attributes, notifications and constructors using the XML format. In addition, you can declare the behavioral features, persistence and caching, that the XMBean implementation supports via the Model MBean descriptors.

The root element for the XML document instance will be an <mbean> tag. The <mbean> tag will contain a collection of MBeanconstructors, operations, attributes, and notifications. For example, a simple document instance that declares a management operation start() and a read-write management attribute Port could be written as shown in Listing 8.13.

LISTING 8.13   Basic XMBean XML Document Instance

```
<!xml version="1.0" encoding="UTF-8"?>
<!DOCTYPE mbean SYSTEM "file:/C:/Examples/xmbean.dtd">

<mbean>
  <operation><name>start</name>
    <impact>ACTION</impact>
  </operation>

  <attribute>
    <name>Port</name>
    <type>int</type>
    <access>read-write</access>
  </attribute>
</mbean>
```

The <operation> element assumes a void return type if nothing is declared explicitly. It also contains a nested element <impact> that declares the impact of the operation: ACTION, INFO or ACTION_INFO. The <attribute> element defines the runtime type of the management attribute and its access (read-only, write-only, read-write) using nested elements <type> and <access>, respectively. A more complete example of the XML document instance is shown in Listing 8.14. It shows the management interface of the User resource introduced in Part I of the book.

LISTING 8.14   User.xml

```
<?xml version="1.0" encoding="UTF-8"?>
<!DOCTYPE mbean SYSTEM "file:/C:/Examples/xmbean.dtd">

<mbean>
  <constructor>
    <name>Default Constructor</name>
  </constructor>

  <attribute>
    <name>ID</name>
```

LISTING 8.14 continued

```xml
    <type>java.lang.String</type>
    <access>read-only</access>
  </attribute>

  <attribute>
    <name>Name</name>
    <type>java.lang.String</type>
    <access>read-write</access>
  </attribute>

  <attribute>
    <name>Address</name>
    <type>java.lang.String</type>
    <access>read-write</access>
  </attribute>

  <attribute>
    <name>PhoneNumbers</name>
    <type>[Ljava.lang.String;</type>
    <access>read-write</access>
  </attribute>

  <attribute>
    <name>Password</name>
    <type>java.lang.String</type>
    <access>write-only</access>
  </attribute>

  <operation>
    <name>printInfo</name>
    <return-type>java.lang.String</return-type>
    <impact>INFO</impact>
  </operation>

  <operation>
    <name>addPhoneNumber</name>
    <parameter>
      <name>number</name>
      <type>java.lang.String</type>
    </parameter>
    <return-type>void</return-type>
    <impact>ACTION</impact>
  </operation>

  <operation>
```

LISTING 8.14   continued

```
    <name>removePhoneNumber</name>
    <parameter>
      <name>index</name>
      <type>int</type>
    </parameter>
    <return-type>void</return-type>
    <impact>ACTION</impact>
  </operation>

</mbean>
```

Parsing the XML Document

As was mentioned at the beginning of this section, the creation of the metadata objects for the MBean's management interface is abstracted as a `MetaDataBuilder` interface (see Listing 8.15). This interface declares one `build()` method that should return a `ModelMBeanInfo` instance containing the MBean's management interface description.

To load, parse, and validate the XMBean XML document, you will use the JDOM library, which offers a Java programming interface for loading and manipulating XML data. The JDOM library is licensed under an Apache-style Open Source license and can be downloaded from `http://www.jdom.org` for free. The version in use at the time of the writing is JDOM Beta 7. See the Appendix A for the detailed instructions on downloading and installing the library.

To load and generate the Model MBean metadata from the XML file, add the following constructor to the XMBean implementation:

```
public XMBean(String url, String resource) throws MBeanException {

  try {
    MetaDataBuilder builder = new XMLMetaDataBuilder(resource, url);
    setModelMBeanInfo(builder.build());
    setManagedResource(DefaultLoaderRepository.loadClass(resource)
        .newInstance(), OBJECT_REF);

    try {
      load();
    } catch (InstanceNotFoundException e) {}
  }
  catch (ClassNotFoundException e) {
    throw new MBeanException(
        e, "Unable to load class " + resource
```

```
      );
    }
    catch (InvalidTargetObjectTypeException e) {
      throw new Error("Invalid resource type 'ObjectReference'.");
    }
    catch (JMException e) {
      throw new MBeanException(e);
    }
    catch (Exception e) {
      e.printStackTrace();
      throw new MBeanException(e);
    }
  }
}
```

The constructor creates an instance of an XMLMetaDataBuilder class which implements the MetaDataBuilder interface to load and create the management interface that conforms to the DTD in Listing 8.16. You can later add new implementations of the MetaDataBuilder interface to generate the MBean metadata from different document types, for example the Common Information Model (CIM) DTD defined by the Distributed Managament Task Force (DMTF). You can also implement builders that retrieve the management interface definition from a database or use existing Java interfaces via introspection to create the MBean metadata.

The implementation of the XMLMetaDataBuilder class is shown in Listing 8.17. It parses the XML file and creates the required metadata objects for the Model MBean. It also creates the descriptors for each metadata object if they have been defined in the XML document. For example, to create an MBean that caches all of its attribute values for 5 seconds, and maps an Active management attribute to an isActive getter operation can be declared as follows:

8

XMBean: Model
MBean
Implementation

```
<?xml version="1.0" encoding="UTF-8"?>
<!DOCTYPE mbean SYSTEM "file:/C:/Examples/xmbean.dtd">

<mbean currencyTimeLimit="5">
  <attribute getMethod="isActive">
    <name>Active</name>
    <type>boolean</type>
    <access>read-only</access>
  </attribute>

  <operation>
    <name>isActive</name>
    <return-type>boolean</return-type>
    <impact>INFO</impact>
  </operation>
</mbean>
```

To compile the modified `XMBean.java` and the new `MetaDataBuilder.java` and `XMLMetaDataBuilder.java` files execute the following command:

```
C:\Examples> javac -d . -classpath .;jmx-1_0_1-ri_bin\jmx\lib\jmxri.jar;
➥jdom-b7\build\jdom.jar;jdom-b7\lib\xerces.jar XMBean.java MetaDataBuilder.java
➥XMLMetaDataBuilder.java
```

Notice that the `jdom.jar` and `xerces.jar` libraries are now required from the `jdom-b7` directory to compile the `XMLMetaDataBuilder` class.

You should also package the XMBean implementation as a separate package that you will use in the next chapters for implementing MBeans for the JMX Distributed Services level.

```
C:\Examples> jar cvf xmbean.jar book/jmx/examples/XMBean*.class
➥book/jmx/examples/*MetaDataBuilder.class
```

This should create a file `xmbean.jar` to your working directory you can later use.

LISTING 8.15   `MetaDataBuilder.java`

```java
package book.jmx.examples;

import javax.management.*;
import javax.management.modelmbean.*;

public interface MetaDataBuilder {

  public ModelMBeanInfo build() throws JMException;

}
```

LISTING 8.16   `xmbean.dtd`

```
<!—                                                            —>
<!— DTD for externalizing the definition of the               —>
<!— JMX management interfaces.                                 —>
<!—                                                            —>

<!—
  The <mbean> element is the root element of the document containing the
  required elements for describing the management interface of one
  MBean (constructors, attributes, operations and notifications). It
  also includes an optional description element that can be used to
  describe the purpose of the MBean and attributes for persistence
  policy and attribute caching.
```

LISTING 8.16   continued

```
—>
<!ELEMENT mbean (description?, constructor*, attribute*, operation*,
        notification*)>
<!ATTLIST mbean persistPolicy
                (Never | OnUpdate | NoMoreOftenThan | OnTimer) "Never"
                persistPeriod      NMTOKEN #IMPLIED
                persistLocation    CDATA   #IMPLIED
                persistName        CDATA   #IMPLIED
                currencyTimeLimit NMTOKEN #IMPLIED>

<!—
  The constructor element describes the constructors of an MBean
  that are exposed to the management application. The optional
  description element can be used to to describe the use of the
  constructor.
—>
<!ELEMENT constructor (description?, name, parameter*)>

<!—
  The <attribute> element describes the management attributes of an
  MBean. The <name> element contains the attribute's name and the <type>
  element contains a fully qualified class name of the attribute's
  type.

  The optional <access> element defines the access type (read-only,
  write-only, read-write) of this attribute. Valid values are:
        <access>read-only</access>
        <access>write-only</access>
        <access>read-write</access>

  If <access> element is not specified, read-write access is assumed.
—>
<!ELEMENT attribute (description?, name, type, access?)>
<!ATTLIST attribute persistPolicy     CDATA #IMPLIED
                    getMethod         CDATA #IMPLIED
                    setMethod         CDATA #IMPLIED
                    persistPeriod     NMTOKEN #IMPLIED
                    currencyTimeLimit NMTOKEN #IMPLIED >

<!—
  The <operation> element describes a management operation of an MBean.
  The <name> element contains the operation's name and the <parameter>
  elements describe the operation's signature. The <return-type> element
  must contain a fully qualified class name of the return type from
```

8

XMBean: MODEL
MBEAN
IMPLEMENTATION

LISTING 8.16 continued

```
this operation.

If <return-type> is not specified, void is assumed.

The impact element describes the operation's impact on the MBean's
state when invoked. The valid values are:
     <impact>ACTION</impact>
     <impact>INFO</impact>
     <impact>ACTION_INFO</impact>

If <impact> is not specified, ACTION_INFO is assumed.

—>
<!ELEMENT operation (description?, name, parameter*, return-type?,
        impact?)>

<!—
    The <notification> element describes a management notification. The <name>
    element contains the fully qualified name of the notification class and
    the <notification-type> element contains the dot-separated notification
    type string.
—>
<!ELEMENT notification (description?, name, notification-type+)>

<!ELEMENT parameter (description?, name, type)>

<!ELEMENT name              (#PCDATA)>
<!ELEMENT description       (#PCDATA)>
<!ELEMENT type              (#PCDATA)>
<!ELEMENT access            (#PCDATA)>
<!ELEMENT impact            (#PCDATA)>
<!ELEMENT return-type       (#PCDATA)>
<!ELEMENT notification-type (#PCDATA)>
```

LISTING 8.17 XMLMetaDataBuilder.java

```
package book.jmx.examples;

import java.net.*;
import java.util.*;
import javax.management.MBeanParameterInfo;
import javax.management.MBeanOperationInfo;
```

LISTING 8.17 continued

```java
import javax.management.MBeanAttributeInfo;
import javax.management.MBeanNotificationInfo;
import javax.management.MBeanConstructorInfo;
import javax.management.JMException;
import javax.management.MBeanException;
import javax.management.MBeanInfo;
import javax.management.Descriptor;
import javax.management.modelmbean.*;

import org.jdom.*;
import org.jdom.input.*;

public class XMLMetaDataBuilder
    implements MetaDataBuilder, XMBeanConstants {

  private URL url            = null;
  private String className = null;


  // Constructors.

  public XMLMetaDataBuilder(String resourceClassName, URL url) {
    this.url = url;
    this.className = resourceClassName;
  }

  public XMLMetaDataBuilder(String resourceClassName, String url)
      throws MalformedURLException {

    this(resourceClassName, new URL(url));
  }


  // MetaDataBuilder implementation.

  public ModelMBeanInfo build() throws JMException {
    try {
      SAXBuilder builder = new SAXBuilder();

      builder.setValidation(true);

      Element root        = builder.build(url).getRootElement();
      List constructors = root.getChildren("constructor");
      List operations   = root.getChildren("operation");
```

LISTING 8.17   continued

```
      List attributes    = root.getChildren("attribute");
      List notifications = root.getChildren("notifications");
      String description = root.getChildText("description");

      Attribute persistPolicy   = root.getAttribute(PERSIST_POLICY);
      Attribute persistPeriod   = root.getAttribute(PERSIST_PERIOD);
      Attribute persistLocation = root.getAttribute(PERSIST_LOCATION);
      Attribute persistName     = root.getAttribute(PERSIST_NAME);
      Attribute currTimeLimit   = root.getAttribute(CURRENCY_TIME_LIMIT);

      // create MBean descriptor
      Descriptor descr = new DescriptorSupport();
      descr.setField("name", className);
      descr.setField("descriptorType", "mbean");

      if (persistPolicy != null)
        descr.setField(PERSIST_POLICY, persistPolicy.getValue());
      if (persistPeriod != null)
        descr.setField(PERSIST_PERIOD, persistPeriod.getValue());
      if (persistLocation != null)
        descr.setField(PERSIST_LOCATION, persistLocation.getValue());
      if (persistName != null)
        descr.setField(PERSIST_NAME, persistName.getValue());
      if (currTimeLimit != null)
         descr.setField(CURRENCY_TIME_LIMIT, currTimeLimit.getValue());

      ModelMBeanInfo info = buildMBeanMetaData(
          description, constructors, operations,
          attributes, notifications, descr
      );

      return info;
    }
    catch (JDOMException e) {
      throw new MBeanException(e, "Error parsing the XML file.");
    }
  }


  // builder methods

  protected ModelMBeanInfo buildMBeanMetaData(String description,
      List constructors, List operations, List attributes,
      List notifications, Descriptor descr) {

    ModelMBeanOperationInfo[] operInfo      =
```

LISTING 8.17   continued

```
        buildOperationInfo(operations);
    ModelMBeanAttributeInfo[] attrInfo      =
        buildAttributeInfo(attributes);
    ModelMBeanConstructorInfo[] constrInfo =
        buildConstructorInfo(constructors);
    ModelMBeanNotificationInfo[] notifInfo =
        buildNotificationInfo(notifications);

    ModelMBeanInfo info = new ModelMBeanInfoSupport(
        className, description, attrInfo, constrInfo,
        operInfo, notifInfo, descr
    );

    return info;
}


protected ModelMBeanConstructorInfo[] buildConstructorInfo(
    List constructors) {

    Iterator it = constructors.iterator();
    List infos = new ArrayList();

    while (it.hasNext()) {
        Element constr = (Element)it.next();
        String name     = constr.getChildTextTrim("name");
        String descr     = constr.getChildTextTrim("description");
        List params      = constr.getChildren("parameter");

        MBeanParameterInfo[] paramInfo =
            buildParameterInfo(params);

        ModelMBeanConstructorInfo info      =
            new ModelMBeanConstructorInfo(name, descr, paramInfo);

        infos.add(info);
    }

    return (ModelMBeanConstructorInfo[])infos.toArray(
        new ModelMBeanConstructorInfo[0]);
}

protected ModelMBeanOperationInfo[] buildOperationInfo(List operations) {

    Iterator it = operations.iterator();
```

8

XMBEAN: MODEL
MBEAN
IMPLEMENTATION

LISTING 8.17   continued

```java
List infos  = new ArrayList();

while (it.hasNext()) {
  Element oper  = (Element)it.next();
  String name   = oper.getChildTextTrim("name");
  String descr  = oper.getChildTextTrim("description");
  String type   = oper.getChildTextTrim("return-type");
  String impact = oper.getChildTextTrim("impact");
  List params   = oper.getChildren("parameter");

  MBeanParameterInfo[] paramInfo =
      buildParameterInfo(params);

  // defaults to ACTION_INFO
  int operImpact = MBeanOperationInfo.ACTION_INFO;

  if (impact.equals("INFO"))
    operImpact = MBeanOperationInfo.INFO;
  else if (impact.equals("ACTION"))
    operImpact = MBeanOperationInfo.ACTION;
  else if (impact.equals("ACTION_INFO"))
    operImpact = MBeanOperationInfo.ACTION_INFO;

  // default return-type is void
  if (type == null)
    type = "void";

  ModelMBeanOperationInfo info = new ModelMBeanOperationInfo(
      name, descr, paramInfo, type, operImpact
  );

  infos.add(info);
}

return (ModelMBeanOperationInfo[])infos.toArray(
    new ModelMBeanOperationInfo[0]);
}


protected ModelMBeanNotificationInfo[]
   buildNotificationInfo(List notifications) {

  Iterator it = notifications.iterator();
  List infos  = new ArrayList();

  while (it.hasNext()) {
```

LISTING 8.17   continued

```
  Element notif   = (Element)it.next();
  String name     = notif.getChildTextTrim("name");
  String descr    = notif.getChildTextTrim("description");
  List notifTypes = notif.getChildren("notification-type");

  Iterator iterator = notifTypes.iterator();
  List types = new ArrayList();

  while (iterator.hasNext()) {
    Element type = (Element)iterator.next();
    types.add(type.getTextTrim());
  }

  ModelMBeanNotificationInfo info = new ModelMBeanNotificationInfo(
      (String[])types.toArray(), name, descr
  );

  infos.add(info);
  }

  return (ModelMBeanNotificationInfo[])infos.toArray(
      new ModelMBeanNotificationInfo[0]
  );
}

protected ModelMBeanAttributeInfo[]
    buildAttributeInfo(List attributes) {

  Iterator it = attributes.iterator();
  List infos  = new ArrayList();

  while (it.hasNext()) {
    Element attr        = (Element)it.next();
    String name         = attr.getChildTextTrim("name");
    String description  = attr.getChildTextTrim("description");
    String type         = attr.getChildTextTrim("type");
    String access       = attr.getChildTextTrim("access");

    Attribute persistPolicy = attr.getAttribute(PERSIST_POLICY);
    Attribute persistPeriod = attr.getAttribute(PERSIST_PERIOD);
    Attribute setMethod     = attr.getAttribute(SET_METHOD);
    Attribute getMethod     = attr.getAttribute(GET_METHOD);
    Attribute currTimeLimit = attr.getAttribute(CURRENCY_TIME_LIMIT);

    Descriptor descr = new DescriptorSupport();
```

8

XMBEAN: MODEL
MBEAN
IMPLEMENTATION

LISTING 8.17   continued

```java
    descr.setField("name", name);
    descr.setField("descriptorType", "attribute");

    if (persistPolicy != null)
      descr.setField(PERSIST_POLICY, persistPolicy.getValue());
    if (persistPeriod != null)
      descr.setField(PERSIST_PERIOD, persistPeriod.getValue());
    if (setMethod != null)
      descr.setField(SET_METHOD, setMethod.getValue());
    if (getMethod != null)
      descr.setField(GET_METHOD, getMethod.getValue());
    if (currTimeLimit != null)
      descr.setField(CURRENCY_TIME_LIMIT, currTimeLimit.getValue());

    // defaults read-write
    boolean isReadable = true;
    boolean isWritable = true;

    if (access.equalsIgnoreCase("read-only"))
      isWritable = false;

    else if (access.equalsIgnoreCase("write-only"))
      isReadable = false;


    ModelMBeanAttributeInfo info = new ModelMBeanAttributeInfo(
        name, type, description, isReadable, isWritable, false, descr
    );

    infos.add(info);
  }

  return (ModelMBeanAttributeInfo[])infos.toArray(
      new ModelMBeanAttributeInfo[0]
  );
}


protected MBeanParameterInfo[] buildParameterInfo(List parameters) {

  Iterator it = parameters.iterator();
  List infos = new ArrayList();

  while (it.hasNext()) {
```

LISTING 8.17 continued

```
    Element param = (Element)it.next();
    String name   = param.getChildTextTrim("name");
    String type   = param.getChildTextTrim("type");
    String descr  = param.getChildTextTrim("description");

    MBeanParameterInfo info = new MBeanParameterInfo(name, type, descr);

    infos.add(info);
  }

  return (MBeanParameterInfo[])infos.toArray(new MBeanParameterInfo[0]);
  }

}
```

Summary

The JMX specification defines a Model MBean and a range of functionality that can be incorporated in the implementation. However, most of the functionality described in the specification is optional and may not be implemented by the JMX implementations. This chapter has shown you how to build your own implementation of the ModelMBean interface and has given you ideas where and how the Model MBean can be extended to suit your own needs.

You built a Model MBean that supported basic attribute caching, method mapping and persistence. In addition, you created an implementation for retrieving the management interface definition from an XML file. You should have a basic understanding of the implementation details to add more comprehensive features to this Model MBean implementation: additional sources for management interface definitions, more robust persistence implementation and improved invocation control with security, logging, transactions, and so on.

The JMX specification defines a very flexible and customizable Model MBean. You should be able to add new descriptor types and functionality relatively easily to this base implementation.

8

XMBEAN: MODEL
MBEAN
IMPLEMENTATION

Connectors and Protocol Adaptors

IN THIS CHAPTER

The JMX specification does not currently define the distributed services level of the management architecture. To remotely manage the MBean server, the management application needs to use either a connector or a protocol adaptor to connect to the server. In this chapter, you will see one possible implementation for an RMI-based JMX connector. Also, you will see how the JMX model can be adapted to a Management Information Base (MIB) model via an SNMP adaptor.

RMI Connector

Java Remote Method Invocation (RMI) is the Java approach to the remote procedure call (RPC) mechanism. In the first part of this chapter, you will build an RMI-based connector that enables you to programmatically connect to a remote JMX agent and manipulate the MBeans registered to it. In Chapter 10, "JMX Distribution Layer with J2EE Services," you will use the same connector framework to implement connectors using other means of transport, namely the Simple Object Access Protocol (SOAP) and Java Message Service (JMS).

The RMI connector implementation will consist of three parts:

- The client-side proxy to the connector
- The server-side connector MBean
- A Command abstraction of the remote invocation

The client-side proxy provides an MBean server-like interface to the client. The RemoteMBeanServer interface will offer the client a programming interface that very closely follows the interface of a local MBean server. The RemoteMBeanServer interface will differ from the MBeanServer only slightly to make it more suitable for remote use.

The server side of the connector is an MBean itself, enabling you to manage the connector server of the JMX agent. The connector server implementation will be a Java remote object that is exported to the RMI subsystem. The RMI subsystem will receive the remote method calls from the connector client and delegate them to the server object.

Finally, you will build an implementation of the Command design pattern that abstracts the remote method invocations. The MethodInvocation class will act as a command implementation. The MethodInvocation encapsulates the relevant information about the remote method invocation, such as the method name, parameter values, the target MBean's object name, and so on. The MethodInvocation instance can also be used to carry other context information with the call, such as transaction context or security credentials and principal. The MethodInvocation object itself is unaware of what the transport mechanism is, so you can later reuse it with other connector implementations. In Chapter 10, you will use it with the SOAP and JMS connector implementations.

Let's now look at each part of the RMI connector implementation in detail.

RMI Connector Client

On the client side, the aim is to provide reasonable transparency of the remote communication to the MBean server. The client should not be encumbered with the details of the remote call implementation and should be able to use the MBean server as if it were a local object. Optimally, you would want to expose the already defined `MBeanServer` interface to the client as is, without any modifications. However, the `MBeanServer` interface does declare operations that are not meaningful to be implemented and add complexity to the implementation, so for the sake of simplicity, the `RemoteMBeanServer` interface has been simplified to contain only those operations that have reasonably straightforward, simple implementations on the client side.

The `RemoteMBeanServer` interface will be exposed by the proxies to the client that uses them to communicate with the server. The declaration of the `RemoteMBeanServer` interface is shown in Listing 9.1. First, however, let's take a look at the differences between the `RemoteMBeanServer` and `MBeanServer` interfaces.

The following methods have been removed from the `MBeanServer` interface when declaring the `RemoteMBeanServer` interface:

- `deserialize()`
- `instantiate()`
- `registerMBean()`

In addition, one new method, `close()`, has been added to the interface that allows the client to notify the connector that any allocated resources can be freed and the connector is no longer used. This will prove useful later with other connector implementations.

The `deserialize()` method is mostly useful for connector servers that want to use specific classloaders to deserialize a stream of bytes on the server. This kind of functionality is not required at the management client level. However, a connector server supporting more advanced classloading than what is shown in the examples of this book can use the `deserialize()` methods in its implementation.

The `instantiate()` and `registerMBean()` methods both deal with direct Java `Object` references. Serializing objects between the client and the server is expensive and restricts the objects to those implementing the `Serializable` interface. The most common need for a management application to create objects on the server is to create new MBeans. In this case, the `createMBean()` method can be used.

9

LISTING 9.1   RemoteMBeanServer.java

```java
package book.jmx.examples;

import javax.management.*;
import java.rmi.*;
import java.util.*;

public interface RemoteMBeanServer {

    public ObjectInstance createMBean(String className,
                                      ObjectName name)
                         throws ReflectionException,
                                InstanceAlreadyExistsException,
                                MBeanRegistrationException,
                                MBeanException,
                                NotCompliantMBeanException;

    public ObjectInstance createMBean(String className,
                                      ObjectName name,
                                      ObjectName loaderName)
                         throws ReflectionException,
                                InstanceAlreadyExistsException,
                                MBeanRegistrationException,
                                MBeanException,
                                NotCompliantMBeanException,
                                InstanceNotFoundException;

    public ObjectInstance createMBean(String className,
                                      ObjectName name,
                                      Object[] params,
                                      String[] signature)
                         throws ReflectionException,
                                InstanceAlreadyExistsException,
                                MBeanRegistrationException,
                                MBeanException,
                                NotCompliantMBeanException;

    public ObjectInstance createMBean(String className,
                                      ObjectName name,
                                      ObjectName loaderName,
                                      Object[] params,
                                      String[] signature)
                         throws ReflectionException,
                                InstanceAlreadyExistsException,
                                MBeanRegistrationException,
                                MBeanException,
                                NotCompliantMBeanException,
```

LISTING 9.1 continued

```
                        InstanceNotFoundException;

public void unregisterMBean(ObjectName name)
                throws InstanceNotFoundException,
                        MBeanRegistrationException;

public ObjectInstance getObjectInstance(ObjectName name)
                throws InstanceNotFoundException;

public boolean isRegistered(ObjectName name);

public Integer getMBeanCount();

public Object getAttribute(ObjectName name,
                        String attribute)
                throws MBeanException,
                        AttributeNotFoundException,
                        InstanceNotFoundException,
                        ReflectionException;

public AttributeList getAttributes(ObjectName name,
                            String[] attributes)
                throws InstanceNotFoundException,
                        ReflectionException;

public void setAttribute(ObjectName name,
                    Attribute attribute)
                throws InstanceNotFoundException,
                        AttributeNotFoundException,
                        InvalidAttributeValueException,
                        MBeanException,
                        ReflectionException;

public AttributeList setAttributes(ObjectName name,
                            AttributeList attributes)
                throws InstanceNotFoundException,
                        ReflectionException;

public Object invoke(ObjectName name,
                    String operationName,
                    Object[] params,
                    String[] signature)
                throws InstanceNotFoundException,
                        MBeanException,
                        ReflectionException;
```

9

CONNECTORS AND
PROTOCOL
ADAPTORS

LISTING 9.1   continued

```java
public String getDefaultDomain();

public void addNotificationListener(
                    ObjectName name,
                    NotificationListener listener,
                    NotificationFilter filter,
                    Object handback)
                    throws InstanceNotFoundException;

public void addNotificationListener(
                    ObjectName name,
                    ObjectName listener,
                    NotificationFilter filter,
                    Object handback)
                    throws InstanceNotFoundException;

public void removeNotificationListener(
                    ObjectName name,
                    NotificationListener listener)
                    throws InstanceNotFoundException,
                            ListenerNotFoundException;

public void removeNotificationListener(
                    ObjectName name,
                    ObjectName listener)
                    throws InstanceNotFoundException,
                            ListenerNotFoundException;

public MBeanInfo getMBeanInfo(ObjectName name)
                    throws InstanceNotFoundException,
                            IntrospectionException,
                            ReflectionException;

public boolean isInstanceOf(ObjectName name,
                            String className)
                    throws InstanceNotFoundException;

public Set queryMBeans(ObjectName name, QueryExp query);

public Set queryNames(ObjectName name, QueryExp query);

public void close();

}
```

As you can see, the `RemoteMBeanServer` closely follows the `MBeanServer` interface without the three methods previously mentioned and with an additional `close()` method.

You will use the `RemoteMBeanServer` interface as a front end, or façade, for the proxies that connect to the server. The proxies themselves can operate on a simpler interface that only exposes one method, `invoke()`. All the invocations the client makes to the `RemoteMBeanServer` interface are wrapped with a `MethodInvocation` object in the proxy and sent to the remote server via the `invoke()` method, as shown in Figure 9.1.

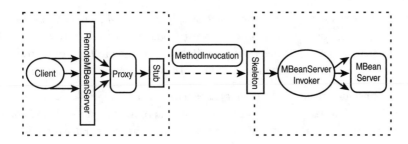

FIGURE 9.1

Design of the RMI connector.

The `MBeanServerInvoker` is the remote interface exported by the RMI subsystem. The client-side proxy invokes the method of this interface "behind-the-scenes" from the management application, which only uses the `RemoteMBeanServer` interface.

The `MBeanServerInvoker` interface is declared in Listing 9.2.

LISTING 9.2   `MBeanServerInvoker.java`

```
package book.jmx.examples;

public interface MBeanServerInvoker extends java.rmi.Remote {

  Object invoke(MethodInvocation mi)
      throws Exception, java.rmi.RemoteException;

}
```

As you can see, the `MBeanServerInvoker` interface is a very simplified interface with one `invoke()` method that makes a reference to a `MethodInvocation` object as its only argument.

9

CONNECTORS AND
PROTOCOL
ADAPTORS

RMIInvocationHandler

With the two interfaces for client and server created, the next step is to build the implementations for the said interfaces. Let's look at the client-side proxy first. As you have most likely realized already, you need an object that implements the RemoteMBeanServer interface on its front-end, which is used by the management client, and invokes methods on the MBeanServerInvoker interface on its back-end, sending the remote procedure calls. In between these two interfaces, you need to construct and initialize the MethodInvocation object that represents the invocation executed by the client.

You can achieve the proxy implementation quite simply by using the Proxy class from java.lang.reflect package. The Proxy class was introduced with the JDK version 1.3 and can be used to generate an object that delegates all the method invocations of its front-end interface to a single invoke() method declared in a InvocationHandler interface.

For the RMI connector, create an RMIInvocationHandler class that implements the InvocationHandler interface. As was mentioned earlier, all the invocations the client makes to the RemoteMBeanServer interface will be delegated to this InvocationHandler object. The method that you are required to implement is declared as follows:

```
public Object invoke(Object proxy, Method method,
                     Object[] args) throws Throwable;
```

This method declaration is quite similar to the invoke() declaration in the MBeanServer and DynamicMBean interfaces. The first argument is a reference to the proxy instance the method was invoked on, the second argument is a reference to a Method object, which gives us the detailed information on what method was invoked. The third argument is an array of Object instances representing the argument values of the method invocation.

Notice that any primitive types, such as int or byte, will be wrapped in the corresponding object types, Integer and Byte. Also, a null array indicates that the method takes no arguments. The return type from invoke() must be the type declared in the interface the proxy implements—in this case, the RemoteMBeanServer interface.

The RMIInvocationHandler implementation itself is quite simple. There is one constructor that initializes the remote connection to the server. A lookup for the remote server returns the stub implementing the MBeanServerInvoker interface declared earlier. In the InvocationHandler implementation, the method argument is passed to the MethodInvocation instance and the invoke() method of the MBeanServerInvoker is called.

The RMIInvocationHandler implementation is shown in Listing 9.3.

LISTING 9.3 RMIInvocationHandler.java

```java
package book.jmx.examples;

import java.util.*;
import java.net.*;
import java.lang.reflect.*;
import java.rmi.*;


public class RMIInvocationHandler
    implements InvocationHandler, RMIConnectorConstants {

  /* Remote reference to the connector server. */
  private MBeanServerInvoker invoker = null;

  /* Property values. */
  private String host = null;
  private String name = null;
  private int port    = 1099;


  /* Constructor */

  public RMIInvocationHandler(Properties props)
      throws NotBoundException, MalformedURLException,
      RemoteException {

    /* Retrieve properties for remote connection. */
    host = props.getProperty(HOST, "localhost");
    port = Integer.parseInt(props.getProperty(PORT, "1099"));
    name = props.getProperty(REMOTE_NAME,"jmx/RMIConnector");

    /* Retrieve the stub implementing MBeanServerInvoker */
    String lookup = "//" + host + ":" + port + "/" + name;
    invoker = (MBeanServerInvoker)Naming.lookup(lookup);
  }


  /* InvocationHandler implementation */

  public Object invoke(Object proxy, Method method,
                       Object[] args) throws Throwable {

    /* Create and initialize serializable MI object. */
    MethodInvocation mi = new MethodInvocation(method);
```

Listing 9.3   continued

```
   mi.setParams(args);

   /* Remote call to the connector server. */
   return invoker.invoke(mi);
  }

}
```

In Listing 9.3, the constructor attempts to retrieve relevant property values, the host name, the port number, and the name of the remote object bound to the RMI registry. The constant strings used to retrieve the connection properties—HOST, PORT, and REMOTE_NAME are defined in the RMIConnectorConstants interface shown in Listing 9.4.

Listing 9.4   RMIConnectorConstants.java

```
package book.jmx.examples;

public interface RMIConnectorConstants {

  static final String HOST = "rmi.host";
  static final String PORT = "rmi.port";
  static final String REMOTE_NAME = "remote.name";

}
```

Before going to the MethodInvocation details, let's look at how to initialize the RMI connector proxy you just created.

ConnectorFactory

With the Java Development Kit (JDK) version 1.3, a new class, Proxy, was introduced to the java.lang.reflect package. The Proxy class allows the creation of objects that implement any given interface, or several interfaces, and delegates all the method invocations to the InvocationHandler object. The Proxy class declares a static newProxyInstance() method that is used to create the proxy instances. Its declaration is as follows:

```
public static Object newProxyInstance(
                        ClassLoader loader,
                        Class[] interfaces,
                        InvocationHandler h)
                    throws IllegalArgumentException;
```

To create a proxy object that implements the RemoteMBeanServer interface and delegates all the method calls to the RMIInvocationHandler object, the following code can be used:

```
RemoteMBeanServer server =

    (RemoteMBeanServer)Proxy.newProxyInstance(
        Thread.currentThread().getContextClassLoader(),
        new Class[] { RemoteMBeanServer.class },
        new RMIInvocationHandler(props)
    );
```

However, you will not expect the client to execute that code every time it needs a new proxy to the MBean server. Instead, you will build a factory class that essentially does this work for the client. For now, the factory class will be able to create only RMI connector proxies, but you will later extend it to return other connector proxies, such as SOAP or JMS connector proxies.

The ConnectorFactory and ConnectorException class implementations are shown in Listings 9.5a and 9.5b.

LISTING 9.5A ConnectorFactory.java

```
package book.jmx.examples;

import java.util.*;
import java.lang.reflect.*;
import java.rmi.*;

import javax.naming.*;


public class ConnectorFactory {

  public static RemoteMBeanServer createConnector(
                                    String transport,
                                    Properties props)
    throws ConnectorException {


    if (transport.equalsIgnoreCase("RMI")) {
      try {
        return (RemoteMBeanServer)Proxy.newProxyInstance(
            Thread.currentThread().getContextClassLoader(),
            new Class[] { RemoteMBeanServer.class },
            new RMIInvocationHandler(props)
        );
      }
```

LISTING 9.5A   continued

```
      catch (Exception e) {
        throw new ConnectorException(
            "Unable to create proxy.", e
        );
      }
    }

    throw new ConnectorException(
        "Unrecognized connector transport: " + transport
    );
  }

}
```

LISTING 9.5B   ConnectorException.java

```
package book.jmx.examples;

import javax.management.JMException;

public class ConnectorException extends JMException {

  private Exception exception = null;

  public ConnectorException() {
    super();
  }

  public ConnectorException(String msg) {
    super(msg);
  }

  public ConnectorException(String msg, Exception e) {
    super(msg);
    this.exception = e;
  }

  public Exception getTargetException() {
    return exception;
  }

}
```

The `ConnectorFactory.createConnector()` method tries to match the submitted transport identifier to its known proxies, in this case the string `"RMI"` to RMI connector proxy. If the transport string is recognized, a proxy instance implementing the `RemoteMBeanServer` interface is returned to the client. Otherwise, a `ConnectorException` is thrown.

You will go through a complete example on how to use the connector factory to connect to a remote MBean server in a few pages. But first, move your attention to the server side and see how the `MethodInvocation` is received on the JMX agent and how the remote invocation is executed on the `MBeanServer` instance.

RMI Connector Server

The server side of the RMI connector consists of two classes. The implementation of `MBeanServerInvoker` interface, which is the RMI remote server object, and the RMI Connector MBean, which exports the RMI server and exposes the management interface of the connector.

As you already saw in the client proxy discussion, the `MBeanServerInvoker` interface is quite simple. It only declares one method, `invoke()`, that takes one parameter, a `MethodInvocation` object. The implementation of the `MBeanServerInvoker` interface, the `RMIServerInvoker` class, is not very complex either.

The RMI subsystem takes care of the details of remote call, so all that is left for you to do is to give the `MethodInvocation` a reference to the MBean server and then call the `invoke()` on the `MethodInvocation` object. The `MethodInvocation` object will then delegate the call originally requested by the client to the MBean server instance.

The implementation of the `RMIServerInvoker` class is shown in Listing 9.6.

LISTING 9.6   `RMIServerInvoker.java`

```java
package book.jmx.examples;

import java.rmi.*;
import javax.management.*;


public class RMIServerInvoker implements MBeanServerInvoker {

  private transient MBeanServer server = null;

  public RMIServerInvoker(MBeanServer server) {
    this.server = server;
  }
```

LISTING 9.6   continued

```
/* MBeanServerInvoker implementation. */

public Object invoke(MethodInvocation mi) throws Exception{

  mi.setMBeanServer(server);
  mi.invoke();


  /* Handle exceptions and errors. */
  if (mi.getStatus() == MethodInvocation.ERROR) {
    Object val = mi.getReturnValue();

    if (val instanceof Exception)
      throw (Exception)val;
    else
      throw new RemoteException(
          "Runtime exception or error at the server.",
          (Throwable)val
      );
  }

  /* Return the result of the invocation. */
  return mi.getReturnValue();
}

}
```

The constructor of the `RMIServerInvoker` takes a reference to the MBean server as an argument. This reference is provided by the connector MBean when initializing and exporting the remote server, as you will see shortly.

RMI Connector MBean

The `RMIConnector` class is an MBean that can be registered to the JMX agent.

You will expose one operation, `startServer()`, that exports the remote server and binds it to the RMI registry. In addition, you will have two management attributes exposed by the RMI connector—`Port` and `Name`. The `Port` attribute allows the `RMIServerInvoker` to be bound to a specific port on the host machine. The `Port` attribute defaults to zero, which indicates that an anonymous port will be used for the server. The `Name` attribute enables you to define what name should be used to bind the remote reference to the RMI registry. If you want to change the default values of these two attributes you must change them before invoking the `startServer()` operation.

The management interface of the RMIConnector is shown in Listing 9.7.

LISTING 9.7   RMIConnectorMBean.java

```java
package book.jmx.examples;

public interface RMIConnectorMBean {

    public void startServer(String agentID)
        throws java.rmi.RemoteException;

    public String getName();
    public void setName(String name);

    public int getPort();
    public void setPort(int port);
}
```

The implementation of the RMIConnector class is shown in Listing 9.8.

LISTING 9.8   RMIConnector.java

```java
package book.jmx.examples;

import java.net.*;
import java.rmi.*;
import java.rmi.server.*;
import java.rmi.registry.*;

import javax.management.*;
import javax.management.modelmbean.*;


public class RMIConnector implements RMIConnectorMBean {

    private String name = "jmx/RMIConnector";
    private int port     = 0; // anonymous port

    private MBeanServer server = null;

    public RMIConnector() { }

    public void startServer(String agentID) throws RemoteException {

        // find the mbean server reference
```

Listing 9.8   continued

```
server = (MBeanServer)MBeanServerFactory
    .findMBeanServer(agentID).get(0);

MBeanServerInvoker invoker = new RMIServerInvoker(server);
UnicastRemoteObject.exportObject(invoker, port);

try {
    Naming.rebind(name, invoker);
}
catch (MalformedURLException e) {
    throw new RemoteException(e.getMessage(), e);
}
}

public String getName() {
  return name;
}

public void setName(String name) {
  this.name = name;
}

public int getPort() {
  return port;
}

public void setPort(int port) {
  this.port = port;
}

}
```

At this point, you have built everything you need on the server side for the basic RMI connector server. You've also seen the code that works on the client side in the proxies. What is left to do is to implement the MethodInvocation class that travels between the client and the server. You will do that next and finish the RMI connector with an example on how to use it.

MethodInvocation

The MethodInvocation class is an abstraction of the invocation that travels between the client and the server. The MethodInvocation is created and initialized in the client proxy to represent the method call made by the client application. As the MethodInvocation arrives to the server, you set the MBean server reference and execute the MethodInvocation invoke() method. This call will then proceed to invoke the corresponding method on the MBean server.

The method invocation abstraction has two key benefits. First, you can reuse the same implementation with all connectors you build, as you will see in Chapter 10. Regardless of the transport protocol, you can send the same `MethodInvocation` objects carrying the logic to invoke an MBean server between the client and the server. As you build more connectors, the parts you will need to reimplement are the protocol-specific `InvocationHandler` and the server-side MBean.

The second advantage to using the `MethodInvocation` is its ability to carry additional context information with the invocation. For example, if you want to make the invocations transactional or you want to attach security principal and credentials, you need a way to attach the relevant information to the remote method call. As the default, `MBeanServer` interface does not allow explicit security or transaction context to be set; the alternative is to attach this information to the current thread of execution. However, because a thread cannot be serialized and sent across the network to the remote system, you need to extract any such information at the proxy implementation before you send the `MethodInvocation`, and add it as a serializable field to the `MethodInvocation` object. The server side that rebuilds the invocation and starts a new thread of execution can associate the additional context information with the thread or process it by some other means.

Now let's take a look at the implementation in more detail. The `MethodInvocation` class has a constructor that takes a `Method` object as a parameter. It also has a `setParams()` method that enables the parameter values to beset the MBean server reference is set via the `setMBeanServer()` by the connector server. In addition, you have a `getReturnValue()` method that allows you to retrieve the result of the invocation and a `getStatus()` method, which indicates whether the invocation was executed successfully or if any errors or exceptions were thrown.

The `MethodInvocation` implementation is shown in Listings 9.9 and 9.10.

LISTING 9.9   MethodInvocation.java

```
package book.jmx.examples;

import java.io.*;
import java.util.*;
import java.lang.reflect.*;
import javax.management.*;

public class MethodInvocation implements Serializable {

  static final long serialVersionUID = 7235369610255097138L;

  /* Status values. */
```

LISTING 9.9 continued

```java
public final static int OK    = 1;
public final static int ERROR = -99;

/* MBean server reference. */
private transient MBeanServer server  = null;

/* MethodInvocation 'payload'. */
private String objectName   = null;
private String methodName   = null;
private Object[] params      = null;
private Object returnValue   = null;
private int status           = OK;


/* Constructors. */

public MethodInvocation() {}

public MethodInvocation(Method m) {
  setMethodName(m.getName());
}


/* Accessor methods. */

public void setParams(Object[] params) {
  if (params == null || params.length < 1)  return;
  this.params = params;
}

public void setMBeanServer(MBeanServer server) {
  this.server = server;
}

public Object getReturnValue() {
  return returnValue;
}

public int getStatus() {
  return status;
}

public String getMethodName() {
  return methodName;
```

LISTING 9.9   continued

```
}

public void setMethodName(String methodName) {
  this.methodName = methodName;
}


/* Invoke implementation. */

public void invoke() {

  ...

}
}
```

The invoke() method of the MethodInvocation is a longish if-else block that matches the
given method name to the known method names of the MBeanServer interface. If the match is
found, the MethodInvocation class invokes the corresponding method on the MBean server.
Because the order and number of the parameters is known from the RemoteMBeanServer interface declaration, you can safely downcast the given object from the params array to the correct
type.

LISTING 9.10   MethodInvocation.java

```
...

/* Invoke implementation. */

public void invoke() {

  try {

    if (methodName.equals("createMBean")) {
      if (params.length == 2) {
        returnValue = server.createMBean(
            (String)params[0],
            (ObjectName)params[1]
        );
      }

      else if (params.length == 3) {
        returnValue = server.createMBean(
```

LISTING 9.10   continued

```
              (String)params[0],
              (ObjectName)params[1],
              (ObjectName)params[2]
        );
    }

    else if (params.length == 4) {
      returnValue = server.createMBean(
              (String)params[0],
              (ObjectName)params[1],
              (Object[])params[2],
              (String[])params[3]
        );
    }

    else if (params.length == 5) {
      returnValue = server.createMBean(
              (String)params[0],
              (ObjectName)params[1],
              (ObjectName)params[2],
              (Object[])params[3],
              (String[])params[4]
        );
    }

  }

  else if (methodName.equals("unregisterMBean")) {
    server.unregisterMBean((ObjectName)params[0]);
  }

  else if (methodName.equals("getObjectInstance")) {
    returnValue = server.getObjectInstance(
          (ObjectName)params[0]
      );
  }

  else if (methodName.equals("isRegistered")) {
    returnValue = new Boolean(server.isRegistered(
          (ObjectName)params[0]
    ));
  }

  else if (methodName.equals("getMBeanCount")) {
```

LISTING 9.10 continued

```
    returnValue = server.getMBeanCount();
}

else if (methodName.equals("getAttribute")) {
  returnValue = server.getAttribute(
      (ObjectName)params[0],
      (String)params[1]
  );
}

else if (methodName.equals("getAttributes")) {
  returnValue = server.getAttributes(
      (ObjectName)params[0],
      (String[])params[1]
  );
}

else if (methodName.equals("setAttribute")) {
  server.setAttribute(
      (ObjectName)params[0],
      (Attribute)params[1]
  );
}

else if (methodName.equals("setAttributes")) {
  returnValue = server.setAttributes(
      (ObjectName)params[0],
      (AttributeList)params[1]
  );
}

else if (methodName.equals("invoke")) {
  returnValue = server.invoke(
      (ObjectName)params[0],
      (String)params[1],
      (Object[])params[2],
      (String[])params[3]
  );
}

else if (methodName.equals("getDefaultDomain")) {
  returnValue = server.getDefaultDomain();
}
```

LISTING 9.10   continued

```java
      else if (methodName.equals("addNotificationListener")) {
      }

      else if (methodName.equals("removeNotificationListener")) {
      }

      else if (methodName.equals("getMBeanInfo")) {
        returnValue = server.getMBeanInfo(
            (ObjectName)params[0]
        );
      }

      else if (methodName.equals("isInstanceOf")) {
        returnValue = new Boolean(server.isInstanceOf(
            (ObjectName)params[0],
            (String)params[1]
        ));
      }

      else if (methodName.equals("queryNames")) {
        returnValue = server.queryNames(
            (ObjectName)params[0],
            (QueryExp)params[1]
        );
      }

      else if (methodName.equals("queryMBeans")) {
        returnValue = server.queryMBeans(
            (ObjectName)params[0],
            (QueryExp)params[1]
        );
      }


    }
    catch (Throwable t) {
      returnValue = t;
      status = ERROR;
    }
  }
```

To compile the class you've written so far, execute the following command:

```
C:\Examples> javac -d . -classpath .;jmx-1_0_1-ri_bin\jmx\lib\jmxri.jar
➥ RemoteMBeanServer.java MBeanServerInvoker.java
➥ RMIInvocationHandler.java RMIConnectorConstants.java
➥ RMIServerInvoker.java ConnectorFactory.java ConnectorException.java
➥ RMIConnectorMBean.java RMIConnector.java MethodInvocation.java
```

Also, you will need to execute the RMI compiler to generate a stub class for the `RMIServerInvoker`:

```
C:\Examples> rmic -d . -classpath . book.jmx.examples.RMIServerInvoker
```

That completes the RMI connector implementation. Next you will go through some examples and see how to use the connector from the client side.

Connector Example

On the client side, you can create the proxy via the `ConnectorFactory`. Using the proxy, you can then invoke the methods on the remote MBean server. A simple client is shown in Listing 9.11.

LISTING 9.11   `ConnectorClient.java`

```java
package book.jmx.examples;

import java.util.*;

public class ConnectorClient implements RMIConnectorConstants {

  public static void main(String[] args) {

    Properties props = new Properties();
    props.put(HOST, "localhost");
    props.put(PORT, "1099");

    try {
      RemoteMBeanServer server =
          ConnectorFactory.createConnector("RMI", props);

      Iterator it = server.queryNames(null, null).iterator();

      while(it.hasNext())
        System.out.println(it.next());
```

Listing 9.11   continued

```
      }
      catch (ConnectorException e) {
        e.printStackTrace();
      }
    }
  }
}
```

For the server to be able to receive the remote method calls from the client, you need to register the RMIConnector MBean. A simple agent with RMI connector is shown in Listing 9.12.

Listing 9.12   RMIAgent.java

```
package book.jmx.examples;

import javax.management.*;

public class RMIAgent {

  final static String SERVER_DELEGATE =
      "JMImplementation:type=MBeanServerDelegate";
  final static String AGENT_ID =
      "MBeanServerId";

  public static void main(String[] args) {
    MBeanServer server =
        MBeanServerFactory.createMBeanServer();

    try {
      String agentID = (String)server.getAttribute(
          new ObjectName(SERVER_DELEGATE), AGENT_ID
      );

      server.createMBean("book.jmx.examples.RMIConnector",
          new ObjectName("Connector:transport=RMI"));
      server.invoke(new ObjectName("Connector:transport=RMI"),
          "startServer",
          new Object[] { agentID },
          new String[] { String.class.getName() }
      );
    }
    catch (JMException e) {
      e.printStackTrace();
    }
  }
}
```

To run the example, compile the files:

```
C:\Examples> javac -d . -classpath .;jmx-1_0_1-ri_bin\jmx\lib\jmxri.jar
➥ RMIAgent.java ConnectorClient.java
```

For locating the remote server, you need to first start the `rmiregistry`.

```
C:\Examples> rmiregistry
```

After the registry is running, you can start the agent application in another window.

```
C:\Examples> java -classpath .;jmx-1_0_1-ri_bin\jmx\lib\jmxri.jar;
➥jdom-b7\build\jdom.jar;jdom-b7\lib\xerces.jar book.jmx.examples.RMIAgent
```

And finally run the client.

```
C:\Examples> java -classpath .;jmx-1_0_1-ri_bin\jmx\lib\jmxri.jar
➥book.jmx.examples.ConnectorClient
```

Notice that the examples assumed a `localhost` setting. If you have a local area network available, you can try the remote communication across different machines. Adjust the properties passed to the `ConnectorFactory` on the client accordingly.

A successful run of the example will print the object names of the MBeans in the agent:

```
JMImplementation:type=MBeanServerDelegate
Connector:transport=RMI
```

SNMP Adaptor

The Simple Network Management Protocol (SNMP) is the de facto protocol standard used by a wide variety of existing network management applications. To provide a bridge to the existing management tools and a JMX-based management architecture a SNMP protocol adaptor can be registered to the JMX agent. You will now learn how some of the existing SNMP tools can be used to manipulate MBeans. Some previous knowledge of SNMP is recommended for the reader.

9

> **NOTE**
>
> For more information about SNMP, please look at the following Web sites:
> - The Simple Web at http://snmp.cs.utwente.nl/
> - Lessons about SNMP at http://www.et.put.poznan.pl/snmp/main/
>   mainmenu.html

The SNMP is widely used to manage network components, such as routers, bridges, hubs, and network servers. JMX specification, on the other hand, addresses the management of software components in addition to the management of devices. Both provide the same basic features enabling components to offer their management interface and clients to manage these components through their management interface.

Both SNMP-based network management systems and the JMX-based management system define a server-side agent allowing components to present their management interface. The agents hide the components from direct client access and act as communication channels between the client and the component. SNMP-based systems define the properties of managed objects via Management Information Bases (MIB) where JMX exposes the management interface through its metadata classes. Both management systems also support events that can be sent back to the management client.

A Comparison Between SNMP and JMX

Both SNMP and JMX agents define a way to make the management interface of their components available to the client. SNMP client uses a Management Information Bases (MIB) that contains the management interface information to manage the components on the SNMP Agent. JMX Agents provide the client with the management interface information on request that is retrieved from the components through reflection on Standard MBeans or the `getMBeanInfo()` method on Dynamic MBeans. This means that SNMP client is limited to the definitions in the MIB, whereas the JMX client can investigate the components at runtime.

Both agents can deliver events (called *notifications* in JMX and *traps* in SNMP) to the client to inform it about changes on the component. In JMX, the client has to register to retrieve events and can filter them on the server side. In SNMP, the client receives them all, or none if disabled.

So, what are the differences? At a first glance, you would think there are not many. Adaptors, which provide a view of the JMX Agent without Java, normally provide a reduced set of supported data types because other protocols and/or presentations are not able to deal with all Java classes. Therefore, they mostly support the basic data types, strings, and maybe some others. The SNMP Adaptor is not able to support even these data types. It is reduced to Strings, Octet and Bit String, Integer and Object Reference. Thus, the MBeans cannot use any other data types than SNMP supports. This indicates that the MBeans programmer must write the management interface with respect to the SNMP Adaptor.

Before a SNMP client can work with a remote SNMP Agent, it has to read the Management Information Bases (MIB) as a file, which means that any structural changes on the SNMP

Agent are not visible to the client. JMX enables the client to investigate the management interface at any time for each MBean separately, allowing the server to reflect changes in the managed components as well as the client to react on these changes. For the SNMP client, this has two important consequences. First, if a component is added to, changed on, or removed from the SNMP Agent, the client does not know about it. Second, the SNMP client has to know which MIB it has to use.

The MIB describes the management interface base as an object tree through which the client can navigate. It is comparable to a group of `MBeanInfo` classes from the JMX API. Note that `MBeanInfo` describes the management interface of one MBean, whereas MIB can describe more than one component, but it does not have to describe all components on a SNMP Agent. JMX groups MBeans into domains and adds properties to each MBean. Except for the fact that the domain and properties as a whole must be unique within the JMX agent, there is no other restriction on the organization of the properties. The client can navigate through the MBeans by first searching for the desired MBeans and then getting their management interface. There is no further organization of the MBeans.

The last major difference is that SNMP does not allow you to invoke a method on the component. The only thing the administrator can do is to set values of the attributes offered by SNMP. This means that the component has to perform operations when the attribute is set, and the client has to retrieve any return values by getting attribute values. For example, the client might want to stop a component. The client can then set the value of the attribute `active` to `false`, and the component will perform the `stop` operation.

Overview of Sun and AdventNet Adaptors

Both the AdventNet and Sun SNMP adaptors work in a similar manner. The SNMP Adaptor creates a static presentation of the JMX Agent or parts of it. The SNMP Adaptor is based on a view that contains the components at the time of the view generation.

In addition, the SNMP adaptors differ from many other protocol adaptors in the following ways:

- SNMP Adaptor and MBeans are generated from a MIB.
- The developer implements the code for the generated MBeans. He or she must implement the necessary conversions from and to the SNMP management model defined by the MIB.
- SNMP Adaptor hides all other MBeans that were not generated from the MIB.
- SNMP Adaptor starts an SNMP Agent that the client uses to work on the SNMP MBeans.

Figure 9.2 shows the participating components when an SNMP Adaptor is used.

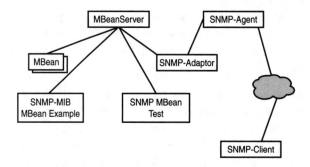

FIGURE 9.2

Network architecture of an SNMP Adaptor.

Protocol adaptors enable a client to work with a remote JMX agent. Their task is to transform the data sent by the client in Java objects, perform the request on their JMX servers, and transform the return values into data that the client understands.

With the SNMP Adaptor, the programmer is required to write the MIB first (see AdventNet and their MIB Editor) that describes the management interface of a SNMP Agent. Then a generator takes this MIB and creates the SNMP Agent and the MBeans. Now the programmer has to code the implementation of the MBeans, which can either be a regular MBean implementation or acting as a proxy for another MBean. Because of the limited number of supported data types and the missing method invocation support, the programmer must make the appropriate transformation if the SNMP MBeans work as proxies.

Creating an SNMP Adaptor

The SNMP adaptor creation involves a MIB declaration and MBean components generated based on the MIB. The Sun JDMK includes a MibGen tool that can be used to read a MIB definition and create corresponding MBean implementations. For instructions for downloading and installing the software required in this section (Sun JDMK and AdventNet tools), see Appendix A, "Environment Setup."

MIB Example

The declaration of the MIB used in this example is as follows:

```
— File Name : example.mib
— Date      : Thu Sep 27 12:38:29 PDT 2001
— Author    : AdventNet Agent Toolkit (Java Edition) - MibEditor 4.2

Example DEFINITIONS ::= BEGIN
```

```
test    MODULE-IDENTITY
        LAST-UPDATED   "200109271233Z"
        ORGANIZATION   "JBoss Group"
        CONTACT-INFO   "Andreas Schaefer"
        DESCRIPTION             "SNMP-Adaptor Test"
        REVISION                "200109271233Z"
        DESCRIPTION             ""
        ::= {  enterprises  1  }

enterprises    OBJECT IDENTIFIER
        ::= {  private  1  }

first   OBJECT-TYPE
        SYNTAX                  Integer32
        MAX-ACCESS              read-write
        STATUS                  current
        DESCRIPTION             "First Attribute"
        ::= {  test  1  }
```

END

This is pretty much the simplest example available, but it should do the trick. It declares a read-write integer attribute named `first` for module `test`. This MIB can be used to generate the required Java files for JMX integration, as you will see next.

SNMP Class Generation

First, you have to create the necessary classes for the SNMP adaptor. The JDMK comes with a MibGen tool that will read the `example.mib` and generate the necessary Java classes for you. To run the MibGen execute the following command:

```
C:\Examples> java -cp .;SUNWjdmk\jdmk4.2\1.2\lib\jdmkrt.jar;
➥SUNWjdmk\jdmk4.2\1.2\lib\jdmktk.jar com.sun.jdmk.tools.MibGen -d . example.mib
```

The previous command will generate the following classes:

- `Example.java`
- `ExampleOID.java`
- `TestMBean.java`
- `Test.java`
- `TestMeta.java`

`Example.java` is the MBean you register in `ServerStartup.java` representing the MIB on which this SNMP adaptor is based. It creates and registers all the MBeans generated out of the

9

CONNECTORS AND
PROTOCOL
ADAPTORS

MIB, which are Standard MBeans. It comes with a default implementation, but you can either add the implementation directly there or add code to transform the request to another MBean, which this MBean is a proxy of.

If you add code directly to the generated MBean class, it will be lost as soon as you recreate the classes with MibGen tool. To avoid this, you write the implementation in a subclass of the generated class. For example, extend the Test class with TestImpl class. Now you can over-write the appropriate methods in TestImpl and adjust the Example class to create instances of TestImpl instead of Test. When the classes are regenerated, the TestImpl class will be unaf-fected. However, you will need to edit the Example class again because it will be regenerated by MibGen.

The generated Test class is shown in Listing 9.13.

LISTING 9.13   Test.java

```
//
// Generated by mibgen version 4.2 (10/20/00) when compiling Example.
//

// java imports
//
import java.io.Serializable;

// jmx imports
//
import javax.management.MBeanServer;
import javax.management.snmp.SnmpString;
import javax.management.snmp.SnmpStatusException;

// jdmk imports
//
import com.sun.jdmk.snmp.agent.SnmpMib;

/**
 * The class is used for implementing the "Test" group.
 * The group is defined with the following oid: 1.3.6.1.4.1.1.
 */
public class Test implements TestMBean, Serializable {

    /**
     * Variable for storing the value of "First".
     * The variable is identified by: "1.3.6.1.4.1.1.1".
     */
```

LISTING 9.13 continued

```java
protected Integer First = new Integer(1);


/**
 * Constructor for the "Test" group.
 * If the group contains a table, the entries created through an SNMP SET
 * will not be registered in JDMK.
 */
public Test(SnmpMib myMib) {
}


/**
 * Constructor for the "Test" group.
 * If the group contains a table, the entries created through an SNMP SET
 * will be AUTOMATICALLY REGISTERED in JDMK.
 */
public Test(SnmpMib myMib, MBeanServer server) {
}

/**
 * Getter for the "First" variable.
 */
public Integer getFirst() throws SnmpStatusException {
    return First;
}

/**
 * Setter for the "First" variable.
 */
public void setFirst(Integer x) throws SnmpStatusException {
    First = x;
}

/**
 * Checker for the "First" variable.
 */
public void checkFirst(Integer x) throws SnmpStatusException {
    //
    // Add your own checking policy.
    //
}

}
```

Completing the Example

In addition to the classes just discussed, you need to create a class to start the JMX server, add the necessary MBeans, and register the Example MIB MBean to the JMX agent and the SNMP adaptor. This is only necessary for the example because in a real-world example, the JMX agent would most likely already be started and you only have to perform the steps in the method addSnmpAdaptor().

The ServerStartup implementation is shown in Listing 9.14.

LISTING 9.14   ServerStartup.java

```java
import java.io.IOException;

import javax.management.ObjectName;
import javax.management.JMException;
import javax.management.MBeanServer;
import javax.management.MBeanServerFactory;
import javax.management.snmp.SnmpStatusException;

import com.sun.jdmk.Trace;
import com.sun.jdmk.comm.HtmlAdaptorServer;
import com.sun.jdmk.comm.SnmpAdaptorServer;

public class ServerStartup {

    public static void main(String args[]) {

        MBeanServer lServer;
        if ((args.length != 0)) {
            usage();
            java.lang.System.exit(1);
        }
        try {
            Trace.parseTraceProperties();
            Trace.send(
                Trace.LEVEL_TRACE,
                Trace.INFO_MISC,
                "ServerStartup",
                "main",
                "Default trace is on"
            );
        } catch(java.io.IOException e) {
            e.printStackTrace();
        }
```

LISTING 9.14   continued

```
try {
    lServer = MBeanServerFactory.createMBeanServer();
    String domain = lServer.getDefaultDomain();

    // Create and start the HTML adaptor. This is necessary
    // to show what the SNMP-Adaptor does not show.
    //
    ObjectName htmlObjName = new ObjectName(
        domain + ":class=HtmlAdaptorServer,protocol=html,port=8082"
    );
    Trace.send(Trace.LEVEL_TRACE, Trace.INFO_MISC, "ServerStartup",
                "main",
                "Adding HTML adaptor to MBean server with name \n\t"
                + htmlObjName);
    java.lang.System.out.println(
        "NOTE: HTML adaptor is bound on TCP port 8082");
    HtmlAdaptorServer htmlAdaptor = new HtmlAdaptorServer( 8082 );
    lServer.registerMBean(htmlAdaptor, htmlObjName);
    htmlAdaptor.start();

    // Add the SNMP-Adaptor
    addSnmpAdaptor( lServer, domain );

    java.lang.System.out.println(
        ">> Press <Ctrl-C> if you want to stop this agent.");

} catch (Exception e) {
    e.printStackTrace();
}
}

/**
* Create and register the SNMP-Adaptor, SNMP-MIB MBean and
* connect this two together. Perform these steps in your
* program to add the SNMP-Adaptor to your server.
**/
public static void addSnmpAdaptor( MBeanServer pServer, String pDomain )
  throws JMException, IOException, SnmpStatusException
{
    int lSnmpPort = 161;
    ObjectName lSnmpObjName = new ObjectName(
        pDomain + ":class=SnmpAdaptorServer,protocol=snmp,port=" + lSnmpPort
    );
    Trace.send(
```

9

LISTING 9.14   continued

```
            Trace.LEVEL_TRACE,
            Trace.INFO_MISC,
            "ServerStartup",
            "main",
            "Adding SNMP adaptor to MBean server with name \n\t" + lSnmpObjName
        );
        java.lang.System.out.println(
            "SNMP Adaptor is bound on UDP port " + lSnmpPort );
        SnmpAdaptorServer lSnmpAdaptor = new SnmpAdaptorServer( lSnmpPort );
        pServer.registerMBean( lSnmpAdaptor, lSnmpObjName );
        lSnmpAdaptor.start();

        // Send a coldStart SNMP Trap.
        java.lang.System.out.print(
            "NOTE: Sending a coldStart SNMP trap to each destination " +
            "defined in the ACL file..."
        );
        lSnmpAdaptor.setTrapPort( new Integer( lSnmpPort + 1 ) );
        lSnmpAdaptor.snmpV1Trap( 0, 0, null );
        java.lang.System.out.println( "Done." );

        // Create the Example and add it to the MBean server.
        //
        ObjectName lMibObjName= new ObjectName( "snmp:class=Example_MIB" );
        Trace.send(Trace.LEVEL_TRACE, Trace.INFO_MISC, "ServerStartup", "main",
                "Adding Example-MIB to MBean server with name \n\t" +
                lMibObjName);

        // Create an instance of the customized MIB
        //
        Example lExample = new Example();
        pServer.registerMBean( lExample, lMibObjName );
        // Add the MBean to the SNMP Adaptor by setting the SNMP Adaptor's
        // Object Name  to the MBean.
        lExample.setSnmpAdaptorName( lSnmpObjName );
    }

    /**
     * Return usage of the program.
     */
    public static void  usage() {
        java.lang.System.out.println("java ServerStartup");
    }
}
```

The `ServerStartup` class registers the `Example` MIB MBean to the MBean server. It also registers an HTTP adaptor so you will be able browse the JMX Agent.

The `addSnmpAdaptor()` method encapsulates the entire code necessary to add the SNMP Adaptor and its MBeans. At the beginning, it creates the `SnmpAdaptorServer` instance, registers it at the JMX Agent, and then starts the adaptor. Last, the `Example` MIB MBean is created and registered to the JMX Agent. The object name of the SNMP Adaptor is passed to the `Example` MIB MBean with the `setSnmpAdaptorName()` method call. This is necessary to inform the MIB MBean about its SNMP Adaptor and to connect these two together. Note that the SNMP Adaptor can support more than one MIB, but the MIB MBean has to know to which SNMP Adaptor it belongs.

Testing the Example

First, you have to compile the example:

```
C:\Examples> javac -classpath .;SUNWjdmk\jdmk4.2\1.2\lib\jdmkrt.jar;
➥SUNWjdmk\jdmk4.2\1.2\lib\jdmktk.jar ServerStartup.java
```

and start the server:

```
java -cp .;SUNWjdmk\jdmk4.2\1.2\lib\jdmkrt.jar;
➥SUNWjdmk\jdmk4.2\1.2\lib\jdmktk.jar ServerStartup
```

You can now point your browser to `http://localhost:8082` (see Figure 9.3). You should be able to find the components shown earlier in Figure 9.2 in the HTTP adaptor view of the JMX agent.

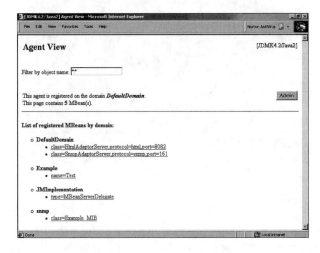

FIGURE 9.3

HTTP adaptor listing all MBeans.

The following domains are listed in Figure 9.3:

- `DefaultDomain`   Contains the HTTP and SNMP adaptors
- `snmp`   Contains the `Example` MIB MBean
- `Example`   Contains all the MBeans represented by the `Example` MIB
- `JMImplementation`   Contains the MBean Server delegate

Now test the remote access. To do this, you need to use the MIB Browser from AdventNet. It is a simple SNMP GUI client that lets you work on a remote SNMP agent. On a Windows system, the default AdventNet installation adds a shortcut under the Start menu Programs folder. Find the AdventNet subfolder and choose Mib Browser under Management Tools. For Linux and Unix systems, the distribution package includes `setenv.sh` and `MibBrowser.sh` files to start the application.

After the MIB Browser has started, adjust the settings for the SNMP agent and SNMP traps port to match the `ServerStart` implementation (notice that in Listing 9.14 the port for the traps is one higher than the SNMP agent port). By default, the SNMP agent port number is 161, and the SNMP traps port number is 162. Also make sure that the SNMP Version is SNMP 2c. You can find the settings dialog under the Edit menu of the MIB browser (see Figure 9.4).

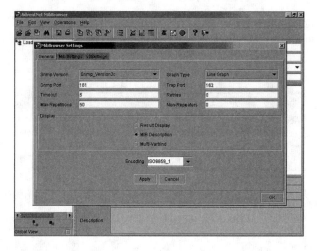

FIGURE 9.4

Shows the MIB Browser's settings.

After you have set up the correct ports and version in the Settings dialog, choose Load MIB from the File menu. Enter the file path to the `example.mib` to the text field in the dialog, for example `C:\Examples\example.mib`. Click OK. You should see the MIB being loaded to the browser, as shown in Figure 9.5. From the tree on the left side of the screen, click or choose Example, Private, Enterprises, Test, and First.

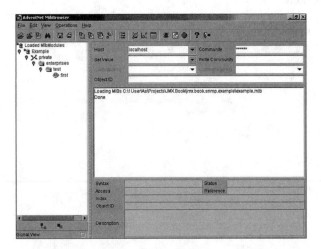

FIGURE 9.5
MIB Browser lists the MIB definition.

Now click the Get SNMP variable icon on the toolbar, or choose Operations, Get from the menu. You will see the MIB browser send a request to localhost port 161 to retrieve the value of the `First` attribute, as illustrated in Figure 9.6.

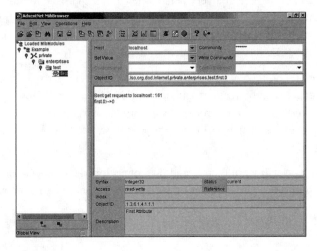

FIGURE 9.6
MIB Browser returns the value of `First` attribute from SNMP adaptor.

9

CONNECTORS AND
PROTOCOL
ADAPTORS

Finally, change the value by entering **123** in the Set value text field and click the Set SNMP variable icon in the toolbar, or choose Operations, Set from the menu. You will see the MIB browser change the value, as shown in Figure 9.7.

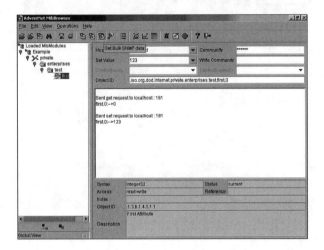

FIGURE 9.7

MIB Browser sets new value.

Summary

In this chapter, you have learned at a very detailed level one approach to implementing JMX connectors. You have also used SNMP-based management applications together with a JMX agent and seen how a SNMP protocol adaptor can be used to integrate existing management technologies with the JMX-based management systems.

Both the connector and protocol adaptor implementations are currently unspecified, so you have to rely on product-specific features and programming interfaces. However, a JSR-160 has been started in the Java Community Process to specify the next version (1.1) of the JMX API, including the client APIs. The client APIs will hopefully standardize the discovery and access to remote JMX agents.

In the next chapter, you will learn more about the connectors, learn how to discover a JMX agent, and see how the J2EE services can be used to implement these features.

JMX Distribution Layer with J2EE Services

IN THIS CHAPTER

This chapter will cover some more connector implementations in detail. You will see example implementations for a SOAP connector and a bare bones implementation of an asynchronous JMS connector. In addition, you will cover some issues with the JMX agent and MBean location transparency and implement a simple mechanism for the management clients to look up the agent or MBean from a naming service.

Location Transparency

When building the management applications, it can be useful to avoid hard coding the location of the MBeans or the MBean servers in the client code. For improved flexibility on the client, both the agent and the MBeans should be accessible using logical names instead of hard-coded addresses. The agent may migrate from one host machine to another during the life span of a management application, and reconfiguring the client to reflect this change can be a nuisance to the user or administrator. More often, an MBean component migrates from one agent to another and the management application must know where the new home of the MBean is, as shown in Figure 10.1.

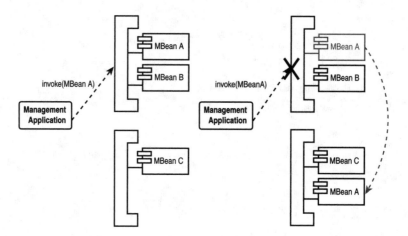

FIGURE 10.1

A management client connecting directly to a JMX agent will not find its target MBean if the MBean has migrated to a different JMX agent.

To achieve a basic location transparency, you can add a step of indirection to the process of connecting to a remote JMX agent. Instead of attempting to connect to a host of the agent directly, you can look up a handle to the agent from a well-known naming service. The handle will be bound to a logical name the management application can use to perform the lookup, and if the location of the agent or an MBean changes, these changes can be reflected on the handle to avoid affecting the client application (see Figure 10.2).

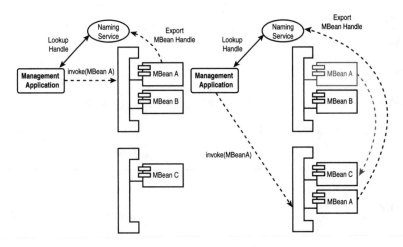

FIGURE 10.2
When the management client looks up a handle that contains the location information of an MBean, it will continue to operate even if the MBean has migrated to a different JMX agent.

You will next create an export manager service implementation. The export manager is capable of connecting to a naming service via Java Naming and Directory Interface (JNDI) and binding a serializable object, an MBeanHandle, to the service. Later in this chapter, you will implement connectors that are able to look up and use the handle objects to determine the host machine address of an agent or MBean and other additional information required to build a remote connection.

MBean Handle

The MBean handle bound to the naming service can be any serializable Java object. The implementation covered in this section is a basic handle consisting of name-value properties. The handle can be used to export values, such as host name and port number, to the name service.

The ConnectorFactory class you built in Chapter 9, "Connectors and Protocol Adaptors," can be modified to accept a JNDI name as an argument for the createConnector() method calls. Instead of receiving the connection properties directly from the client, the factory class will attempt to retrieve them from the name service in the form of the MBeanHandle instance.

The MBeanHandle interface is shown in Listing 10.1. It contains one method, getProperties(), that the connector factory can use to retrieve the properties it needs to form a connection. The implementation of the MBeanHandle interface is shown in Listing 10.2.

LISTING 10.1   `MBeanHandle.java`

```java
package book.jmx.examples;

import java.util.*;

public interface MBeanHandle extends java.io.Serializable {

  public Properties getProperties();

}
```

LISTING 10.2   `MBeanHandleImpl.java`

```java
package book.jmx.examples;

import java.util.*;

public class MBeanHandleImpl implements MBeanHandle {

  private Properties props = new Properties();

  public void addProperties(Properties props) {
    this.props.putAll(props);
  }

  public Properties getProperties() {
    return (Properties)props.clone();
  }
}
```

The modification to the `ConnectorFactory` class is shown in Listing 10.3. The class contains an overloaded `createConnector()` method that takes a JNDI name as its second argument instead of taking a `Properties` object directly. The overloaded `createConnector()` attempts to create a JNDI `InitialContext` reference to the naming service and look up an `MBeanHandle` based on the given name. If the handle is successfully retrieved, the implementation will call the `getProperties()` method of the `MBeanHandle` interface and call the version of the `createConnector()` method with the `Properties` object.

LISTING 10.3   ConnectorFactory.java

```java
package book.jmx.examples;

import java.util.*;
import java.lang.reflect.*;
import java.rmi.*;
import javax.naming.*;

public class ConnectorFactory  {

  public static RemoteMBeanServer createConnector(String transport,
      String jndiName) throws ConnectorException {

    Context ctx = null;
    MBeanHandle handle = null;

    try {
      ctx = new InitialContext();
      handle = (MBeanHandle)ctx.lookup(jndiName);
    }
    catch (NamingException e) {
      throw new ConnectorException(
        "Unable to find the handle", e
      );
    }

    return createConnector(transport, handle.getProperties());
  }

  public static RemoteMBeanServer createConnector(String transport,
      Properties props)   throws ConnectorException {

    if (transport.equalsIgnoreCase("RMI")) {
      try {
        return (RemoteMBeanServer)Proxy.newProxyInstance(
            Thread.currentThread().getContextClassLoader(),
            new Class[] { RemoteMBeanServer.class },
            new RMIInvocationHandler(props)
        );
      }
      catch (Exception e) {
        throw new ConnectorException(
            "Unable to create proxy.", e
        );
      }
    }
```

LISTING 10.3 Continued

```
    }

    throw new ConnectorException(
        "Unrecognized connector transport: " + transport
    );
  }
}
```

Next, you need to write the export manager implementation that takes care of binding the relevant connection properties for the MBeans.

Export Manager

The export manager takes care of binding an MBean handle to the naming service. As was shown in the previous section, the handle contains named properties that the connector factory uses on the client side to determine how to construct the connection.

What needs to be decided next is what properties the handle should contain. The JMX specification does not restrict the distributed services level to a specific RPC implementation, such as RMI, to connect to a remote JMX agent. Instead, the management client can use many different means to connect to the agent. Some possibilities include RMI, SOAP, JMS, and SNMP. So how does the export manager know what kind of properties are required to be exposed in the handle? Several different remote call mechanisms can be used to connect to an MBean server. Furthermore, new connectors can be added to and removed from the server dynamically at runtime. The answer is that the export manager doesn't know. However, because each JMX connector should have a connector server MBean registered to the agent, the manager can query the server for those MBeans for their export properties. Each connector server MBean can be expected to know what information is required to connect to it. For example, an RMI connector server knows the host name and port to which it is listening. Similarly, a SOAP connector server knows the HTTP address that it is using to receive the SOAP requests. A JMS connector server knows what queue or topic the client needs to connect to so it can receive the messages.

To build the handle, the export manager implementation used in this chapter queries each connector server for their individual export properties and adds them as part of the handle. The export manager implementation will assume that the connector servers are registered under the Connector:* object name domain. This restricts all the connector server implementations that want to export their properties as part of the handle to register themselves to this known management domain. As usual, you are free to change the implementation to support a more configurable naming scheme.

In addition, the export manager registers with the MBean server delegate to receive notifications on MBean registration and unregistration events. If new MBeans are added to the Connector domain, the export manager attempts to retrieve the value of the ExportProperties attribute. If the attribute exists, its content is added as part of the properties that are attached to the MBean handle. Similarly, when connector server MBeans are unregistered from the server, their export properties are removed from the export manager.

By registering to listen to the registration events of connector server MBeans, the export manager is able to adapt to the changes in connector configuration of an MBean server. Notice however, that the implementation of the export manager shown here does not keep track of or update existing handles that have already been exported to the name server. When new connector servers are added to a running system, you could rebind the existing handles to reflect the changes. However, the conditions of when and how to make the rebinding varies based on the application, so that part of the implementation is left as an exercise for the reader. Adding a policy descriptor for rebinding behavior might be one option for the implementation.

The implementation of the ExportManager is shown in Listing 10.4. The connectorMap field holds a map with MBean object names as keys and a list of properties as its value. The start() method creates the initial naming context reference and registers a listener to the MBean server delegate. It also queries the MBean server for already existing MBeans in the Connector domain and adds them to the map if necessary. The export() method can be used by the agent or an individual MBean to bind a logical name to the naming service. The MBeanHandleImpl object contains the properties that the connectors can use to create a connection to the agent where the MBean resides.

LISTING 10.4   ExportManager.java

```java
package book.jmx.examples;

import java.util.*;
import javax.naming.*;
import javax.management.*;


public class ExportManager {

  final static String SERVER_DELEGATE =
      "JMImplementation:type=MBeanServerDelegate";

  // maps connector object name to export properties
  private HashMap connectorMap = new HashMap();
```

LISTING 10.4   Continued

```java
// stores the naming context
private Context ctx          = null;

// reference to the mbean server
private MBeanServer server   = null;


// default constructor
public ExportManager() { }


public void start(String agentID) throws NamingException {

  ctx = new InitialContext();
  ObjectName serverDelegate = null;

  try {
    server = (MBeanServer)MBeanServerFactory.
        findMBeanServer(agentID).get(0);

    // listen for MBean registration notifications
    serverDelegate = new ObjectName(SERVER_DELEGATE);

    server.addNotificationListener(
      serverDelegate,
      new RegistrationListener(),
      null,
      null
    );

    // query for existing connector servers
    ObjectName connectorQuery = new ObjectName("Connector:*");
    Set connectors = server.queryNames(connectorQuery, null);
    Iterator it = connectors.iterator();

    while (it.hasNext()) {
      ObjectName name = null;

      try {
        name = (ObjectName)it.next();

        // try to retrieve export properties
        connectorMap.put(name,
            server.getAttribute(name, "ExportProperties"));
```

LISTING 10.4   Continued

```
      }
      catch (JMException e) {
        System.out.println(
            name + " does not have ExportProperties attribute."
        );
      }
    }
  }
  catch (JMException e) {
    e.printStackTrace();
  }
}

public void export(String exportName) throws NamingException {

  MBeanHandleImpl handle = new MBeanHandleImpl();
  Iterator it = connectorMap.values().iterator();

  // add the known export properties to the handle
  while (it.hasNext())
    handle.addProperties((Properties)it.next());

  // bind to naming service
  ctx.rebind(exportName, handle);
}


// This notification listener updates the export properties based
// on connector server registration and unregistration events
class RegistrationListener implements NotificationListener {

  public void handleNotification(Notification n, Object hb) {

    if (!(n instanceof MBeanServerNotification))
      return;

    MBeanServerNotification notif = (MBeanServerNotification)n;
    ObjectName name     = notif.getMBeanName();
    String notifType = notif.getType();
    String domain    = name.getDomain();

    if (!domain.equalsIgnoreCase("Connector"))
      return;
```

LISTING 10.4 Continued

```
        if (notifType.equals(
            MBeanServerNotification.REGISTRATION_NOTIFICATION)) {

          try {
            connectorMap.put(name,
                server.getAttribute(name, "ExportProperties"));
          }
          catch (JMException e) {
            System.out.println(
                name + " does not have ExportProperties attribute."
            );
          }
        }

        else if (notifType.equals(
            MBeanServerNotification.UNREGISTRATION_NOTIFICATION)) {

          connectorMap.remove(name);
        }
      }
    }
  }
}
```

Also, to be able to register the export manager as an MBean to the server, it needs a management interface. To use the XMBean Model MBean implementation, you will need the management interface declaration in XML. One such suggestion for the management interface is shown in Listing 10.5.

LISTING 10.5 ExportManager.xml

```xml
<?xml version="1.0" encoding="UTF-8"?>
<!DOCTYPE mbean SYSTEM "file:/C:/Examples/xmbean.dtd">

<mbean>
  <operation>
    <name>export</name>
    <parameter>
      <name>ExportName</name>
      <type>java.lang.String</type>
    </parameter>
    <impact>ACTION</impact>
  </operation>
```

LISTING 10.5 Continued

```
<operation>
  <name>start</name>
  <parameter>
    <name>AgentID</name>
    <type>java.lang.String</type>
  </parameter>
  <impact>ACTION</impact>
</operation>
</mbean>
```

Notice the location of the DTD file. You may need to modify it to reflect the location of the `xmbean.dtd` on your system.

Next, you need to create a connector implementation that can work with the export manager MBean to relay its connection properties to the handle.

SOAP Connector

In Chapter 9, you built a generic connector framework that used the Java RMI as the remote call mechanism. It is quite easy to modify that basic approach to building a connector to include other means of transporting the method invocation to the remote JMX agent. In this chapter, you will see how to add a SOAP-based JMX connector to your collection of distributed services.

Recall from Chapter 9 that to build a new connector with different transport mechanism requires you to implement an invocation handler for the client-side proxy and a connector server MBean to the server side. You will next implement a SOAP invocation handler and a SOAP connector server MBean, as shown in Figure 10.3.

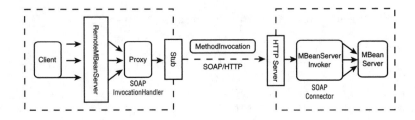

FIGURE 10.3

SOAP connector needs to replace the proxy implementation with a `SOAPInvocationHandler` on the client and add a SOAP connector server to the agent.

For the SOAP implementation, the GLUE framework is used, available from `http://` `www.themindelectric.com` (see Appendix A, "Environment Setup," for installation instructions). The `SOAPInvocationHandler` class (see Listing 10.6) implements the `InvocationHandler` interface and sends the `MethodInvocation` instance through a SOAP envelope.

The SOAP connector also uses the `MBeanServerInvoker` interface as its remote interface to the connector server. The client-side implementation of the proxy is quite simple. In the `SOAPInvocationHandler` constructor, you retrieve the reference to the invoker, and you set the `MethodInvocation` as the payload of the SOAP message in the `invoke()` method. The GLUE library handles the details of sending the invocation to the receiving HTTP server. The relevant two lines of code are highlighted in Listing 10.6.

LISTING 10.6   SOAPInvocationHandler.java

```java
package book.jmx.examples;

import java.util.*;
import java.net.*;
import java.lang.reflect.*;
import java.rmi.*;
import electric.registry.*;


public class SOAPInvocationHandler
    implements InvocationHandler, SOAPConnectorConstants {

  // the remote interface
  private MBeanServerInvoker invoker = null;

  public SOAPInvocationHandler(Properties props)
      throws RegistryException {

    System.setProperty("electric.xml.io.serialize", "yes");

    // retrieve the connection properties
    String host = props.getProperty(HOST, "localhost");
    String port = props.getProperty(PORT, "8085");
    String name = props.getProperty(NAME);
    String path = props.getProperty(PATH, "");

    // retrieve the stub
    String url = "http://" + host + ":" + port + "/" + path + "/" + name;
    invoker = (MBeanServerInvoker)Registry.bind(url, MBeanServerInvoker.class);
  }
```

LISTING 10.6   Continued

```java
public Object invoke(Object proxy, Method method,
                     Object[] args) throws Throwable {

  String methodName = method.getName();

  MethodInvocation mi = new MethodInvocation(method);
  mi.setParams(args);

  return invoker.invoke(mi);
  }


}
```

The connector server is as easy to implement as the client proxy (see Listing 10.7). The start() method again makes use of the GLUE framework to start an HTTP server that receives the SOAP invocations. The invoke() method of the SOAPConnector is called whenever a SOAP request arrives to the HTTP server for the given path and WSDL (Web Service Definition Language) file. In addition, the SOAPConnector class implements a getExportProperties() method that the export manager can use to retrieve the connection properties. For the SOAP connector, you include the host name, port number, and the WSDL filename and path. The property names are declared in the SOAPConnectorConstants interface, as shown in Listing 10.8.

LISTING 10.7   SOAPConnector.java

```java
package book.jmx.examples;

import java.rmi.RemoteException;
import java.util.*;
import java.io.*;
import java.net.*;
import javax.management.*;
import javax.management.modelmbean.*;

import electric.server.http.*;
import electric.registry.*;

public class SOAPConnector
    implements MBeanServerInvoker, SOAPConnectorConstants {

  private int port = 8085;
  private String path = "jmx";
  private String name = "urn:soapconnector";
```

LISTING 10.7   Continued

```java
private MBeanServer server = null;

public SOAPConnector() {
  System.setProperty("electric.xml.io.serialize", "yes");
}

public void start(String agentID)
    throws IOException, RegistryException {

  HTTP.startup("http://localhost:" + port + "/" + path);
  Registry.publish(name, this, MBeanServerInvoker.class);

  // find the mbean server reference
  server = (MBeanServer)MBeanServerFactory
      .findMBeanServer(agentID).get(0);
}

public int getPort() {
  return port;
}

public void setPort(int port) {
  this.port = port;
}

public String getName() {
  return name;
}

public void setName(String name) {
  this.name = name;
}

public String getPath() {
  return path;
}

public void setPath() {
  this.path = path;
}

public Object invoke(MethodInvocation mi) throws Exception {

    mi.setMBeanServer(server);
    mi.invoke();
```

LISTING 10.7 Continued

```
      if (mi.getStatus() == MethodInvocation.ERROR) {
        Object val = mi.getReturnValue();

        if (val instanceof Exception)
          throw (Exception)val;
        else throw new RemoteException(
            "Error at the server.", (Throwable)val
        );
      }

      return mi.getReturnValue();
  }


  /* Export Manager */
  public Properties getExportProperties() throws UnknownHostException {
    Properties props = new Properties();
    props.put(HOST, InetAddress.getLocalHost().getHostAddress());
    props.put(PORT, "" + getPort());
    props.put(PATH, path);
    props.put(NAME, getName() + ".wsdl");
    return props;
  }
}
```

LISTING 10.8 SOAPConnectorConstants.java

```
package book.jmx.examples;

public interface SOAPConnectorConstants {

    final static String NAME = "urn.name";
    final static String PATH = "http.path";
    final static String HOST = "http.host";
    final static String PORT = "soap.port";

}
```

To make the new connector accessible to the clients, you need to also add a new proxy instance creation to the ConnectorFactory class, as shown in Listing 10.9.

LISTING 10.9 ConnectorFactory.java (SOAP Connector)

```java
// Modify the existing ConnectorFactory.java with the
// the highlighted changes below...


public static RemoteMBeanServer createConnector(String transport,
    Properties props)  throws ConnectorException {

  if (transport.equalsIgnoreCase("RMI")) {
    try {
      return (RemoteMBeanServer)Proxy.newProxyInstance(
          Thread.currentThread().getContextClassLoader(),
          new Class[] { RemoteMBeanServer.class },
          new RMIInvocationHandler(props)
      );
    }
    catch (Exception e) {
      throw new ConnectorException(
          "Unable to create proxy.", e
      );
    }
  }

  else if (transport.equalsIgnoreCase("SOAP")) {
    try {
      return (RemoteMBeanServer)Proxy.newProxyInstance(
          Thread.currentThread().getContextClassLoader(),
          new Class[] { RemoteMBeanServer.class },
          new SOAPInvocationHandler(props)
      );
    }
    catch (Exception e) {
      throw new ConnectorException(
          "Unable to create proxy.", e
      );
    }
  }

  throw new ConnectorException(
      "Unrecognized connector transport: " + transport
  );
}
```

Also, to register the SOAP connector as an MBean, you will need to declare a management interface for it. An XML declaration for the XMBean is shown in the `SOAPConnector.xml` file in Listing 10.10. Again, notice that the DTD is pointing to a file in the local file system. You may need to modify the second line to point to where you have placed your DTD.

LISTING 10.10 SOAPConnector.xml

```xml
<?xml version="1.0" encoding="UTF-8"?>
<!DOCTYPE mbean SYSTEM "file:/C:/Examples/xmbean.dtd">

<mbean>

  <attribute getMethod="getExportProperties"
             currencyTimeLimit="-1">
    <name>ExportProperties</name>
    <type>java.util.Properties</type>
    <access>read-only</access>
  </attribute>

  <operation>
    <name>start</name>
    <parameter>
      <name>AgentID</name>
      <type>java.lang.String</type>
    </parameter>
  </operation>

  <operation>
    <name>getExportProperties</name>
    <return-type>java.util.Properties</return-type>
  </operation>

</mbean>
```

To compile the SOAP connector classes, execute the following command:

```
C:\Examples> javac -d . -classpath .;electric\lib\GLUE-STD.jar;
➥jmx-1_0_1-ri_bin\jmx\lib\jmxri.jar
➥SOAPInvocationHandler.java SOAPConnector.java SOAPConnectorConstants.java
➥MethodInvocation.java MBeanServerInvoker.java
➥ConnectorFactory.java ConnectorException.java
```

Next, you will see how to use the SOAP connector with the export manager to look up and invoke a remote JMX agent.

SOAP Example

The following example will show you how to use the SOAP connector from an external JVM or from a remote host to find the location of an agent and invoke the methods of the MBean server.

The example consists of three parts:

- An agent implementation
- A client implementation
- A name server.

The agent implementation will contain two MBeans—one for the export manager implementation and another for the SOAP connector server. The client will look up the agent from the name server by using a logical name with the help of the modified `ConnectorFactory` you saw in Listing 10.9. The name server implementation will be provided by the JBoss server. The components of the example are shown in Figure 10.4.

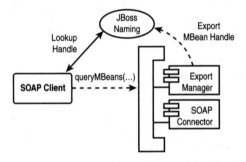

FIGURE 10.4

Components of the SOAP example.

The agent registers two Model MBeans—one for the SOAP connector and another for the export manager. The management interfaces for each are described in Listings 10.5 and 10.10. When the `start()` operation is invoked on the SOAP connector, it will start the HTTP server and register a WSDL description of the `MBeanServerInvoker` interface to the Web server. After that happens, the `start()` operation on the export manager will discover the SOAP connector registered at the `Connector` domain and query it for the `ExportProperties` attribute. With the `export()` operation, the agent binds a handle under name `MyAgent` to the naming service that contains the required connection properties for the client-side connection factory to build a SOAP connection to the server.

The source for the `ExportAgent` class is shown in Listing 10.11.

LISTING 10.11   ExportAgent.java

```java
package book.jmx.examples;

import javax.management.*;
import javax.management.modelmbean.*;
import java.rmi.*;
import java.rmi.registry.*;

public class ExportAgent {

  final static String SERVER_DELEGATE =
      "JMImplementation:type=MBeanServerDelegate";
  final static String AGENT_ID =
      "MBeanServerId";
  final static String XMBEAN =
      "book.jmx.examples.XMBean";
  final static String[] XMBEAN_CONSTRUCTOR_SIGNATURE =
      { String.class.getName(), String.class.getName() };

  public static void main(String[] args) {

    try {
      MBeanServer server = MBeanServerFactory.createMBeanServer();
      String agentID = (String)server.getAttribute(
          new ObjectName(SERVER_DELEGATE), AGENT_ID
      );

      ObjectName exportManager =
          new ObjectName("Service:name=ExportManager");
      ObjectName soapConnector =
          new ObjectName("Connector:transport=SOAP");

      server.createMBean(XMBEAN, soapConnector,
          new Object[] {
              "file:/C:/Examples/SOAPConnector.xml",
              "book.jmx.examples.SOAPConnector" },
          XMBEAN_CONSTRUCTOR_SIGNATURE
      );

      server.createMBean(XMBEAN, exportManager,
          new Object[] {
              "file:/C:/Examples/ExportManager.xml",
              "book.jmx.examples.ExportManager" },
          XMBEAN_CONSTRUCTOR_SIGNATURE
      );
```

10

JMX DISTRIBUTION
LAYER WITH J2EE
SERVICES

LISTING 10.11   Continued

```
            server.invoke(soapConnector, "start",
                new Object[] { agentID },
                new String[] { String.class.getName() }
            );

            server.invoke(exportManager, "start",
                new Object[] { agentID },
                new String[] { String.class.getName() }
            );

            server.invoke(exportManager, "export",
                new Object[] { "MyAgent" },
                new String[] { String.class.getName() }
            );
        }
        catch (RuntimeMBeanException e) {
          e.getTargetException().printStackTrace();
        }
        catch (MBeanRegistrationException e) {
          e.getTargetException().printStackTrace();
        }
        catch (RuntimeErrorException e) {
          e.getTargetError().printStackTrace();
        }
        catch (ReflectionException e) {
          e.getTargetException().printStackTrace();
        }
        catch (MBeanException e) {
          e.getTargetException().printStackTrace();
        }
        catch (Exception e) {
          e.printStackTrace();
        }
      }
    }
}
```

The client code is shown in Listing 10.12. It requests the connection factory for a connector implementation with the "SOAP" identifier and requests a handle bound to the "MyAgent" name. It then executes a simple query for all MBean names in the agent.

LISTING 10.12   SOAPClient.java

```java
package book.jmx.examples;

import java.util.*;

public class SOAPClient {

  public static void main(String[] args) {

    RemoteMBeanServer server = null;

    try {
      // Lookup and connect to "MyAgent"
      server = ConnectorFactory.createConnector("SOAP", "MyAgent");

      // invoke queryNames on the remote mbean server
      Iterator it = server.queryNames(null, null).iterator();

      while(it.hasNext())
        System.out.println(it.next());
    }
    catch (ConnectorException e) {
      e.printStackTrace();
    }
  }
}
```

To compile and run the example, first start the JBoss server. This is required for the naming service. The JBoss server can be started with the run.bat or run.sh scripts in its bin directory (JBoss-2.4.1\bin). See Appendix A for more detailed instructions for setup.

```
C:\Examples> cd JBoss-2.4.1\bin
```

```
C:\Examples\JBoss-2.4.1\bin> run
```

When the server starts, you will see a long list of services being started. You will later make use of some of them, mostly the Java Message Service, but for now, all you need is the naming service.

When the JBoss server has started, you will see a line similar to the following printed on the console.

```
[Default] JBoss 2.4.1 Started in 0m:33s
```

Next, in a different command shell, compile and start the ExportAgent application. It will start the GLUE HTTP server and bind a "MyAgent" reference to the name server. For the initial naming context lookup to work, a file called jndi.properties must be located in the classpath (shown in Listing 10.13)

LISTING 10.13 jndi.properties

```
java.naming.factory.initial=org.jnp.interfaces.NamingContextFactory
java.naming.factory.url.pkgs=org.jboss.naming:org.jnp.interfaces
java.naming.provider.url=localhost:1099
```

Save the jndi.properties to your working directory (C:\Examples in the context of this example) and execute the following two commands:

```
C:\Examples> javac -d . -classpath jmx-1_0_1-ri_bin\jmx\lib\jmxri.jar
➥ExportAgent.javaExportManager.java MBeanHandleImpl.java MBeanHandle.java
C:\Examples> java -classpath .;jmx-1_0_1-ri_bin\jmx\lib\jmxri.jar;
➥electric\lib\GLUE-STD.jar;electric\lib\servlet.jar;
➥electric\lib\jnet.jar;xmbean.jar;
➥jdom-b7\lib\xerces.jar;
➥jdom-b7\build\jdom.jar;JBoss-2.4.1\client\jnp-client.jar
➥book.jmx.examples.ExportAgent
```

The libraries GLUE-STD.jar, servlet.jar, and jnet.jar under the electric directory are required by the GLUE SOAP implementation. The xmbean.jar is the packaged XMBean implementation from Chapter 8, "XMBean: Model MBean Implementation," and requires the jdom.jar (JDOM API) and the xerces.jar for XML parsing. Finally, the jnp-client.jar is required from the JBoss client directory to interact with the JBoss naming service.

After you add all of the previously mentioned libraries successfully and get your export agent application started, you should see the following line printed on your console window:

```
GLUE 1.2 (c) 2001 The Mind Electric
startup server on http://192.168.0.3:8085/jmx
```

You can also confirm that the handle can be found from the JBoss naming service. Point your browser to http://localhost:8082 and you will see the HTTP adaptor view of the JBoss server. Find a JNDIView MBean (see Figure 10.5) and execute its list() operation by clicking the corresponding button. You should then be able to find the "MyAgent" reference bound to the global naming space (see Figure 10.6).

FIGURE 10.5

The JNDIView *MBean displays the contents of the JBoss Name Service.*

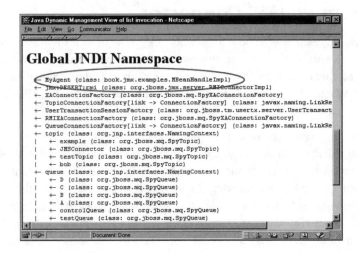

FIGURE 10.6

The global namespace should list the MBean handle for "MyAgent".

The last step is to compile and run the client code that executes the query to the MBean server. Again, to run the client the GLUE libraries are required (GLUE-STD.jar, servlet.jar, and jnet.jar) and the JBoss naming client library (jnp-client.jar and the jndi.properties file).

```
C:\Examples> javac -d . -classpath .;jmx-1_0_1-ri_bin\jmx\lib\jmxri.jar;
➥electric\lib\GLUE-STD.jar SOAPClient.javaC:\Examples> java -classpath .;
➥jmx-1_0_1-ri_bin\jmx\lib\jmxri.jar;electric\lib\GLUESTD.jar;
➥electric\lib\servlet.jar;electric\lib\jnet.jar;JBoss-2.4.1\client\
➥jnp-client.jar
➥ book.jmx.examples.SOAPClient
```

When you successfully run the client, it should print out the object names of the agent to which it connected:

```
Connector:transport=SOAP
JMImplementation:type=MBeanServerDelegate
Service:name=ExportManager
```

This output means you have successfully executed a method on the MBean server using the SOAP connector.

Next, you will look at a slightly different kind of connector that sends its MBean invocations asynchronously.

Asynchronous JMS Connector

One of the common features with both the connectors you have seen so far has been the fact that the invocation semantics have been synchronous. This means that when a method is being invoked from the client side to the MBean server, the client-side thread initiating the call sequence will block until the response from the MBean is returned by the MBean server back to the client.

Next you will see an implementation of an asynchronous connector. An asynchronous connector allows the client thread initiating the call sequence to continue to work, regardless of the network latency and execution time between the client and the MBean server. The synchronous invocation can be slowed down by the network traffic or, in the worst case, its inability to reach the remote host. The client-side thread initiating the invocation is blocked until the invocation is returned, or the invocation times out because either the host was unreachable, or the return value did not arrive in time. It may also be the case that the invocation starts a resource-intensive task on the server side and can take a long time to finish before any return value can be delivered back to the client.

The asynchronous connector resolves the aforementioned issues by not requiring the client to block on the method invocation. The timeout threshold for an asynchronous invocation can be set higher because the client is free to continue to work and there is no resource waste on blocked threads. It may not be relevant for the management application to know when the invocation has been received by the remote host, so there is increased tolerance for system downtime and network problems.

Messaging services are often used to implement asynchronous invocation semantics. The invocation is abstracted as a message and left to be delivered by a message service that implements asynchronous delivery. The receiver of the message can optionally send another message back to the caller to indicate it has received the message or to deliver possible return values. If the client side implements a callback mechanism, the message service can deliver the receipt or a return value when it is available to the caller.

The J2EE platform provides a Java Message Service (JMS) that you can use for asynchronous messaging. The next connector implementation, to implement an asynchronous connector, is based on the JMS.

Design of the JMS Connector

The asynchronous JMS connector consists of the following classes and interfaces:

- `JMSInvocationHandler` class
- `JMSConnector` class
- `AsyncMBeanServer` interface
- `Callback` interface

The `JMSConnector` and `JMSInvocationHandler` classes are again the corresponding connector server and client proxy implementation classes shown in Figure 10.7. The `AsyncMBeanServer` interface is a replacement for the `RemoteMBeanServer` interface used as a façade for the proxies. The asynchronous call semantics require a slightly modified remote MBean server interface. The return values are now replaced with `Callback` instances instead of the actual return types. Changing the interface exposed to the client is quite easy because all you need to do is to provide a different class instance to the `java.reflect.Proxy` instance. Other than the changed return values, the `AsyncMBeanServer` is an exact copy of the `RemoteMBeanServer` interface.

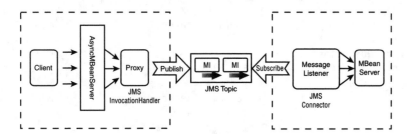

FIGURE 10.7

The JMS connector requires a `JMSInvocationHandler` *proxy implementation, JMS connector server, and a modified interface façade for the client.*

You will also modify the `ConnectorFactory` class to add factory methods for a JMS connector. Additionally, you will define the management interface of the `JMSConnector` in an XML file conforming to the `XMBean` DTD.

Asynchronous `MBean` Server Interface

The asynchronous MBean server interface shown in Listing 10.13 replaces all the method return types with a `Callback` interface. The returned `Callback` instances from all the methods can be queried for the return values at any time. Consequently, the client thread is not required to block on the MBean server invocation to receive the return value.

LISTING 10.13   AsyncMBeanServer.java

```
package book.jmx.examples;

import javax.management.*;

public interface AsyncMBeanServer {

  /* returns ObjectInstance */
  public Callback createMBean(String className,
                             ObjectName name);

  /* returns ObjectInstance */
  public Callback createMBean(String className,
                             ObjectName name,
                             ObjectName loaderName);

  /* return ObjectInstance */
  public Callback createMBean(String className,
                             ObjectName name,
                             Object[] params,
                             String[] signature);

  /* returns ObjectInstance */
  public Callback createMBean(String className,
                             ObjectName name,
                             ObjectName loaderName,
                             Object[] params,
                             String[] signature);

  public void unregisterMBean(ObjectName name);

  /* returns ObjectInstance */
  public Callback getObjectInstance(ObjectName name);
```

LISTING 10.13 Continued

```
/* returns boolean */
public Callback isRegistered(ObjectName name);


/* returns Integer */
public Callback getMBeanCount();


/* returns Object */
public Callback getAttribute(ObjectName name,
                             String attribute);


/* returns AttributeList */
public Callback getAttributes(ObjectName name,
                              String[] attributes);


public void setAttribute(ObjectName name,
                         Attribute attribute);


/* returns AttributeList */
public Callback setAttributes(ObjectName name,
                              AttributeList attributes);


/* returns Object */
public Callback invoke(ObjectName name,
                       String operationName,
                       Object[] params,
                       String[] signature);


/* returns String */
public Callback getDefaultDomain();


public void addNotificationListener(
                 ObjectName name,
                 NotificationListener listener,
                 NotificationFilter filter,
                 Object handback);


public void addNotificationListener(
                 ObjectName name,
                 ObjectName listener,
                 NotificationFilter filter,
                 Object handback);


public void removeNotificationListener(
                 ObjectName name,
                 NotificationListener listener);
```

LISTING **10.13**   Continued

```
public void removeNotificationListener(
                          ObjectName name,
                          ObjectName listener);

/* returns MBeanInfo */
public Callback getMBeanInfo(ObjectName name);

/* returns boolean */
public Callback isInstanceOf(ObjectName name,
                             String className);

/* returns Set */
public Callback queryMBeans(ObjectName name, QueryExp query);

/* returns Set */
public Callback queryNames(ObjectName name, QueryExp query);

public void close();


}
```

Callback Interface

The Callback implementation is created on the client-side proxy of the connector when the message that contains the invocation has been left for the JMS to deliver. The Callback is returned to the client immediately and the client is free to handle the Callback instances as it sees fit. The client may not use them at all or it can store them for later use.

Because you cannot determine beforehand when the return value from the asynchronous invocation is received, the Callback interface declares two methods that allows you to investigate the state of the invocation—peek() and get().

The peek() method allows you to check the Callback object to see whether the return value has been received. The important thing to notice with the peek() method implementation is that it returns the state of the invocation immediately and does not block to wait for a return value in case one has not arrived yet. Therefore, the peek() method should be used when the client wants to store the Callback instance, and periodically check whether or not the JMX invocation has been executed and if the return value has been received.

The get() method allows you to retrieve the return value when it has arrived. The get() method *does* block if the return value has not been received yet. This behavior has two implications to the client using the connector. First, to continue the execution of the thread without blocking, the client should always check the Callback with peek() before invoking get() to retrieve the value.

Second, if the client thread needs to retrieve the value of the invocation before it can continue its work, it may safely block on the get() method to guarantee the thread execution will not proceed until the remote invocation has returned. In essence, calling the get() method immediately on the Callback object after each invocation will give you synchronous invocation semantics at the client.

The Callback interface declaration is shown in Listing 10.14.

LISTING 10.14   Callback.java

```
package book.jmx.examples;

import java.rmi.*;
import java.io.*;

public interface Callback extends Serializable {

  int peek();

  Object get() throws RemoteException;

}
```

The concrete implementations of the Callback interface are returned by the JMS connector proxy.

ConnectorFactory

You will next modify the existing ConnectorFactory to support the new connector type. Add the factory methods to create the JMS connector proxies based on an explicitly passed properties and a factory method that accepts the JNDI reference to an MBeanHandle object.

The modified implementation of the ConnectorFactory class is shown in Listing 10.15.

LISTING 10.15   ConnectorFactory.java

```
package book.jmx.examples;

import java.util.*;
import java.lang.reflect.*;
import java.rmi.*;

import javax.naming.*;
import javax.jms.*;
```

LISTING 10.15   Continued

```java
public class ConnectorFactory  {

  public static RemoteMBeanServer createConnector(String transport,
      String jndiName) throws ConnectorException {

    Context ctx = null;
    MBeanHandle handle = null;

    try {
      ctx = new InitialContext();

      handle = (MBeanHandle)ctx.lookup(jndiName);
    }
    catch (NamingException e) {
      throw new ConnectorException(
        "Unable to find the handle", e
      );
    }

    return createConnector(transport, handle.getProperties());
  }

  public static RemoteMBeanServer createConnector(String transport,
      Properties props)  throws ConnectorException {

    if (transport.equalsIgnoreCase("RMI")) {
      try {
        return (RemoteMBeanServer)Proxy.newProxyInstance(
            Thread.currentThread().getContextClassLoader(),
            new Class[] { RemoteMBeanServer.class },
            new RMIInvocationHandler(props)
        );
      }
      catch (Exception e) {
        throw new ConnectorException(
            "Unable to create proxy.", e
        );
      }
    }

    else if (transport.equalsIgnoreCase("SOAP")) {
      try {
        return (RemoteMBeanServer)Proxy.newProxyInstance(
            Thread.currentThread().getContextClassLoader(),
```

LISTING 10.15 Continued

```
                new Class[] { RemoteMBeanServer.class },
                new SOAPInvocationHandler(props)
        );
    }
    catch (Exception e) {
      throw new ConnectorException(
          "Unable to create proxy.", e
      );
    }
  }

  throw new ConnectorException(
      "Unrecognized connector transport: " + transport
  );
}


public static AsyncMBeanServer createAsyncConnector(
    String transport, String jndiName) throws ConnectorException {

  try {
    Context ctx = new InitialContext();

    MBeanHandle handle = (MBeanHandle)ctx.lookup(jndiName);

    return createAsyncConnector(transport, handle.getProperties());
  }
  catch (NamingException e) {
    throw new ConnectorException(
        "Error connecting to Naming Service.", e
    );
  }

}

public static AsyncMBeanServer createAsyncConnector(
    String transport, Properties props) throws ConnectorException {

  if (transport.equalsIgnoreCase("jms")) {
    try {
      return (AsyncMBeanServer)Proxy.newProxyInstance(
          Thread.currentThread().getContextClassLoader(),
          new Class[] { AsyncMBeanServer.class },
          new JMSInvocationHandler(props)
```

LISTING 10.15 Continued

```
        );
    }
    catch (JMSException e) {
      throw new ConnectorException(
          "Error connecting to Java Message Service", e
      );
    }
    catch (NamingException e) {
      throw new ConnectorException(
          "Error connecting to Naming Service", e
      );
    }
  }

  throw new ConnectorException("Unknown transport " +
      transport);

  }
}
```

The JMS connector proxy requires its own InvocationHandler implementation. The JMSInvocationHandler class will transform all invocations to JMS messages and then publish them to the given message topic. It will also subscribe to the topic to receive the messages containing the return values that are sent back from the remote agent. The JMSInvocationHandler implementation is shown in Listing 10.16.

In the JMSInvocationHandler constructor, the connection to a JMS topic is created using the connection properties from the MBean handle. The JMSInvocationHandler will act as a publisher of messages that contain the invocation and as a subscriber to messages that contain the return values of the invocations. The invocation messages are matched to the return values with a messageID counter.

Just as with the RemoteMBeanServer interface, all the invocations that are made to the AsyncMBeanServer interface are delegated to the invoke() method of the JMSInvocationHandler instance. The change of the interface does not require any other changes to the way you implement the connector. Just remember to return the correct runtime types from the invoke() operation. In the invoke() implementation, the MethodInvocation is attached as the payload of the message that is published to the topic. The MethodInvocation object contains all the required information for the receiving connector MBean on the remote agent to invoke the corresponding management operation on the target MBean server.

With each published invocation a JMSCallback instance is created. This Callback object is matched with the messageID of the published message. When the onMessage() method of the JMSInvocationHandler receives a reply from the remote agent, it looks up the corresponding Callback object from callbackBuffer and sets its return value. At the same time, the Callback object notifies all threads that may be waiting on its get() method.

LISTING 10.16   JMSInvocationHandler.java

```
package book.jmx.examples;

import java.util.*;
import java.lang.reflect.*;
import java.rmi.*;
import javax.jms.*;
import javax.naming.*;
import javax.management.*;

public class JMSInvocationHandler
    implements MessageListener, InvocationHandler, JMSConnectorConstants {

  // JMS Topic
  private Topic topic              = null;
  private TopicConnection con      = null;
  private TopicSession session     = null;
  private TopicPublisher publisher = null;
  private TopicSubscriber subscriber = null;
  private Context ctx              = null;

  // keeps track of the message IDs
  static long messageID = 1;

  // Stores the references to the callback objects. When a reply
  // matching to the ID is received the return value is inserted
  // to the callback instance and any threads waiting on it will
  // be notified.
  private Map callbackBuffer =
      Collections.synchronizedMap(new HashMap());


  // constructor
  public JMSInvocationHandler(Properties props)
      throws NamingException, JMSException {

    // retrieve connection properties
    String conFactory =
        props.getProperty(JMS_TOPIC_CONNECTION_FACTORY);
```

LISTING 10.16 Continued

```
String topicName =
    props.getProperty(JMS_TOPIC);

// lookup connection factory and create topic connection
// and topic session
ctx = new InitialContext();
TopicConnectionFactory factory =
    (TopicConnectionFactory)ctx.lookup(conFactory);

con = factory.createTopicConnection();

session = con.createTopicSession(
    false,        /* not a transacted session */
    Session.AUTO_ACKNOWLEDGE
);

// Proxy acts as a publisher of invocations and subscribes
// for reply messages
topic = (Topic)ctx.lookup(topicName);
publisher   = session.createPublisher(topic);
subscriber  = session.createSubscriber(topic, "JMSType='REPLY'", true);

// topic is non persistent.
publisher.setDeliveryMode(DeliveryMode.NON_PERSISTENT);
publisher.setDisableMessageTimestamp(true);
subscriber.setMessageListener(this);

con.start();
}


public Object invoke(Object proxy, Method method,
                     Object[] args) throws Throwable {

// initialize MethodInvocation
String methodName   = method.getName();
MethodInvocation mi = new MethodInvocation(method);
mi.setParams(args);

// create message ID and callback object.
// Map ID to callback in callbackBuffer.
String ID           = "" + messageID++;
Callback cb         = new JMSCallback(ID, mi);
callbackBuffer.put(ID, cb);
```

LISTING 10.16   Continued

```
    // wrap MethodInvocation in JMS Object message
    ObjectMessage msg   = session.createObjectMessage(mi);
    msg.setJMSType("SEND");
    msg.setStringProperty("ID", ID);

    if (methodName.equals("close")) {
      close();
      return null;
    }

    // send
    publisher.publish(msg);
    return cb;
  }

  private void close() {
    try {
      con.close();
    }
    catch (JMSException e) {
      e.printStackTrace();
    }
  }


  // subscriber for reply messages

  public void onMessage(Message message) {

    try {
      // extract the MethodInvocation and message ID
      ObjectMessage msg   = (ObjectMessage)message;
      MethodInvocation mi = (MethodInvocation)msg.getObject();
      String ID           = msg.getStringProperty("ID");

      // find the corresponding callback object (ID is the key)
      JMSCallback cb       = (JMSCallback)callbackBuffer.get(ID);
// JPL: REMOVE FROM QUEUE!

      // setMI() implementation in JMS Callback will set the
      // return value and notify all waiting threads
      cb.setMethodInvocation(mi);
```

Listing 10.16   Continued

```
    }
    catch (JMSException e) {
      e.printStackTrace();
    }
  }


  // JMS callback implementation

  class JMSCallback implements Callback {

    private int status          = UNKNOWN;
    private String ID           = null;
    private MethodInvocation mi = null;


    JMSCallback(String ID, MethodInvocation mi) {

      status = SENDING;

      this.ID = ID;
      this.mi = mi;
    }

    // notifies all threads that the answer has arrived
    protected void setMethodInvocation(MethodInvocation mi) {
      synchronized (this) {
        this.mi = mi;
        status = FINISHED;

        notifyAll();
      }
    }

    // returns status, won't block
    public int peek() {
      return status;
    }

    // blocks on status -- status set to FINISHED after
    // return value has been set and before threads are
    // notified.
    public Object get() throws RemoteException {
```

LISTING 10.16 Continued

```java
    synchronized (this) {
      while (status != FINISHED) {
        try {
            wait();
        }
        catch (InterruptedException e) {}
      }
    }

    // if an exception was thrown, wrap it in RemoteExc.
    // and throw to the client
    if (mi.getStatus() == MethodInvocation.ERROR) {
      Throwable t = (Throwable)mi.getReturnValue();

      if (t instanceof RuntimeMBeanException) {
        RuntimeMBeanException e = (RuntimeMBeanException)t;
        throw new RemoteException(e.getMessage(), e.getTargetException());
      }

      throw new RemoteException("", (Throwable)mi.getReturnValue());
    }

    // return value
    return mi.getReturnValue();
  }
}

}
```

LISTING 10.17 JMSConnectorConstants.java

```java
package book.jmx.examples;

public interface JMSConnectorConstants {

  final static String JMS_TOPIC  =
      "jms.topic";
  final static String JMS_TOPIC_CONNECTION_FACTORY =
      "jms.topic.connection.factory";


  final static int UNKNOWN  = -999;
  final static int SENDING  = 1000;
  final static int FINISHED = 1;
}
```

JMSConnector

The JMSConnector is both a subscriber and publisher to the JMS topic, just like the JMSInvocationHandler is on the client side. The onMessage() method receives the messages from the JMS topic and extracts the MethodInvocation object. The JMSConnector then sets the agent reference to the MethodInvocation object before calling its invoke() method. The MethodInvocation handles the invocation and stores the return value or a possible exception.

The source for the JMSConnector is shown in Listing 10.18. The start() method looks up the JMS connection factory and topic and creates the subscriber listener before starting the connection. The getExportProperties() method returns the connection factory and topic JNDI names to the export manager when it queries for the connection properties.

The ConnectorListener inner class creates a publisher for the return messages for JMS invocations. The return messages have a matching ID value that the JMSInvocationHandler on the client side has set and uses to find the corresponding Callback object. Also, the returned message contains the complete MethodInvocation instance this time. Although this adds to the message size somewhat, it can be a useful mechanism for sending additional information about the invocation back to the client. If you recall from Chapter 9, the MethodInvocation object can carry any context information with it. Some of the context information, such as measurement data or an invocation trace, can be useful to be sent back to the client. This can be easily achieved by returning the MethodInvocation object itself. Asynchronous calls are convenient for gathering such data and the additional overhead in message size is less of a factor compared to synchronous calls.

LISTING 10.18 JMSConnector.java

```
package book.jmx.examples;

import java.io.*;
import java.util.*;
import javax.management.*;
import javax.jms.*;
import javax.naming.*;


public class JMSConnector implements JMSConnectorConstants {

    // JMS topic
    private TopicConnection connection = null;
    private TopicSubscriber subscriber = null;
    private Topic topic              = null;
```

LISTING 10.18 Continued

```java
// JNDI names for connection factory and topic
private String connFactory = "TopicConnectionFactory";
private String topicName   = "topic/JMSConnector";


// reference to the target MBean server
private MBeanServer server = null;


// constructor
public JMSConnector() { }


public void start(String agentID) throws NamingException, JMSException {

  server = (MBeanServer)MBeanServerFactory
      .findMBeanServer(agentID).get(0);

  // lookup topic and create topic connection
  InitialContext ctx = new InitialContext();
  TopicConnectionFactory fact =
      (TopicConnectionFactory)ctx.lookup(connFactory);
  topic = (Topic)ctx.lookup(topicName);
  connection = fact.createTopicConnection();

  // subscribe to invocation messages
  TopicSession session = connection.createTopicSession(
      false, Session.AUTO_ACKNOWLEDGE);
  subscriber  = session.createSubscriber(topic, "JMSType='SEND'", true);
  subscriber.setMessageListener(new ConnectorListener());

  connection.start();
}

/* Export Manager */
public Properties getExportProperties() {
  Properties props = new Properties();
  props.put(JMS_TOPIC_CONNECTION_FACTORY, connFactory);
  props.put(JMS_TOPIC, topicName);

  return props;
}


// message listener for invocations
```

LISTING 10.18   Continued

```
class ConnectorListener implements MessageListener {

    TopicSession session     = null;
    TopicPublisher publisher = null;


    // constructor

    ConnectorListener() throws JMSException {
      // create a publisher session for return values
      session   = connection.createTopicSession(false,
Session.AUTO_ACKNOWLEDGE);
      publisher = session.createPublisher(topic);

      publisher.setDeliveryMode(DeliveryMode.NON_PERSISTENT);
      publisher.setDisableMessageTimestamp(true);
    }


    // onMessage invoke when a message arrives
    public void onMessage(Message message) {

      try {

        // extract MethodInvocation and message ID
        ObjectMessage msg     = (ObjectMessage)message;
        MethodInvocation mi = (MethodInvocation)msg.getObject();
        String ID             = msg.getStringProperty("ID");

        // set the target mbean server reference and invoke the method
        mi.setMBeanServer(server);
        mi.invoke();

        // Wrap the invoked MI as JMS object message and send it back.
        // The MI will contain the return value. Attach the same ID
        // to the return message.
        ObjectMessage reply = session.createObjectMessage(mi);
        reply.setJMSType("REPLY");
        reply.setStringProperty("ID", ID);

        // send message
        publisher.publish(reply);
```

LISTING 10.18 Continued

```
      } catch (JMSException e) {
          e.printStackTrace();
      }
    }
  }
}
```

The JMSConnector requires a management interface as well so it can be registered to the MBean server. Listing 10.19 shows a declaration of a management interface using the XMBean DTD.

LISTING 10.19 JMSConnector.xml

```xml
<?xml version="1.0" encoding="UTF-8"?>
<!DOCTYPE mbean SYSTEM "file:/C:/Examples/xmbean.dtd">

<mbean>

  <attribute getMethod="getExportProperties"
             currencyTimeLimit="-1">
    <name>ExportProperties</name>
    <type>java.util.Properties</type>
    <access>read-only</access>
  </attribute>

  <operation>
    <name>start</name>
    <parameter>
      <name>AgentID</name>
      <type>java.lang.String</type>
    </parameter>
  </operation>

  <operation>
    <name>getExportProperties</name>
    <return-type>java.util.Properties</return-type>
  </operation>

</mbean>
```

JMS Connector Example

To build a test application for the JMS connector, you can reuse the ExportAgent class you wrote for the SOAP connector earlier in this chapter. Register an additional connector server MBean, JMSConnector, to the agent and start the connector server. The modified application code is shown in Listing 10.20.

LISTING 10.20   ExportAgent.java

```java
package book.jmx.examples;

import javax.management.*;
import javax.management.modelmbean.*;
import java.rmi.*;
import java.rmi.registry.*;

public class ExportAgent {

  final static String SERVER_DELEGATE =
      "JMImplementation:type=MBeanServerDelegate";
  final static String AGENT_ID =
      "MBeanServerId";
  final static String XMBEAN =
      "book.jmx.examples.XMBean";
  final static String[] XMBEAN_CONSTRUCTOR_SIGNATURE =
      { String.class.getName(), String.class.getName() };

  public static void main(String[] args) {

    try {
      MBeanServer server = MBeanServerFactory.createMBeanServer();
      String agentID = (String)server.getAttribute(
          new ObjectName(SERVER_DELEGATE), AGENT_ID
      );

      ObjectName exportManager =
          new ObjectName("Service:name=ExportManager");
      ObjectName soapConnector =
          new ObjectName("Connector:transport=SOAP");
      ObjectName jmsConnector =
          new ObjectName("Connector:transport=JMS");

      server.createMBean(XMBEAN, soapConnector,
          new Object[] {
              "file:/C:/Examples/SOAPConnector.xml",
```

LISTING 10.20   Continued

```
            "book.jmx.examples.SOAPConnector" },
        XMBEAN_CONSTRUCTOR_SIGNATURE
    );

    server.createMBean(XMBEAN, jmsConnector,
        new Object[] {
            "file:/C:/Examples/JMSConnector.xml",
            "book.jmx.examples.JMSConnector" },
        XMBEAN_CONSTRUCTOR_SIGNATURE
    );

    server.createMBean(XMBEAN, exportManager,
        new Object[] {
            "file:/C:/Examples/ExportManager.xml",
            "book.jmx.examples.ExportManager" },
        XMBEAN_CONSTRUCTOR_SIGNATURE
    );

    server.invoke(soapConnector, "start",
        new Object[] { agentID },
        new String[] { String.class.getName() }
    );

    server.invoke(jmsConnector, "start",
        new Object[] { agentID },
        new String[] { String.class.getName() }
    );

    server.invoke(exportManager, "start",
        new Object[] { agentID },
        new String[] { String.class.getName() }
    );

    server.invoke(exportManager, "export",
        new Object[] { "MyAgent" },
        new String[] { String.class.getName() }
    );
}
catch (RuntimeMBeanException e) {
    e.getTargetException().printStackTrace();
}
catch (MBeanRegistrationException e) {
    e.getTargetException().printStackTrace();
}
```

LISTING 10.20   Continued

```
    catch (RuntimeErrorException e) {
      e.getTargetError().printStackTrace();
    }
    catch (ReflectionException e) {
      e.getTargetException().printStackTrace();
    }
    catch (MBeanException e) {
      e.getTargetException().printStackTrace();
    }
    catch (Exception e) {
      e.printStackTrace();
    }
  }
}
```

You can then run a little example to see if the JMS connector works. First, make sure that the JBoss server has a topic JMSConnector configured in the JBoss-2.4.1/conf/default/ jboss.jcml configuration file. For details where to find this entry and how to set up the JMS topic, see Appendix A.

Compile the JMS connector classes:

```
C:\Examples> javac -d . -classpath .;jmx-1_0_1-ri_bin\jmx\lib\jmxri.jar;
➥JBoss-2.4.1\client\jboss-j2ee.jar;electric\lib\GLUE-STD.jar JMSConnector.java
➥ JMSConnectorConstants.java JMSInvocationHandler.java ConnectorFactory.java
➥ ConnectorException.java AsyncMBeanServer.java Callback.java ExportAgent.java
```

Notice that to run the ExportAgent application that uses JBossMQ (JBoss JMS implementation), you will need to add the classes from the JBoss-2.4.1\client directory to your classpath. Libraries jboss-j2ee.jar, jbossmq-client.jar, log4j.jar, and jta-spec1_0_1.jar are required in addition to the classes shown in the SOAP example.

Listing 10.21 shows how to create a client with both a synchronous SOAP connector and an asynchronous JMS connector. It creates a User MBean (from Chapter 3, "Standard MBeans") and invokes a setAttribute() method in a loop of 5,000 times for each connector. The asynchronous JMS connector thread should finish quite a bit before the synchronous SOAP connector thread. The JMS connector is finished as soon as it has published the messages to the JMS topic. After that, the workload is moved to the JMS implementation to handle the delivery of the messages.

LISTING 10.21   ConnectorClient.java

```java
package book.jmx.examples;

import java.util.*;
import javax.management.*;

public class ConnectorClient {

  public static void main(String[] args) {


    try {
      final ObjectName user = new ObjectName("test:name=user");

      final AsyncMBeanServer aServer =
          ConnectorFactory.createAsyncConnector("JMS", "MyAgent");
      final RemoteMBeanServer rServer =
          ConnectorFactory.createConnector("SOAP", "MyAgent");

      rServer.createMBean("book.jmx.examples.User", user);

      Thread jms = new Thread(new Runnable() {

        Attribute attr = new Attribute("Name", "Testing...");

        public void run() {
          try {
            System.out.println("JMS Started.");

            for (int i = 0; i < 5000; ++i)
              aServer.setAttribute(user, attr);

            System.out.println("JMS Ended.");
          }
          catch (Exception e) {
            e.printStackTrace();
          }
        }
      });

      Thread soap = new Thread(new Runnable() {

        Attribute attr = new Attribute("Name", "Testing...");
```

LISTING 10.21   Continued

```
        public void run() {
          try {
            System.out.println("SOAP Started.");

            for (int i = 0; i < 5000; ++i)
              rServer.setAttribute(user, attr);

            System.out.println("SOAP Ended.");
          }
          catch (Exception e) {
            e.printStackTrace();
          }
        }
      });

      soap.start();
      jms.start();
    }
    catch (ConnectorException e) {
      e.getTargetException().printStackTrace();
    }
    catch (JMException e) {
      e.printStackTrace();
    }
  }
}
```

Summary

This chapter covered some slightly more advanced implementations of how to connect and
communicate with remote JMX agents. It provided examples of bare-bones implementations
of two new connectors—a synchronous SOAP connector and an asynchronous JMS connector.
You also saw how to use the Java Naming service to locate your JMX agents and MBeans.
These implementations can be used as a base for more robust and advanced connectors.
However, you can take a little breather from all the coding now as you move on to the next
chapters that discuss how the future of JMX and J2EE management looks. Also discussed are
the JBoss server and how JMX has been used in a state-of-the-art application server.

JMX for the Administrator

IN THIS CHAPTER

For many network administrators, daily activities involve managing a wide variety of hardware devices. An enterprise setting requires the routers, gateways, bridges, and network servers to be managed and be manageable. For network administration, the Simple Network Management Protocol (SNMP) has emerged and established itself as the de facto management protocol. Because service-based architectures, such as J2EE, become more common in these same enterprise environments, a need to manage large software systems has become apparent.

You saw earlier in this book how JMX enables you to manage software components and applications locally as well as remotely. However, the requirements of large software installments, where several dozen or even hundreds of servers, JVMs, and MBean servers are involved, have not been addressed. The efforts to find a uniform way of managing such large systems are the focus in this chapter.

In comparison to the number of devices the network administrator has to manage, the number of software components can become considerably larger. For such systems to be manageable, you need to find ways to present the management information to the administrator in a model that allows him or her to filter and categorize the management information.

Management of Server Farms

The JMX specification itself does not define a management model for large systems, such as those previously described. Issues, such as MBean server federation or management of clustered servers, are not addressed as part of the specification. However, a Java Specification Request has been created for defining a management model for the J2EE platform. The expert group working on this specification, JSR-77, aims to define a management model for large installments of J2EE servers. The specification request reached a public review status in the of Fall 2001 and, hopefully, by the time you are reading, it has reached the final status.

In the second part of this chapter, you will go through what the JSR-77 expert group has specified at this stage of the process. It should give you a good idea regarding how the expert group sees the management of the potentially complex, service-based J2EE platform.

Federation of Servers

As was mentioned, the JMX specification does not have any notion of a set of computers or a set of software components that are distributed across several JVMs. If a management client needs to manipulate several resources that are all distributed across different physical nodes and MBean servers, you need to individually connect to all the relevant servers from the management client. This complicates the implementation of the client, because it has to deal with the complexity of communicating to several MBean servers at the same time.

What would be more desirable from the management client's point of view would be the ability to have one common logical view of the entire distributed system (see Figure 11.1). This would allow the client to deal with one connection and MBean server only and keep the implementation simpler at the management client. On the server side, the added complexity of a distributed environment can be handled transparently to the client application. A single MBean server would be able to service all the requests of the client and forward them to the correct nodes and MBean servers that host the requested resources.

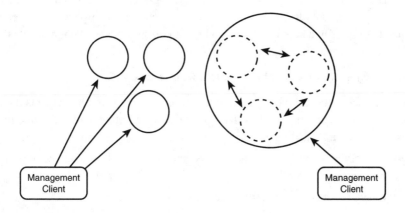

FIGURE 11.1
Management clients are simplified by providing a logical view to the group of servers.

To implement a federation between MBean servers, a simple proxy-based design can be used. You can build a common view of all distributed components of a system by having a proxy represent each component. The proxies can then forward any requests for specific components to the server that actually hosts the required component. This enables the client to be unaware of the topology and the location of managed resources across distributed MBean servers.

The federation itself does not reduce the number of software components the administrator needs to manage. A federated management system gives a single view to the entire group of servers. In many cases, however, it would be desirable to actually lessen the number of individual manageable components. If the individual components can be represented as logical groups, it will allow management operations to be easily performed to a group of resources. For example, the administrator can target a specific group of user resources instead of executing the same management operation one-by-one on a single managed user resource.

Logical Views

To ease the task of the administrator, you need to reduce the number of components that must be managed. You can achieve this by forming groups of managed components that represent the same type of resource with identical or similar management interfaces. You can then expose the group of components to the administrator as one logical entity that the administrator can manipulate.

A group of managed resources represented as a single logical entity allows the administrator to perform group operations on them. A group can be managed in synchronization instead of as several separate units. You can build groups and hierarchies of managed components that are easily managed via simpler interfaces.

To implement the logical view, you have the following three options:

- The client management tool connects to all servers, and creates and presents the logical view to the user. This enables the client to connect to different applications/components and still provide a logical view.

- A separate server connects to all the servers, and creates and presents the logical view to the client management tool.

- A component on the cluster presents the logical view.

The first implementation is a little bit tricky, because the tool can miss a server when the client did not add all servers to the cluster. Either the client can look up all the participating servers on a JNDI-server or at least find an object delivering this information.

The second implementation does not rely on the cluster because the application or component presenting the logical view runs outside the cluster. Consequently, you can manage the cluster without having the cluster running. The downside is that when the server goes down, there is no administration anymore.

The third implementation runs inside the cluster and can also be clustered to increase the uptime of the administration as well, but the cluster has to run to be able to manage the application.

JSR-77—J2EE Management

As was mentioned at the beginning of this chapter, the JMX specification does not define the model for forming logical groups or hierarchies of managed resources. Such a model would be required for management applications to be able to discover group management information without relying on management domain specific conventions. Advanced configuration and management of software systems that involves clusters of servers and services are, therefore, left outside the scope of the JMX specification.

The J2EE specification defines a distributed, service-based platform architecture. However, as far as management of the platform goes, there has not been an effort to standardize the management architecture or model for the J2EE platform implementations so far.

In the J2EE specification, the System Administrator is mentioned as one of the platform roles, but the administration of the platform is not defined. As a result, there is no vendor-neutral J2EE system administration today. Instead, the administrators are focusing on specific implementations of the J2EE platform, because no management model that would allow all the J2EE implementations to be managed in a consistent manner exists (see Figure 11.2).

FIGURE 11.2
The JSR-77 specification will allow J2EE System Administrators to emerge.

The JSR-77 took on the task of defining a management model for the J2EE platform. The specification was created to meet the following requirements:

- Support to manage any resources defined in the J2EE specification, such as EJB-Container, Web-Container, JMS, Connector and Connection Pools (JDBC as well as EIS), and so on
- Support to deploy applications (EJBs, servlets and JSPs, Connectors)
- Support to start and stop any resources and applications at runtime
- Support to get runtime information about the performance and resources of the application server, such as memory, heap size, number of threads, size of bean pool, size of active beans, and so on
- Support for management of clustered systems

> **NOTE**
>
> At the time of this writing, the JSR-77 had just been closed for the community review but had not yet entered the public review state. You can follow the progress of each specification request at `http://www.jcp.org`.

The JSR-77 expert group created a specification for a management interface for J2EE application servers.

What then is the idea is behind JSR-77? The Java 2 Platform, Enterprise Edition Management Specification will provide server vendors and tool vendors with a standard model for managing the J2EE Platform.

In a little more in detail, the Specification proposes a standard management model for exposing and accessing the management information, operations, and parameters of the Java 2 Platform, Enterprise Edition components.

The management model will:

- Allow rapid development of management solutions for J2EE
- Provide integration with existing management systems
- Enable a single management tool to manage multiple vendor implementations of the platform
- Enable a specific implementation of a platform to use any compliant management tool

The JSR-77 specification defines a model layer (or metadata layer) defining the information layer and describing the format and semantics of the data. All models combined build up the meta model of the J2EE platform. It also describes the meta model layer (or meta-metadata layer) defining the model layer, describing the structure and semantics of the metadata. This meta model is described by the associations and cardinalities of the J2EE Management Model components.

JSR-77 does not deliver objects from the J2EE application server but instead delivers a representation of the logical view of the J2EE application server. Most parts of the specification do not talk about a particular server but of the logical view grouping all the participating servers together. You can manage one or many servers under the one logical representation. This enables the management provider to build the application accordingly because it is guaranteed that the J2EE server has to be compliant.

The specification is composed of four parts:

- Managed Objects required by the J2EE management model
- Event model required by the managed objects that emits events, whereas the implementation is optional
- State management model required by managed objects to optionally support state manipulation and, if so, it also emits events
- Performance monitoring model required by managed objects that optionally supports state manipulation

Each managed object specifies if it emits events, maintains a state (state management), or provides performance-monitoring data. Every managed object maintaining a state also automatically emits events.

Management Model

Every object represented by JSR-77 implements the J2EEManagedObject, which provides its name and states which of the optional models (events, state management, and performance monitoring) it implements or supports.

A JSR-77 represents one management domain containing a list of applications, servers, and deployments, which is a temporary object available during the deployment of an application. The application contains modules, such as a Web module, EJB module, and Connector module. Each of these modules represents an appropriate archive—Web Archive (WAR), Java Archive (JAR), and Resource adapter Archive (RAR), whereas the application represents the Enterprise Application Archive (EAR) (but can also be the container for one single module archive). The server represents an application server cluster containing the deployed applications, resources (JNDI, JMS, URL, JTA, JavaMail, JDBC, RMI, and IIOP) and the nodes, which are the physical computer.

Event Model

All J2EEManagedObject emitting events implement the EventProvider interfaces specifying a list of event types that they emit. The event (J2EEManagementEvent) contains the source (J2EEManagedObject), time, sequence, type, and message. The type is a dot-separated list of names (like the package name in Java). All types prefixed with j2ee. are reserved for events emitted by the components of the management system implementation, such as j2ee.object.created. All types prefixed with state. are reserved for state manageable objects, such as state.starting. Otherwise, the event source is free to be named as you want.

State Management Model

A `J2EEManagedObject` supports the state management and must implement the `StateManageable` interface delivering the current state, the time the object was started, and the operations `start()`, `startRecursive()`, and `stop()`.

Performance Monitoring Model

The performance data framework allows the client to get information about the performance of the managed objects. Each `J2EEManagedObject` providing performance data must implement the `StatisticsProvider` interface providing a list of `Stats`. Note that the performance data of a managed object are bundled in a `Stats`. Each `Stats` contains a list of `Statistic` objects that represents a statistic value. There are the following types of statistics: `Count-`, `Boundary-`, `Range-`, `BoundedRange-` and `TimeStatistic`. The `StatisticsProvider` interface provides a list of `Stats` instances.

Management EJB Component (MEJB)

The JSR-77 requires each implementation to provide an implementation of the Management EJB, which must be deployed on at least one server. The design of the MEJB is nearly a 100% copy of the JMX `MBeanServer` with some changes made by adding the `J2EE` prefix to some class names.

Maybe you are a little bit puzzled why anyone would go the whole nine yards to come up with something similar to JMX but not utilize JMX. One of the reasons is that the JSR-77 group didn't want to bind JSR-77 together with JMX because there are not requirements in the J2EE specification to do so. On the other hand, an EJB can be deployed on each J2EE-compliant application server, but it also provides a distinction between these two. JMX hosts any JMX-compliant MBeans, but the MEJB should only provide J2EE managed objects compliant to JSR-77. Note that in the MEJB, the MBeans are replaced by `J2EEManagedObjects`, Notifications are replaced by events, and state management and performance monitoring are additional.

As said earlier, the MEJB does not return any J2EE-related instances but only information about the specified managed objects. That is why JSR-77 talks about a model and not about Java instances. The following is an example:

1. Client obtains the remote interface of the MEJB Session Bean, which represents the management domain the client wants to manage.
2. Client retrieves all the attributes of the management domain, which is the list of deployed applications, the participating clusters (logical server), and applications in the process of deployment.

3. All items in this list are themselves managed objects, so the MEJB only returned their object names. Thus, the client can navigate through the list of deployed applications. Each of them is of type object name.

4. Client retrieves the attribute of the managed object referred by the object name (as in JMX where the client retrieves the attributes of an MBean by the object name).

5. The attribute of the deployed application is a list of modules that are managed objects as well, so an object name is returned instead.

6. Client retrieves the attributes of a cluster, which is a list of deployed applications, resources, nodes, ports, and JVMs. In addition, it also supplies the name of the J2EE server vendor. All attributes (except the name of the server vendor) are a list of object names. The server vendor name is returned as String because its value describes an attribute of the cluster and not another managed object.

The JSR-77 client has to do the following simple steps:

- Get the remote interface of the MEJB of the management domain on which the user wants to work.

- Get the attributes of the management domain.

- Check if an attribute is an object name and, if so, prepare to retrieve its attributes when requested.

- Allow the client to set attributes on the managed object. The JSR-77 client has to convert a reference to another managed object into an object name.

- Allow the user to invoke methods on the managed objects, which is an invocation of the method on the managed object referenced by the object name.

- Allow the user to listen for events emitted from any managed object emitting events, but the user has to register a listener to receive those events.

Of course, the programmer can hide all these conversions and mapping behind a set of Java instances that would create a nearly transparent view to the management domain. Now a JSR-77 client works on an application server like a management tool running in the same JVM (works like a JMX Connector).

On the other hand, an HTML client can be easily created by displaying the object names as links to another page and the other attributes as simple text on the current page, which would look like the HTML-Adaptor of JMX-RI.

J2EE Management SNMP

To enable JSR-77 to be manageable by SNMP, JSR-77 has to define a management information base (MIB) that can be used by an SNMP client to manage JSR-77 compliant application servers. In addition, the service of the SNMP implementation has to transform the data into an MIB- and SNMP-compliant form.

Summary

JSR-77 does not really provide an API (except the classes for the MEJB and the appendixes), but it provides a model the client can use to investigate and work on the application server it manages. Thus, any JSR-77 client can let a user manage any JSR-77–compliant J2EE application server. This allows companies specializing in building management tools to create one management tool to manage all compliant application servers. When JSR-77 becomes part of the J2EE specification, this will mean all application servers.

On the other hand it frees the J2EE application server vendors from creating a management tool of their own. They can simply provide a JSR-77 implementation and rely on existing management tools implemented by third-party vendors.

Finally it enables an application server administrator to manage different vendors with the same tool, the same knowledge, and from the same place.

JMX Use Case: The JBoss Server

The JBoss server is a collaborative effort of a worldwide group of developers to create a J2EE application server in Open Source. The goal of the project is to commoditize the J2EE service stack and make it available free of charge for everyone to use. Started in 1999, JBoss is currently the leading Open Source effort to implement the enterprise Java APIs.

The JBoss application server was the first J2EE server to embrace the JMX API. In fact, the architecture of the JBoss application server has been built on top of the JMX infrastructure. This chapter will go briefly through the JBoss arhitecture for those parts where JMX is involved and explain the reasons and benefits of using JMX in the server core.

You can download the JBoss server for free from `http://www.jboss.org`. See Appendix A for more detailed download and installation instructions.

Microkernel Architecture

"The Microkernel architectural pattern applies to software systems that must be able to adapt to changing system requirements. It separates a minimal functional core from extended functionality and customer-specific parts. The microkernel also serves as a socket for plugging in these extensions and coordinating their collaboration."

(*Pattern-Oriented Software Architecture: A System of Patterns* by Buschmann, Meunier, Rohnert, Sommerlad, and Stal)

The J2EE platform is a service based platform. The platform contains services for naming, messaging, transactions, persistence, security, logging, and so on. It also defines server-side component models, such as Enterprise Java Beans and Java servlets. Both servlets and the EJBs require their own containers for the components to be deployed on the server. The containers also need to be able to interact with all the other services in the platform.

Many application servers are built as monolithic applications, containing all the services of the J2EE platform at all times. Whether or not you are using the Java Message Service (JMS) or the Java Connector Architecture (JCA), or Java servlets, these service implementations are always present on the server.

JBoss takes a different approach to implementing the J2EE platform. Instead of building a monolithic server application, JBoss implements a microkernel architecture of MBean components, each of which implements different J2EE services or other server infrastructure components. The fact that the server itself is built on top of the JMX infrastructure makes both the applications deployed to the server easily manageable and also makes the server itself extremely flexible in how it can be configured.

The quotation at the beginning of this section very clearly defines in a couple of sentences the design goals of the JBoss server and the reasons why a microkernel approach to implement the server were chosen. The microkernel definition given by Buschmann et al. also closely matches the design of a JMX based management system. The J2EE platform is used for a variety of different purposes; from simple Web sites to handling critical business transactions. Being able to adapt to changing requirements, allowing for customer specific extensions and enabling high availability during maintenance are important factors when you choose your platform implementation.

Adapt to Changing System Requirements

As you have learned throughout the course of this book, the JMX agent level was designed to be adaptable to a range of runtime environments, from J2ME to J2EE. The core of the JMX agent level, the MBean server, is a rather simple and lightweight object. The MBean server decouples the MBeans from each other and allows components to be managed or switched at run-time.

The JBoss server can be configured and built with a set of MBean components, each implementing a different J2EE service. For example, several different servlet containers can be embedded to the JBoss server, from Tomcat to Jetty Web Server and servlet container. Similarly, it is possible to choose different JMS implementation or transaction manager for the server, if necessary. All of this enables you to more easily adapt the server to match your requirements. If one service implementation cannot provide the functionality required by your application, you are able to choose another service implementation for the server. You do not need to find a whole new J2EE platform implementation which, in practice, is often an expensive operation to go through—in some cases, it may also turn out to be technically very difficult to do.

Minimal Core

Both the JMX agent and the JBoss server have a very small core—the MBean server. The MBean server itself is merely an invocation bus containing a registry of the MBean components and their management interfaces. Registering agent service MBeans, such as the M-Let service, Relation Service, or connector MBeans can extend the core functionality.

Also the core of the server is able to adapt as requirements change. The JMX agent level allows run-time configuration to some extent through the agent service MBeans. Also the MBean server can be switched by choosing a different JMX implementation. For example, the JBoss server has been run on MBean server implementations provided by both Sun Microsystems and IBM Tivoli teams. A new JMX compliant agent core can be installed as a base to the JBoss platform if the runtime system so requires.

Extended Functionality and Customer-Specific Parts

By virtue of the JMX-based implementation, the JBoss server is extremely easy to extend with new functionality. Adding new services, or application specific components, to the server is a matter of creating a new MBean and registering it to the MBean server. For example, extending the server to report platform statistics and resource usage requires you to implement the code as an MBean, just as you would with any other MBean server. You can easily extend the server with parts that are specific to your installation only. The mechanism to do this is standardized by the JMX specification.

Collaboration Between Components

The MBean server allows queries that are to be executed to find different service implementations. For example, a JMS MBean or the EJB Container MBean can query the MBean server to find a Naming service that both components use. The notification mechanism also allows the components to broadcast information to other interested components in the system. The standard agent services (monitoring, timers, and relation service) allow additional collaboration between the MBean components via the notification mechanism.

The Server Spine

At the core of the JBoss server is the JMX MBean server. The MBean server acts as the spine of the JBoss server, allowing different J2EE service implementations to register to the server, as shown in Figure 12.1. Depending on your needs, the server can contain the full J2EE platform, parts of the J2EE platform, or nothing except the MBean server in the initial startup.

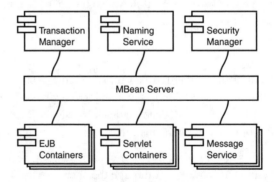

FIGURE 12.1

Different services in the JBoss platform are implemented as MBeans.

The default configuration of the JBoss server loads up all services—the servlet container, EJB containers, message service, naming service, connection pools, log service, and so on. However, you can quite easily configure the server to leave out the messaging service if you do not utilize it in any way. Or maybe the message service really is the only J2EE service your application requires; in this case, you can quite effortlessly leave out the EJB container. All that is required is for you to register one less MBean at startup.

JBoss utilizes the JMX M-Let service in its configuration and initial startup. As you explored in Chapter 7, "Standard Agent Services," the M-Let service can be used to build applications that have very minimal bootstrap code and load the rest of their configuration and components from the network, as requested. This allows the centralized administration and maintenance of the application components.

The JBoss server can be used exactly this way. It is possible to start the server with only the JMX spine installed. Everything else, including the configuration services, EJB containers, messaging service, naming service, pools, and so on, can be loaded from a central configuration server. This enables an easy maintenance of a farm of servers, for example in an Application Service Provider (ASP) environment, where dozens of servers need to be both maintained and new ones installed. The configuration is stored in one location where each server will find it and install and configure the required components to the host machine (see Figure 12.2).

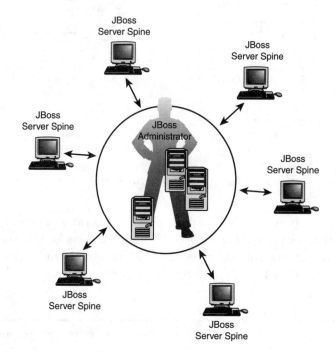

FIGURE 12.2

The administrator can easily control how each server is configured and which versions of the components are installed.

Configuration Service

One of the core components loaded the JBoss M-Let service is a Configuration Service implementation. The `ConfigurationService` MBean allows the JBoss bootstrap to download and configure the server using an XML based configuration file format. The XML file `jboss.jcml` includes a list of the downloadable MBean components and their initial configuration values. After the `ConfigurationService` MBean has been loaded and registered to the MBean server, it takes over the server startup sequence from the JMX M-Let service implementation. It loads the containers, databases, connection pools, and so on and configures them, as shown in Figure 12.3.

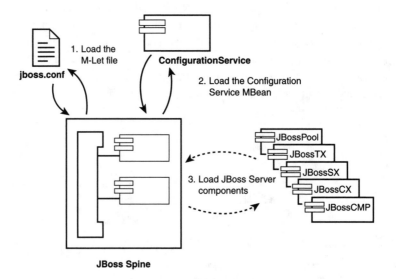

FIGURE 12.3

As part of the JBoss core application, the M-Let service loads a ConfigurationService *MBean, which is then used to load individual J2EE service components to the server.*

The M-Let file from the JBoss 2.4.1 installation is shown as an example in Listing 12.1. At the end of the file, you can see the `ConfigurationService` MBean being loaded, which then reads in the XML based configuration file in Listing 12.2. Both `jboss.conf` and `jboss.jcml` files can be found under the `JBoss-2.4.1/conf/default` directory.

LISTING 12.1   `jboss.conf` M-Let Text File

```
<! — ============================================================== —>
<! —                                                                —>
<! —   JBoss JMX Boot-strap Configuration                           —>
<! —                                                                —>
```

LISTING 12.1   continued

```
<!— ============================================================ —>

<MLET CODE = "org.jboss.logging.Logger"
      ARCHIVE="jboss.jar"
      CODEBASE="../../lib/ext/">
</MLET>

<!— The log4j based logging service   —>
<MLET CODE = "org.jboss.logging.Log4jService"
      ARCHIVE="jboss.jar,log4j.jar"
      CODEBASE="../../lib/ext/">
</MLET>

<!— location of log.properties —>
<MLET CODE = "org.jboss.util.ClassPathExtension"
      ARCHIVE="jboss.jar"
      CODEBASE="../../lib/ext/">
   <ARG TYPE="java.lang.String" VALUE="../../log/">
</MLET>

<!— Place the config directory in the classpath —>
<MLET CODE = "org.jboss.util.ClassPathExtension"
      ARCHIVE="jboss.jar"
      CODEBASE="../../lib/ext/">
   <ARG TYPE="java.lang.String" VALUE="./">
</MLET>

<MLET CODE = "org.jboss.util.Info"
      ARCHIVE="jboss.jar"
      CODEBASE="../../lib/ext/">
</MLET>

<MLET CODE = "org.jboss.util.ClassPathExtension"
      ARCHIVE="jboss.jar"
      CODEBASE="../../lib/ext/">
   <ARG TYPE="java.lang.String" VALUE="../../tmp/">
</MLET>

<MLET CODE = "org.jboss.util.ClassPathExtension"
      ARCHIVE="jboss.jar"
      CODEBASE="../../lib/ext/">
   <ARG TYPE="java.lang.String" VALUE="../../db/">
</MLET>

<MLET CODE = "org.jboss.configuration.ConfigurationService"
```

LISTING 12.1   continued

```
        ARCHIVE="jboss.jar,../xml.jar"
        CODEBASE="../../lib/ext/">
</MLET>

<MLET CODE = "org.jboss.util.Shutdown"
      ARCHIVE="jboss.jar"
      CODEBASE="../../lib/ext/">
</MLET>

<MLET CODE = "org.jboss.util.ServiceControl"
      ARCHIVE="jboss.jar"
      CODEBASE="../../lib/ext/">
</MLET>
```

LISTING 12.2   Partial MBean XML Configuration file (jboss.jcml)

```
<?xml version="1.0" encoding="UTF-8"?>
<!— This is where you can add and configure your MBeans
  ATTENTION: The order of the listing here is the same order as
    the MBeans are loaded. Therefore if a MBean depends on another
    MBean to be loaded and started it has to be listed after all
    the MBeans it depends on.
—>

<server>
  <!— =========================================================== —>
  <!— Classloading                                                —>
  <!— =========================================================== —>
  <mbean code="org.jboss.web.WebService"
         name="DefaultDomain:service=Webserver">
    <attribute name="Port">8083</attribute>
  </mbean>

  <!— =========================================================== —>
  <!— JNDI                                                        —>
  <!— =========================================================== —>
  <mbean code="org.jboss.naming.NamingService"
         name="DefaultDomain:service=Naming">
    <attribute name="Port">1099</attribute>
  </mbean>

  <mbean code="org.jboss.naming.JNDIView"
         name="DefaultDomain:service=JNDIView" />
```

LISTING 12.2   continued

```
<!-- ============================================================ -->
<!-- Transactions                                                 -->
<!-- ============================================================ -->
<mbean code="org.jboss.tm.TransactionManagerService"
       name="DefaultDomain:service=TransactionManager">
  <attribute name="TransactionTimeout">300</attribute>
</mbean>



<!-- ============================================================ -->
<!-- Security                                                     -->
<!-- ============================================================ -->

<!-- JAAS security manager and realm mapping -->
<mbean code="org.jboss.security.plugins.JaasSecurityManagerService"
       name="Security:name=JaasSecurityManager">
  <attribute name="SecurityManagerClassName">
      org.jboss.security.plugins.JaasSecurityManager
  </attribute>
</mbean>



<!-- ============================================================ -->
<!-- J2EE deployment                                              -->
<!-- ============================================================ -->

<mbean code="org.jboss.ejb.ContainerFactory"
       name=":service=ContainerFactory">
  <attribute name="VerifyDeployments">true</attribute>
  <attribute name="ValidateDTDs">false</attribute>
  <attribute name="MetricsEnabled">false</attribute>
  <attribute name="VerifierVerbose">true</attribute>
  <attribute name="BeanCacheJMSMonitoringEnabled">false</attribute>
</mbean>


<!-- ============================================================ -->
<!-- Auto deployment                                              -->
<!-- ============================================================ -->
<mbean code="org.jboss.ejb.AutoDeployer"
       name="EJB:service=AutoDeployer">
  <attribute name="Deployers">
    J2EE:service=J2eeDeployer;
    JCA:service=RARDeployer
  </attribute>
```

LISTING 12.2   continued

```
    <attribute name="URLs">../deploy,../deploy/lib</attribute>
  </mbean>


  <!— ============================================================ —>
  <!— JMX adaptors                                                 —>
  <!— ============================================================ —>

  <mbean code="org.jboss.jmx.server.JMXAdaptorService"
         name="Adaptor:name=RMI" />

  <mbean code="org.jboss.jmx.server.RMIConnectorService"
         name="Connector:name=RMI" />

  <mbean code="com.sun.jdmk.comm.HtmlAdaptorServer"
         name="Adaptor:name=html">
    <attribute name="MaxActiveClientCount">10</attribute>
    <attribute name="Parser" />
    <attribute name="Port">8082</attribute>
  </mbean>


  <!— ============================================================ —>
  <!— Mail Connection Factory                                      —>
  <!— ============================================================ —>
  <mbean code="org.jboss.mail.MailService" name=":service=Mail">
    <attribute name="JNDIName">Mail</attribute>
    <attribute name="ConfigurationFile">mail.properties</attribute>
    <attribute name="User">user_id</attribute>
    <attribute name="Password">password</attribute>
  </mbean>


  <!— ================================================================== —>
  <!— Add your custom MBeans here                                        —>
  <!— ================================================================== —>

</server>
```

Should you want to replace or remove one of the services, you can easily do so by editing the XML file. However, you can also do this at run-time through a Web interface, as explained in the next section.

Remote Management

By choosing to implement the JMX management architecture as part of the server core, the JBoss platform has had remote management capabilities virtually from the beginning. The server can be managed through HTTP adaptors, or custom management tools can be created using the standard JMX programming interface.

By default, the JBoss server enables automatic management of the server via an HTML adaptor. Both the default platform services and the customer-specific extensions to the server become manageable automatically through the MBean server. For example, an MBean extension to run a periodic batch reporting task on the server can easily be exposed to Web management and executed by the administrator from his or her Web browser. In fact, bringing new component implementations to the JBoss server and registering and managing them can easily be achieved through the basic HTTP adaptor interface. This means the administrator can customize the server and add new code and service implementations without ever having to leave his or her seat. A simple Web browser will do. In the next section, "Extending the JBoss Server," you will first build a simple MBean component and then install it to a live server through the Web browser.

Extending the JBoss Server

To demonstrate the extensibility of the JMX based server, you will

1. Write an MBean that starts a new thread in the server and periodically polls the Java runtime for the amount of used memory and thread count (see Listing 12.3).

2. Expose a management attribute that allows you to set the polling interval (see Listing 12.4).

3. Attach it to a running JBoss server instance.

LISTING 12.3   JBossMonitorMBean.java

```
package book.jmx.examples;

public interface JBossMonitorMBean {

  void setInterval(int interval);
  int  getInterval();

}
```

LISTING 12.4 JBossMonitor.java

```java
package book.jmx.examples;

import javax.management.*;

public class JBossMonitor implements JBossMonitorMBean,
    MBeanRegistration, Runnable {

  Thread monitor = null;
  int interval = 10000;

  public ObjectName preRegister(MBeanServer server,
                                ObjectName name) throws Exception {

    if (name == null)
      return new ObjectName(":className=" + getClass().getName());

    else return name;
  }

  public void postRegister(Boolean registrationSuccessful) {
    monitor = new Thread(this);
    monitor.setDaemon(true);
    monitor.setName("My JBoss Thread");
    monitor.start();
  }

  public void preDeregister() throws Exception {
    monitor.interrupt();
  }

  public void postDeregister() {}

  public void setInterval(int interval) {
    this.interval = interval;
  }

  public int getInterval() {
    return interval;
  }

  public void run() {

    boolean running = true;

    while (running) {
      try {
```

LISTING 12.4   continued

```
            Thread.sleep(interval);
            System.out.println(getMem());
            System.out.println(getThreads());
                }
    catch (InterruptedException e) {
      running = false;
    }
  }
}

  private String getMem() {
    return "Total Mem: " + Runtime.getRuntime().totalMemory() + "    " +
           "Free Mem:  " + Runtime.getRuntime().freeMemory();
  }

  private String getThreads() {
    ThreadGroup root = null;
    root = Thread.currentThread().getThreadGroup();

    while (root.getParent() != null)
      root = root.getParent();

    return "Thread Count: " + root.activeCount();
  }

}
```

The thread in Listing 12.4 prints the memory and thread values to the console when it is run.

To compile and package the MBean, execute the following commands:

```
C:\Examples> javac -d . -classpath jmx-1_0_1-ri_bin\jmx\lib\jmxri.jar
➥JBossMonitor.java JBossMonitorMBean.java

C:\Examples>  jar -cvf mon.jar book/jmx/examples/JBossMonitor*.class
```

Next, start the JBoss server by invoking the run.bat or run.sh command:

```
C:\Examples> cd JBoss-2.41
C:\Examples\JBoss-2.4.1> cd bin
C:\Examples\JBoss-2.4.1\bin> run
```

When you have started the JBoss server, you can point your Web browser to http://local-
host:8082. It should open the Web management view to JBoss components. Find the link to
the M-Let MBean (see Figure 12.4).

FIGURE 12.4
Locate the JBoss server M-Let class loader.

Use the M-Let to add your new classes to the server. Execute the M-Let's addURL() operation to add the mon.jar to the class loader (see Figure 12.5).

To create the MBean on the MBean server, go back to the Agent View page at the beginning. On the top-right corner, you can see an Admin link (see Figure 12.6). Click it.

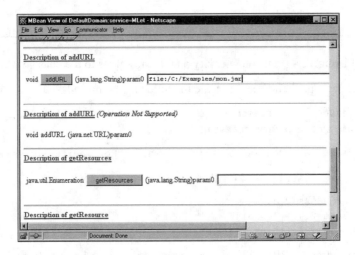

FIGURE 12.5
Add your new compiled classes to the server at runtime via M-Let class loaders addURL() *method.*

JMX Use Case: The JBoss Server

CHAPTER 12

357

12

JMX USE CASE:
THE JBOSS
SERVER

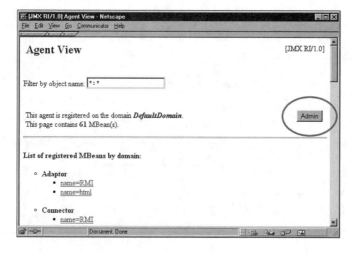

FIGURE 12.6

Locate the Admin link on the Agent View page to create a new MBean.

On the Admin page, you can create new MBeans and register them to the server. Fill in the requested fields:

- Set domain to **Example**
- Set keys to **name=MyComponent**
- Set Java Class Name to **book.jmx.examples.JBossMonitor**

You can leave the Classloader field blank. Select the Create action and click Send Request (see Figure 12.7). The Web page should change to inform you that the create operation was successful. Now you can go back to the Agent View at the beginning, find the newly created MBean under the Example domain, and select it (see Figure 12.8). If you check the JBoss console, it should be printing out the information from the MBean.

```
[Service Control] Started 48 services
[Default] JBoss 2.4.1 Started in 0m:6s
[Default] Total Mem: 4112384  Free Mem:  1694272
[Default] Thread Count: 25
[Default] Total Mem: 4112384  Free Mem:  2133984
[Default] Thread Count: 25
```

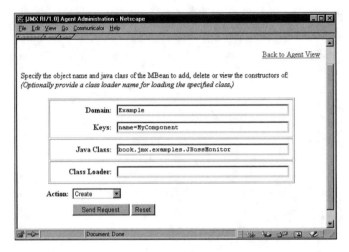

FIGURE 12.7

Fill in the object name domain, keys, and the MBean classname before executing the Create action.

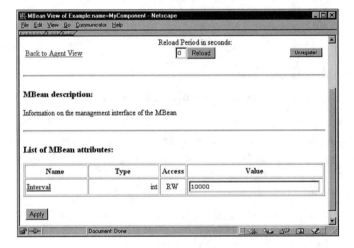

FIGURE 12.8

The Web management view of the JBossMonitor MBean.

You can change the interval setting to set the pace at which the output is being printed on the console. For a more sophisticated implementation, find the JMS implementation under the JBossMQ management domain. Change your MBean implementation to invoke createTopic() or createQueue() operations at startup. You can now change the MBean thread implementation to push the information to a JMS topic or a queue. The code to accomplish this is left as an exercise to the reader.

To add the MBean permanently as part of the server startup sequence, add the code in Listing 12.3 to the end of the `jboss.jcml` file .

LISTING 12.3   jboss.jcml

```
<!— ===================================================================== —>
<!— Add your custom MBeans here                                          —>
<!— ===================================================================== —>
<mbean code="book.jmx.examples.JBossMonitor"
       name="Example:name=MyExtension">
</mbean>
```

Integration and Development Process

The JBoss project has grown to become one of the most successful open-source Java projects. During its lifetime, several dozen developers have worked to create new features, maintain, and improve the existing services.

To support the distributed development of JBoss, a common infrastructure was needed. The developers of JBoss needed to be able to concentrate on their own area of interest without being disturbed by development efforts occurring on other parts of the server. This requirement to isolate the implementation effort is highlighted by the fact that developers are scattered across the globe and only have the electronic means of e-mail and mailing lists to communicate with each other.

A unified approach to registering and using the services was needed because many components need to communicate with other parts of the platform. The JMX API offered an easy-to-use and lightweight solution to the development problem. MBeans are easy to create and quick to implement. The MBean server interface is simple to understand and offers the basic "pluggability" for the platform components.

The JMX approach has allowed the JBoss platform to incorporate several other service implementations as part of the platform with little effort. The JBoss server can be easily configured to use different servlet containers—Tomcat 3 series, Tomcat 4 (Catalina), or Jetty Web Server and servlet container. The transaction manager can be switched between the JBossTX and Tyrex implementations; the Log4j logging framework has been embedded to the server as an MBean, as is CastorJDO, a Java Data Objects (JDO) implementation. All of the mentioned products are independently developed, without a specific focus on the JBoss server. However, by building an MBean component wrapper for each service implementation, the JBoss platform has been able to leverage the independent work of other projects. The JBoss platform has become an umbrella of independently developed J2EE service implementations with the help

12

JMX USE CASE:
THE JBOSS
SERVER

of the microkernel design and the JMX API. As the J2EE platform has grown bigger with new service specifications, the JBoss project has been able to adapt to the new requirements by integrating third-party implementations of those services. The users of the JBoss server today are able to mix and match these service implementations to build the exact kind of server platform their application requires.

Summary

The technical aspects of flexibility, extensibility, and manageability are the reasons the JBoss platform is built on top of the JMX infrastructure. The flexibility offered by the JMX—decoupled and non-typed invocation mechanism and the metadata based management interface—enables the integration of server components and automated management of the server through a Web interface.

The instrumentation level of the JMX specification defines a standardized mechanism to extend the server functionality. Anyone can extend the JBoss server by implementing custom code as an MBean. There is no need for server-specific "startup classes" in JBoss or server-specific timer or scheduler services. For scheduled batch jobs, the JMX Timer service can be used to notify application components at a given date and time. The startup classes can be implemented as MBeans and added either to the standard M-Let service file or the JBoss Configuration Service XML file. The JMX agent allows any JMX-compliant management application to be built to manage the JBoss server. Again, customer-specific tools can be built because all management operations are based on the standardized JMX API. Also, generic management tools, such as the HTTP adaptor, can be used for the rapid development of management applications.

The fact that the JBoss platform has been built as a collaborative project of hundreds of developers all around the world has required a standard component model to be used in building the platform. For JBoss, that component model has been the one defined by the JMX specification, and it has proven itself to be the right choice. Without the flexibility and ease-of-use of the MBean server and the MBean components, the JBoss project would not have been able to maintain the number of developers it enjoys today.

Appendixes

PART

III

IN THIS PART

Environment Setup

IN THIS APPENDIX

The code examples in Part I, "Java Management Extensions Specification," require you to install Sun Java SDK, Standard Edition, version 1.3 or later and a Java Management Extensions (JMX) implementation. The examples have been tested with two JMX implementations—the Sun JMX Reference Implementation, version 1.0, and IBM Tivoli JMX implementation, version 1.2. The following instructions apply to the Microsoft Windows NT 4.0 and 2000 platforms. Users of other platforms will need to make proper adjustments to ensure the examples work correctly.

Java SDK Installation

Download and install the Sun Microsystems Java SDK from http://java.sun.com/j2se and install it according to the supplied instructions. Most of the examples are compiled and run from the command line, so make sure the installation process adds the required commands, located in the bin directory of the Java SDK installation, to your PATH environment variable. You can check that the PATH settings are correct by trying to execute the java command from the command prompt. If the java command is found correctly, you should see the following output on the console window:

```
C:\Examples> java
Usage: java [-options] class [args...]
           (to execute a class)
   or  java -jar [-options] jarfile [args...]
           (to execute a jar file)
```

If the java command does not work, modify the PATH environment setting to point to the bin directory of the SDK installation. For example,

```
C:\Examples> set PATH=%PATH%;C:\Java1.3\bin
```

Modify the directory path in the previous example to match your Java SDK installation directory. To make the PATH environment setting permanent, go to the Windows Control Panel and modify the System settings.

Those of you wanting to use an Integrated Development Environment (IDE) to run the examples will have to adjust these instructions to your corresponding IDEs. Unix and Linux users should set up the environment settings as documented in their command shells.

Sun JMX Reference Implementation Installation

Download the JMX Reference Implementation from http://java.sun.com/products/JavaManagement/index.html. Create a new empty directory for the examples in this book, for example C:\Examples. Unpack the downloaded package into this directory. Notice that if you are using a tool such as WinZip to unpack the downloaded file, you should ensure that the Use Folder Names option has been checked. After you have unpacked the JMX Reference Implementation package, all the files should appear under the `C:\Examples\jmx-1 0 1-ri_bin` directory.

When compiling and running the examples, you will need the libraries under the `C:\Examples\jmx-1 0 1-ri_bin\jmx\lib` directory—the `jmxri.jar` and `jmxtools.jar` files. The `jmxri.jar` file contains the JMX API classes, and the `jmxtools.jar` file contains JMX extensions, such as the HTTP Adaptor.

IBM Tivoli JMX Implementation

To configure the second JMX implementation used in this book, download the Tivoli JMX implementation from the IBM AlphaWorks Web site at `http://www.alphaworks.ibm.com/tech/TMX4J`. Again, unzip the package into the `C:\Examples` directory. You should see all the files in the package appear in the `C:\Examples\tmx4j` directory. The libraries required to compile and run the examples can be found under `C:\Examples\tmx4j\base\lib`—the `jmxx.jar`, `jmxc.jar` and `log.jar` files. In addition, JMX extension libraries can be found under the `C:\Examples\tmx4j\ext\lib` directory.

Example Source Code

All the source code in the book can be compiled and run from the directory that you created in the `C:\Examples` directory. If specific classpath settings are required, they are mentioned in the text. Usually all classpath settings are passed to the runtime environment using a `classpath` switch or a similar mechanism.

All the source code is also packaged in a `book.jmx.examples` package. This requires you to specify the full package names when running the examples. When compiling the source code, use the `-d` switch to specify the target directory as the current work directory. This will create a directory structure under the work directory that matches the Java package declaration in the source files. When running the code with `java` command, this directory structure is expected by the runtime system.

To compile a Java source file, the following command line should be used:

```
C:\Examples> javac -d . -classpath .;jmx-1_0_1-ri_bin\jmx\lib\
➥jmxri.jar;jmx-1_0_1-ri_bin\jmx\lib\jmxtools.jar <Java source file>
```

If the `Java source` file contains the package declaration `book.jmx.examples`, a corresponding directory structure is created under the work directory, as indicated by the `-d` switch.

A

ENVIRONMENT
SETUP

To run the compiled classes, the full package name must be included. The code should be executed from the same working directory where it was compiled. For example, to run the previous example, the following command line should be executed:

```
C:\Examples> java –classpath .;jmx-1_0_1-ri_bin/jmx/lib/
➥jmxri.jar;jmx-1_0_1-ri_bin/jmx/lib/jmxtools.jar book.jmx.examples.MyClassName
```

The previous two example commands use the Sun JMX Reference Implementation. To switch to the IBM Tivoli JMX implementation, replace the `jmxri.jar` with the three Jar packages found under `tmx4j\base\lib`—`jmxx.jar`, `jmxc.jar` and `log.jar`. Replace the `jmxtools.jar` with `jmxext.dir` found in the `C:\Examples\tmx4j\ext\lib` directory.

```
C:\Examples> javac -d . –classpath .;tmx4j/base/lib/jmxc.jar;tmx4j/base/lib/
➥jmxx.jar;tmx4j/ext/lib/jmxext.jar <Java source file>
C:\Examples> java –classpath .;tmx4j/base/lib/jmxc.jar;tmx4j/base/lib/
➥jmxx.jar;tmx4j/base/lib/log.jar;tmx4j/ext/lib/jmxext.jar
book.jmx.examples.Agent
```

JBoss Setup

In Part II, "JMX in the J2EE Platform," you will look at some examples that use the J2EE services with JMX. The examples use the JBoss version 2.4.1 implementation, which is available as Open Source and for free from `http://www.jboss.org`.

To install JBoss, download the package and unpack it to the directory you have created. If you are following the directory setup shown previously, the directory will be `C:\Examples`. After you have unpacked the JBoss distribution, you will have a directory `C:\Examples\ JBoss-2.4.1` in your file system. If you change the directory to `C:\Examples\JBoss-2.4.1\bin`, you will find the `run.bat|sh` files that you can execute to start the JBoss server.

In Chapter 10, "JMX Distribution Layer with J2EE Services," you will build an asynchronous connector that can be used for remote communication between a management application and the MBean server. The message transport for this connector is implemented using Java Message Service (JMS). The JBoss server starts an implementation of JMS—the JBossMQ—automatically when you execute the server start scripts. However, a JMS topic needs to be added and configured for the JBossMQ server. Using the previous file structure, you can find the configuration file `jboss.jcml` from under the `C:\Examples\JBoss-2.4.1\conf\default` directory. About half way through the configuration file, you can find the JBossMQ configuration shown next:

```
<!— ========================================================= —>
<!— JBossMQ                                                   —>
<!— ========================================================= —>
<mbean code = "org.jboss.mq.server.JBossMQService"
```

```
            name = "JBossMQ:service=Server"/>


<!— The StateManager is used for JMS persistent state data.    —>
<!— For example: what durable subscriptions are active.        —>
<mbean code = "org.jboss.mq.server.StateManager"
        name = "JBossMQ:service=StateManager">
    <attribute name="StateFile">jbossmq-state.xml</attribute>
</mbean>


<!— The PersistenceManager is used to store messages to disk. —>
<mbean code = "org.jboss.mq.pm.rollinglogged.PersistenceManager"
        name = "JBossMQ:service=PersistenceManager">
    <attribute name="DataDirectory">../../db/jbossmq/</attribute>
</mbean>


<!— InvocationLayers are the different transport methods that —>
<!— can be used to access the server.                         —>
<mbean code = "org.jboss.mq.il.jvm.JVMServerILService"
        name = "JBossMQ:service=InvocationLayer,type=JVM">
    <attribute name = "ConnectionFactoryJNDIRef">
        java:/ConnectionFactory
    </attribute>
    <attribute name = "XAConnectionFactoryJNDIRef">
        java:/XAConnectionFactory
    </attribute>
</mbean>


<mbean code = "org.jboss.mq.il.rmi.RMIServerILService"
        name = "JBossMQ:service=InvocationLayer,type=RMI">
    <attribute name = "ConnectionFactoryJNDIRef">
        RMIConnectionFactory
    </attribute>
    <attribute name = "XAConnectionFactoryJNDIRef">
        RMIXAConnectionFactory
    </attribute>
</mbean>


<mbean code = "org.jboss.mq.il.oil.OILServerILService"
        name = "JBossMQ:service=InvocationLayer,type=OIL">
    <attribute name = "ConnectionFactoryJNDIRef">
        ConnectionFactory
    </attribute>
    <attribute name = "XAConnectionFactoryJNDIRef">
        XAConnectionFactory
    </attribute>
</mbean>
```

A

ENVIRONMENT
SETUP

```
<mbean code = "org.jboss.mq.il.uil.UILServerILService"
       name = "JBossMQ:service=InvocationLayer,type=UIL">
    <attribute name = "ConnectionFactoryJNDIRef">
        UILConnectionFactory
    </attribute>
    <attribute name = "XAConnectionFactoryJNDIRef">
        UILXAConnectionFactory
    </attribute>
</mbean>

<!- The following three line create 3 topics named: testTopic, ->
<!- example, and bob                                           ->
<mbean code = "org.jboss.mq.server.TopicManager"
       name = "JBossMQ:service=Topic,name=testTopic"/>
<mbean code = "org.jboss.mq.server.TopicManager"
       name = "JBossMQ:service=Topic,name=example"/>
<mbean code = "org.jboss.mq.server.TopicManager"
       name = "JBossMQ:service=Topic,name=bob"/>
```

To add a new topic to the JBossMQ server, insert the following lines at the end of the previous listing.

```
<!- The following three line create 3 topics named: testTopic, ->
<!- example, and bob                                           ->
<mbean code = "org.jboss.mq.server.TopicManager"
       name = "JBossMQ:service=Topic,name=testTopic"/>
<mbean code = "org.jboss.mq.server.TopicManager"
       name = "JBossMQ:service=Topic,name=example"/>
<mbean code = "org.jboss.mq.server.TopicManager"
       name = "JBossMQ:service=Topic,name=bob"/>
<mbean code = "org.jboss.mq.server.TopicManager"
       name = "JBossMQ:service=Topic,name=JMSConnector"/>
```

Adding the last two lines in jboss.jcml will create the JMSConnector topic at startup.

SOAP Configuration

In Chapter 10, you will build a SOAP connector to invoke and manipulate MBeans from a remote host using the SOAP protocol. The SOAP connector implementation uses the GLUE library available from http://www.themindelectric.com. There is a free binary distribution available for GLUE from the Web site. A registration is required to download the standard edition of the library.

Unpack the 1.2 version of the Standard GLUE library in to the same directory to which you have unpacked the other files. If you are following the naming used in this chapter, the directory is `C:\Examples`. After you have unpacked the GLUE package, you will see a `C:\Examples\electric` on library your file system and under that a directory a `C:\Examples\electric\lib` directory that contains the Java archive file `GLUE-STD.jar` that you will use in the SOAP examples.

JDOM Configuration

The examples in Part II of the book use XML on several occasions. All the examples use the JDOM library for the XML read and write operations. You can download the JDOM library from `http://www.jdom.org`. The examples have been compiled and run using the JDOM Beta 7 release.

Unpack the JDOM package into `C:\Examples` directory. At the time of this writing, the Beta 7 release of JDOM library was the latest stable release. After unpacking, you will find the library under the `C:\Examples\jdom-b7\build` directory. In addition, there are other required XML related libraries under the `C:\Examples\jdom-b7\lib` directory, namely the `jaxp.jar` and `crimson.jar` libraries.

SNMP Configuration

The SNMP examples in Chapter 9, "Connectors and Protocol Adaptors," require that both AdventNet JMX implementation and Sun JDMK implementation be installed.

You can download a free evaluation version of the AdventNet JMX implementation from `http://www.adventnet.com`. Install the software under the `C:\Examples` directory.

Similarly, download the Sun JDMK from `http://www.sun.com/software/java-dynamic/` and unpack it under the `C:\Examples` directory.

After you have finished installing all this software, the directory structure of your setup should look similar to the Explorer view shown in Figure A.1.

A

ENVIRONMENT
SETUP

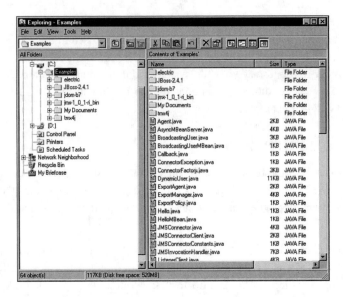

FIGURE A.1

Microsoft Windows File Explorer view of the expected file structure for the examples in this book.

Open MBeans

IN THIS APPENDIX

At the time when the first version of the JMX specification was released (1.0), the Open MBean specification was still incomplete and the Open MBeans were not fully specified. However, there are plans now to include an Open MBean implementation as part of the Maintenance Release of the Sun JMX Reference Implementation scheduled to be released sometime in the early 2002. This appendix will briefly touch on some of the main features of Open MBeans described in the JMX specification. Keep in mind, though, that Open MBeans are currently not required by the JMX implementations, and the JMX specification states that claiming a compliance at this time with regard to Open MBeans is not possible. There are plans to make Open MBeans a mandatory part of the specification in its next release.

Overview of Open MBeans

The main goal of the Open MBeans is to allow management applications to discover and understand new management object types at runtime. Normally, when you define custom classes as part of the management interface of an MBean, all the management applications require the same classes to be available to them to be able to use the management operations. On the other hand, Open MBeans rely on a predefined set of basic and universal data types that can be used to describe the management interface and management objects for complex types as well as the basic Java primary and string types.

Relying on the predefined types allows for increased flexibility in MBean component collaboration. A generic management application or another MBean can communicate with existing MBean components without requiring the custom runtime classes representing complex management data objects to be loaded to the system.

Open MBeans are extensions of the `DynamicMBean` interface. They do not require any additional interfaces to be implemented but do have to conform to the predefined data types to represent their management interfaces. Open MBeans also expose their management interface through specific metadata class implementations. An Open MBean uses `OpenMBeanInfo`, `OpenMBeanAttributeInfo`, `OpenMBeanOperationInfo`, `OpenMBeanConstructorInfo`, and `OpenMBeanParameterInfo` classes to expose its management interface.

Predefined Data Types

The predefined data types an Open MBean can use in its management interface are the object wrapper classes for the basic Java primary types (`Integer`, `Long`, `Byte`, `Boolean`, `Float`, `Double`, `Short` and `Character`), Java `String` class, and JMX `ObjectName` class. For complex data types, the JMX Open MBean specification defines two interfaces that can be used—CompositeData and TabularData. For arrays, the Open MBean specification defines an ArrayType class that can be used to represent either single or multi-dimensional arrays of the Open MBean data types.

The CompositeData and TabularData interfaces are used to represent complex types in Open MBeans. Both data types can contain any number and combination of the object wrappers of the primary types, strings, object names, arrays, or other CompositeData and TabularData objects. The implementation of the CompositeData interface is an equivalent of a hash map implementation. The contained types are added and retrieved based on a unique string key in the map.

The TabularData objects represent a table structure with any number of rows having any number of columns per row. Each row in a TabularData object must be a CompositeData object. Each CompositeData object must represent an identically structured data type. The TabularData object contains an index that is a subset of the types within each CompositeData object. The index must be a unique identifier for the row in a TabularData object and each method of the TabularData implementation must ensure the uniqueness of the index is preserved when new rows are added.

The CompositeData object must be immutable once it has been instantiated. This differs from the TabularData object, which allows rows to be added or removed even for existing instances.

Summary

The Open MBeans rely on a small, predefined set of data types that they must use to describe their management interface. This allows new management data and operations to be added at runtime without recompilation or dynamic linking. Open MBeans enables maximum flexibility of discovery of new management objects; administrators will be able to use new management data objects automatically through generic management tools.

However, the specification for the Open MBeans is not currently finished, so the Open MBean type is not mandatory for a compliant JMX implementation. Neither the Sun Reference Implementation or the Tivoli JMX implementation support the Open MBeans at the time of this writing.

B

OPEN MBEANS

References and Resources

This appendix offers listings and brief descriptions of various Web sites related to the JMX technology covered in this book.

JMX home page at Sun Microsystems:

`http://java.sun.com/products/JavaManagement/index.html`

Includes JMX specifications and Reference Implementation binaries and source code.

JSR-160, Java Management Extensions (JMX) 1.1 Specification:

`http://jcp.org/jsr/detail/160.jsp`

The second phase of the JMX specification that defines the client APIs and agent discovery among other things.

JSR-77, J2EE Management: `http://jcp.org/jsr/detail/077.jsp`

Specification request for defining management model for the J2EE platform.

JSR-70, IIOP Protocol Adaptor for JMX: `http://jcp.org/jsr/detail/070.jsp`

Specification request for IIOP based JMX adaptor to allow CORBA clients to access JMX agents.

JSR-48, Java WBEM Services Specification: `http://jcp.org/jsr/detail/048.jsp`

Specification request for Java API for WBEM.

Tivoli JMX, IBM AlphaWorks: `http://www.alphaworks.ibm.com/tech/TMX4J`

Tivoli JMX Implementation.

JMX-Forum: `http://archives.java.sun.com/archives/jmx-forum.html`

Java Management extensions (JMX) discussion list.

JBoss: `http://www.jboss.org/`

A JMX-based J2EE application server.

AdventNet: `http://www.adventnet.com`

Tools for building Java and JMX compliant SNMP agents.

GLUE framework for SOAP: `http://www.themindelectric.com/`

A Java SOAP library.

Apache AXIS: `http://xml.apache.org/axis/index.html`

Apache implementation of the SOAP specification.

Log4j: `http://jakarta.apache.org/log4j/doc/`

Open Source logging package for Java.

Jetty: `http://jetty.mortbay.com/`

Open Source Web Server and Java servlet container.

Tomcat: `http://jakarta.apache.org/tomcat/index.html`

Open Source reference implementation of the Java servlet specification.

JDOM: `http://www.jdom.org/`

Open Source Java API for XML processing.

Xerces: `http://xml.apache.org/xerces2-j/index.html`

Apache XML parser.

JBossMX

IN THIS APPENDIX

The JBossMX project is a work-in-progress JMX implementation for the JBoss application server. The goal of JBossMX is to provide a standards-compliant JMX implementation that acts as the core of the JBoss application server microkernel architecture. The JBossMX is optimized for speed in the MBean server invocation bus and supports many of the advanced features mentioned in this book.

The core of the JBossMX implementation is based on many parts on the code you have read about and studied in this book. In addition, the JBossMX project will further extend the implementation with features such as security, transactions, MBean server federation, and MBean fail-over.

To find out more about JBossMX and to see the code level details of advanced JMX implementations, point your Web browser to `http://www.jboss.org/developers/jboss-jbossmx.jsp`.

Feel free to join the JBoss team with your ideas, input, and code(!). The discussion forums for JBossMX are available at `http://www.jboss.org/forums/index.jsp`.

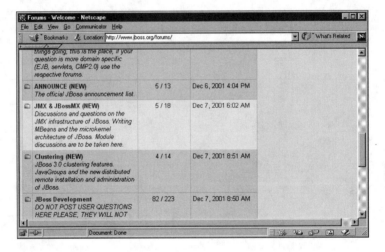

FIGURE D.1
Join the JBossMX discussion forums.

Project Goals

In addition to the base JMX implementation, the JBossMX will implement many of the more advanced features mentioned in the book. These features cover all the levels of the JMX management architecture—instrumentation, agent, and distributed services level.

Agent Level

The agent implementation will support security for all MBean invocations through invocation interceptors. The interceptors are pluggable and can be configured to include security, logging, and transaction demarcation for all MBeans. In addition, the MBean server methods for MBean creation, registration, and unregistration can be restricted via security interceptors.

The agent level will also support advanced class loaders developed as part of the JBoss project. The advanced class loading mechanism will allow you to easily deploy different versions of the same component, reload new Java class versions based on scope, and delegate class loading between several loaders to avoid class loading conflicts between different loaders.

The JBossMX MBean server will be in a critical location in the application server invocation path. Consequently, the server invocation mechanism will be optimized for speed and scalability. In addition, a federation of MBean servers will be supported to form an MBean view that spans across several servers and will be the base for handling clustered resources.

Instrumentation Level

The JBossMX server will allow interceptors with security, transaction, and logging functionality to be added for all MBean types. Also, the Model MBean implementation in this book is extended with component configurable interceptors, different kinds of persistence mechanisms (transactional persistence through existing persistence components, such as EJB entities), different forms of metadata generation, and other features.

Distributed Services Level

The connector implementation you studied in Chapter 9, "Connectors and Protocol Adaptors," and Chapter 10, "JMX Distribution Layer with J2EE Services," will be extended to support secure communication between the management application and the MBean server. The connector proxies will support fail-over behavior for MBean resources and support remote notifications.

The HTTP adaptor implementation will support Model MBeans with the capability of investigating the management interface descriptors (such as the presentation string) and adjust itself accordingly. Also, the possibility to expose the MBeans as Web Services through a WSDL adaptor in cooperation with the JBoss.NET project will be investigated.

Summary

The JBossMX project is a JMX implementation for the JBoss application server and should adapt to all the requirements demanded by a high-performance, distributed platform. This provides interesting possibilities to investigate the internal design and implementation of a JMX server and components. As JBoss is a free, open-source project, anyone is welcome to participate. We hope to see you on the forums soon!

INDEX

A

Other Related Titles

Jini and JavaSpaces Application Development
Robert Flenner
0-672-32258-7
$49.99 U.S.

Wireless Java Programming with Java 2 Micro Edition
Yu Feng and Dr. Jun Zhu
0-672-32135-1
$49.99 U.S.

Developing Java Servlets, Second Edition
James Goodwill
0-672-32107-6
$39.99 U.S.

Java 2 Micro Edition Application Development
Stefan Haustein and Michael Kroll
0-672-32095-9
$49.99 U.S.

Java Web Application Cookbook
Jamie Jaworski
Publishing in February 2002
0-672-32283-8
$49.99 U.S.

JBoss Administration and Development
The JBoss Group
Publishing in March 2002
0-672-32347-8
$49.99 U.S.

EJB: Rapid Enterprise Development
Peter Thaggard
Publishing in March 2002
0-672-32178-5
$49.99 U.S.

Java Connector Architecture: Building Custom Connectors and Adaptors
Atul Apte
Publishing in March 2002
0-672-32310-9
$49.99 U.S.

J2EE Unleashed
Paul Allen and Joseph Bambara
0-672-32180-7
$59.99 U.S.

Java Deployment (JNLP, WebStart, J2EE, J2SE)
Mauro Marinilli
0-672-32182-3
$39.99 U.S.

SAMS
www.samspublishing.com

All prices are subject to change.